D1155073

A Reader's
Hebrew-English Lexicon
of the Old Testament

A Reader's Hebrew-English Lexicon of the Old Testament

Volume I Genesis-Deuteronomy

Terry A. Armstrong

Douglas L. Busby

Cyril F. Carr

ZONDERVAN PUBLISHING HOUSE OF THE ZONDERVAN CORPORATION GRAND RAPIDS, MICHIGAN 49506

A Reader's Hebrew-English Lexicon
of the Old Testament. Volume 1
(Genesis—Deuteronomy)

Copyright © 1980 by The Zondervan Corporation
Grand Rapids, Michigan

Library of Congress Cataloging in Publication Data

Armstrong, Terry A   1944-
    A reader's Hebrew-English lexicon of the Old Testament.

    CONTENTS: v. 1. Genesis—Deuteronomy.
    1.   Bible. O.T. Hebrew—Glossaries, vocabularies, etc.
2.   Hebrew language—Dictionaries—English.   3.   Hebrew language
—Word frequency.   I.   Busby, Douglas L., 1946-   joint author.
II.   Carr, Cyril F., 1949-   joint author.   III.   Title.
PJ4833.A69   221.4'4'03   79-13294
ISBN 0-310-37020-5

Printed in the United States of America

CONTENTS

PREFACE

A Reader's Hebrew-English Lexicon of the Old Testament is an attempt to meet the need for an Old Testament translation tool on the level of Sakae Kubo's *Reader's Greek-English Lexicon of the New Testament*. With the student and pastor in view, it has been developed as a means to a more rapid reading of the Hebrew text. The *Reader's Lexicon* should not, therefore, be considered a replacement to a standard lexicon.

The format of the *Reader's Lexicon,* then, serves the purpose of eliminating most of the time-consuming lexical work from basic translation. Words that occur fifty or fewer times in the Old Testament are listed verse by verse in the order of their occurrence. Nouns and adjectives appear in their vocabulary form. Verbs appear in their perfect third masculine singular form of the stem used at that point in the text (e.g., וַיַּבְדֵּל appears in Genesis 1:4; in the *Reader's Lexicon* it is listed as הִבְדִּיל). This form is pointed when it occurs, as listed, somewhere in the Old Testament. When such a form is not extant, the form is left unpointed. In the case of middle weak verbs whose third masculine singular form is not extant, all three radicals are listed.

Particles such as adverbs, conjunctions, prepositions, interjections and their compounds appear in the *Reader's Lexicon* as they appear in the text but without pronominal suffixes (e.g., מִלְמַעְלָה in Genesis 6:16 is written as such; not as מַעַל, which is its basic part).

In rare situations, forms other than those described will appear in the *Reader's Lexicon.* In each case clarity is the governing principle. This lexicon does not include numerals or proper nouns.

Along with the definition of the Hebrew words, their respective frequencies are given. For words other than verbs, the first number indicates the frequency of that word in the given book of the Old Testament; the second gives the frequency in the whole of the Old Testament. In the case of verbs, the first number indicates the frequency of the given stem in the Bible book in which it is being studied. The second number gives the number of occurrences of that stem in the entire Old Testament. The third number gives the frequency of all the stems of a given verb in the entire Old Testament.

Example: Genesis 1:22 פרה (10-22-29)

10 ..... The Qal stem occurs ten times in Genesis.

22 ..... The Qal stem occurs twenty-two times in the Old Testament.

29 ..... The cumulative occurrence of all stems in the Old Testament is twenty-nine times.

Konkordanz zum Hebräischen Alten Testament by Gerhard Lisowsky has been relied upon for verb, noun, and adjective frequencies. Frequencies for words in other categories come from *Veteris Testamenti Concordantiae Hebraicae Atque Chakdaicae* by Soloman Mandelkern. Occasionally Lisowsky departed from *A Hebrew and English Lexicon of the Old Testament* by Francis Brown, S.R. Driver, and Charles A. Briggs (hereafter designated by BDB) in accepting one root, whereas BDB saw two roots (or vice versa). An example of this is Genesis 3:15 where Lisowsky takes two occurrences of שׁוף as two different words, while BDB lists but one root. This difference is especially prominent where Lisowsky counts a participle used as a substantive, as if it were a noun in its own right. A question mark following the frequency listing indicates this disharmony.

Frequencies for particles and prepositions posed a problem. The decision was made to list compound forms in the *Reader's Lexicon* even where the simple form existed in excess of fifty times (e.g., מִלְמַעְלָה, Gen. 6:16, which occurs only twenty-four times, though its simple form, מַעְלָה, occurs more than fifty times). Thus each compound was treated on its own and the numbers appearing with it indicate the frequency of that particle or compound only.

Definitions have been taken from BDB and checked against the text for meaning in context. Question marks following definitions indicate the interrogative. Suggested meanings are indicated by "perh." while questionable definitions are designated as "(dub.)." The number at the end of the entry gives the page number in BDB where the given definitions for a word may be found.

As an exegetical tool, this work allows the user immediately to (1) estimate accurately the work involved in any given word study he might wish to pursue, (2) gain a feel for the degree of certainty of a given definition, and (3) go directly to the correct page of a standard Hebrew lexicon of the Old Testament for further investigation. All this is in addition to the main function of making rapid reading of the Hebrew text possible. In using this lexicon, students of Hebrew will be enabled to examine the syntax of the language and, by extensive reading in the language, gain an understanding of the contexts in which a given word occurs.

It is our prayer that this tool will make Hebrew exegesis and Hebrew reading more delightful and more common among students and pastors who have a high regard for the Word of God as given in the Old Testament.

GENESIS

Chapter 1

תֹּהוּ	2 formlessness (1·20)	1062
בֹּהוּ	emptiness (1·3)	96
תְּהוֹם	deep (4·36)	1062
רחף	to hover (1·2·3)	934
הִבְדִּיל	4 to divide (5·31·41)	95
רָקִיעַ	6 expanse (9·17)	956
הִבְדִּיל	to divide (5·31·41)	95
רָקִיעַ	7 expanse (9·17)	956
הִבְדִּיל	to divide (5·31·41)	95
רָקִיעַ	8 expanse (9·17)	956
נקוה	9 to be collected (1·2·2)	876
יַבָּשָׁה	dry land (2·14)	387
יַבָּשָׁה	10 dry land (2·14)	387
מִקְוֶה	collection (1·7)	876
הדשׁיא	11 to cause to sprout (1·1·2)	205
דֶּשֶׁא	grass (2·14)	206
עֵשֶׂב	herb (7·33)	793
מִין	species (11·22)	568
דֶּשֶׁא	12 grass (2·14)	206
עֵשֶׂב	herb (7·33)	793
מִין	species (11·22)	568
מָאוֹר	14 luminary (5·19)	22
רָקִיעַ	expanse (9·17)	956
הִבְדִּיל	to divide (5·31·41)	95
מָאוֹר	15 luminary (5·19)	22
רָקִיעַ	expanse (9·17)	956
הֵאִיר	to cause to shine (2·34·40)	21
מָאוֹר	16 luminary (5·19)	22
מֶמְשָׁלָה	dominion (5·17)	606
כּוֹכָב	star (5·37)	456
רָקִיעַ	17 expanse (9·17)	956
הֵאִיר	to cause to shine (2·34·40)	21
הִבְדִּיל	18 to divide (5·31·41)	95
שָׁרַץ	20 to swarm (5·14·14)	1056

שֶׁרֶץ	coll. swarming things, swarm (2·15)	1056
עוֹפֵף	to fly about (1·5·25)	733
רָקִיעַ	expanse (9·17)	956
תַּנִּין	21 sea monster (1·15)	1072
רמשׂ	to move about, to glide about (10·16·16)	942
שָׁרַץ	to swarm (5·14·14)	1056
מִין	species (11·22)	568
פרה	22 to be fruitful (10·22·29)	826
מִין	24 species (11·22)	568
רֶמֶשׂ	creeping things (9·16)	943
מִין	25 species (11·22)	568
רֶמֶשׂ	creeping things (9·16)	943
צֶלֶם	26 image (5·17)	873
דְּמוּת	likeness (3·25)	198
רדה	to rule (2·22·23)	921
דָּגָה	fish (2·15)	185
רֶמֶשׂ	creeping things (9·16)	943
רמשׂ	to creep (10·16·16)	942
צֶלֶם	27 image (5·17)	853
נְקֵבָה	female (6·22)	666
פרה	28 to be fruitful (10·22·29)	826
כבשׁ	to subdue (1·8·14)	461
רדה	to rule (2·22·23)	921
דָּגָה	fish (2·15)	185
רמשׂ	to creep (10·16·16)	942
עֵשֶׂב	29 herb (7·33)	793
אָכְלָה	food (4·18)	38
רמשׂ	30 to creep (10·16·16)	942
יֶרֶק	green (1·8)	438
עֵשֶׂב	herb (7·33)	793
אָכְלָה	food (4·18)	38

Chapter 2

תּוֹלְדוֹת	4 account of, generations (13·39)	410
שִׂיחַ	5 shrub (2·4)	967
טֶרֶם	not yet (5·16)	382

עֵשֶׂב	herb (7·33) 793		נָחָשׁ	4 serpent (6·31) 638
צָמַח	to sprout (3·15·33) 855		נִפְקַח	5 to be opened (2·3·20) 824
הִמְטִיר	to make rain fall (3·16·17) 565		מַאֲכָל	6 food (4·30) 38
אֵד	6 mist (1·2) 15		תַּאֲוָה	desirable (2·21) 16
יָצַר	7 to form, fashion (3·41·44) 427		נֶחְמָד	to be desirable (2·4·21) 326
נָפַח	to blow (1·9·12) 655		נִפְקְחָה	7 to be opened (2·3·20) 824
נְשָׁמָה	breath (2·24) 675		עֵירֹם	naked (3·10) 735
גַּן	8 garden (14·41) 171		תָּפַר	to sew together (1·3·4) 1074
יָצַר	to form, fashion (3·41·44) 427		עָלֶה	leaves (2·17) 750
הִצְמִיחַ	9 to cause to grow, sprout (1·14·33) 855		תְּאֵנָה	fig [tree] (1·38) 1061
נֶחְמָד	to be desirable (2·4·21) 326		חֲגוֹרָה	loin covering, girdle (1·5) 292
מַאֲכָל	food (4·30) 38		גַּן	8 garden (14·41) 171
גַּן	garden (14·41) 171		הִתְחַבֵּא	to hide oneself (1·10·34) 285
גַּן	10 garden (14·41) 171		אֵי	9 where? (3·39) 32
נִפְרָד	to divide (7·12·26) 825		גַּן	10 garden (14·41) 171
בְּדֹלַח	12 bdellium (1·2) 95		עֵירֹם	naked (3·10) 735
שֹׁהַם	onyx (1·11) 995		נֶחְבָּא	to hide oneself (2·16·34) 285
קִדְמָה	14 in front of (2·4) 870		עֵירֹם	11 naked (3·10) 735
גַּן	15 garden (14·41) 171		נָחָשׁ	13 serpent (6·31) 638
גַּן	16 garden (14·41) 171		נִשָּׁא	to deceive (1·14·15) 674
עֵזֶר	18 helper (2·21) 740		נָחָשׁ	14 serpent (6·31) 638
כְּנֶגֶד	corresponding to (2·2) 617		גָּחוֹן	belly (1·2) 161
יָצַר	19 to form, fashion (3·41·44) 427		אֵיבָה	15 enmity, personal hostility (1·5) 33
עֵזֶר	20 helper (2·21) 740		שׁוּף	to bruise (1·1·1[?]) 1003
כְּנֶגֶד	corresponding to (2·2) 617		שׁוּף	to bruise (1·3·3[?]) 1003
תַּרְדֵּמָה	21 deep sleep (2·7) 922		עָקֵב	heel (3·14) 784
יָשֵׁן	to sleep (2·24·25) 445		עִצָּבוֹן	16 pain (3·3) 781
צֵלָע	rib (2·39) 854		הֵרוֹן	pregnancy, conception (1·1) 248
צֵלָע	22 rib (2·39) 854		עֶצֶב	pain (1·6) 780
לְזֹאת	23 this one (1·2) 260		תְּשׁוּקָה	longing (2·3) 1003
עָרוֹם	25 naked (1·16) 736		בַּעֲבוּר	17 because of (15·46) 721

Chapter 3

			עִצָּבוֹן	pain (3·3) 781
נָחָשׁ	1 serpent (6·31) 638		קוֹץ	18 thorn [bush] (1·11) 881
עָרוּם	crafty (1·11) 791		דַּרְדַּר	thistles (1·2) 205
גַּן	garden (14·41) 171		הִצְמִיחַ	to cause to grow, sprout (2·14·33) 855
נָחָשׁ	2 serpent (6·31) 638		עֵשֶׂב	herb (7·33) 793
גַּן	garden (14·41) 171		זֵעָה	19 sweat (1·1) 402
גַּן	3 garden (14·41) 171		כֻּתֹּנֶת	21 tunic (9·30) 509

גַּן 23 garden (14·41) 171

גרש 24 to drive out (3·35·48) 176

גַּן garden (14·41) 171

לַהַט flame (1·1) 529

Chapter 4

הָרָה 1 to conceive, become pregnant (20·38·40) 247

שָׁעָה 4 to regard, gaze (2·12·15) 1043

שָׁעָה 5 to regard, gaze (2·12·15) 1043

שְׂאֵת 7 acceptance, forgiveness, uplifting [dub.] (2·7) 673

רָבַץ to lie down, lie, make its lair (5·24·30) 918

תְּשׁוּקָה longing (2·3) 1003

אֵי 9 where? (3·9) 32

פצה 11 to open wide (1·15·15) 822

נוע 12 to totter (2·22·38) 631

נוד to wander (2·19·26) 626

גרש 14 to drive out, drive away (3·33·48) 176

נוע to totter (2·22·38) 631

נוד to wander (2·19·26) 626

נקם 15 to take vengeance (2·3·34) 667

קִדְמָה 16 in front of (2·4) 870

הָרָה 17 to conceive, become pregnant (20·38·40) 247

כִּנּוֹר 21 lyre (2·41) 490

עוּגָב flute (1·4) 721

לטש 22 to hammer (1·4·5) 538

הַאֲזִין 23 to listen (1·41·41) 24

אִמְרָה word, utterance (1·30) 57

פֶּצַע wound (1·8) 822

חַבּוּרָה stripe, blow (1·8) 289

נקם 24 to take vengeance (2·3·34) 667

Chapter 5

תּוֹלְדוֹת 1 generations (13·39) 410

דְּמוּת likeness (3·25) 198

נְקֵבָה 2 female (6·22) 666

דְּמוּת 3 likeness (3·25) 198

צֶלֶם image (5·17) 853

עִצָּבוֹן 29 pain (3·3) 781

Chapter 6

רבב 1 to be many (2·23·24) 912

דון 3 to contend [dub.] (1·1·1) 192

שׁגג to go astray (1·5·5) 992

נְפִילִים 4 giants (1·3) 658

יֵצֶר 5 imagination (2·9) 428

הִתְעַצֵּב 6 to grieve (2·2·15) 780

מחה 7 to blot out (3·22·35) 562

רֶמֶשׂ creeping things (9·16) 943

תּוֹלְדוֹת 9 generations (13·39) 410

תֵּבָה 14 ark (26·28) 1061

גֹּפֶר gopher [dub.] (1·1) 172

קֵן cell (1·13) 890

כֹּפֶר pitch (1·1) 498

תֵּבָה 15 ark (26·28) 1061

קוֹמָה height (1·45) 879

צֹהַר 16 roof (1·1) 844

תֵּבָה ark (26·28) 1061

מִלְמַעְלָה above (2·24) 751

צַד side (1·32) 841

תַּחְתִּי lower (1·18) 1066

מַבּוּל 17 flood (12·13) 550

גָּוַע to perish (6·24·24) 157

תֵּבָה 18 ark (26·28) 1061

תֵּבָה 19 ark (26·28) 1061

נְקֵבָה female (6·22) 666

מִין 20 species (11·22) 568

רֶמֶשׂ creeping thing (9·16) 943

מַאֲכָל 21 food (4·30) 38

אָכְלָה food (4·18) 38

Chapter 7

תֵּבָה 1 ark (26·28) 1061

3

נְקֵבָה 3 female (6·22) 666

הַמְטִיר 4 to make rain fall (3·16·17) 565

מחה to blot out (3·22·35) 562

יְקוּם substance, existance (2·3) 879

מַבּוּל 6 flood (12·13) 550

תֵּבָה 7 ark (26·28) 1061

מַבּוּל flood (12·13) 550

רמשׁ 8 to creep (10·16·16) 942

תֵּבָה 9 ark (26·28) 1061

נְקֵבָה female (6·22) 666

מַבּוּל 10 flood (12·13) 550

מַעְיָן 11 spring (2·23) 745

תְּהוֹם deep (4·36) 1062

אֲרֻבָּה lattice, window (2·8) 70

גֶּשֶׁם 12 rain (2·36) 177

תֵּבָה 13 ark (26·28) 1061

מִין 14 species (11·22) 568

רֶמֶשׂ creeping thing (9·16) 943

רמשׂ to creep (10·16·16) 942

צִפּוֹר bird[s] (2·40) 861

תֵּבָה 15 ark (26·28) 1061

נְקֵבָה 16 female (6·22) 666

מַבּוּל 17 flood (12·13) 550

תֵּבָה ark (26·28) 1061

גָּבַר 18 to prevail (5·17·25) 149

תֵּבָה ark (26·28) 1061

גָּבַר 19 to prevail (5·17·25) 149

גָּבֹהַּ high (1·41) 147

מִלְמַעְלָה 20 above (2·24) 751

גָּבַר to prevail (5·17·25) 149

גָּוַע 21 to perish (6·24·24) 157

רמשׂ to creep (10·16·16) 942

שֶׁרֶץ swarming thing (2·15) 1056

שָׁרַץ to swarm (5·14·14) 1056

נְשָׁמָה 22 breath (2·24) 675

חָרָבָה dry ground (1·8) 351

מחה 23 to blot out (3·22·35) 562

יְקוּם substance, existance (2·3) 879

רֶמֶשׂ creeping thing (9·16) 943

תֵּבָה ark (26·28) 1061

גָּבַר 24 to prevail (5·17·25) 149

Chapter 8

תֵּבָה 1 ark (26·28) 1061

שָׁכַךְ to abate, decrease (1·4·5) 1013

נסכר 2 to be stopped (1·2·4) 698

מַעְיָן spring (2·23) 745

תְּהוֹם deep (4·36) 1062

אֲרֻבָּה opening, window (2·8) 70

נכלא to restrain (1·3·17) 476

גֶּשֶׁם rain (2·36) 177

חָסֵר 3 to lack, decrease (3·20·24) 341

תֵּבָה 4 ark (26·28) 1061

חָסֵר 5 to lack, decrease (3·20·24) 341

חַלּוֹן 6 window (2·30) 319

תֵּבָה ark (26·28) 1061

עֹרֵב 7 raven (1·12) 788

יוֹנָה 8 dove (5·35) 401

יוֹנָה 9 dove (5·35) 401

מָנוֹחַ resting place (1·7) 629

תֵּבָה ark (26·28) 1061

חול 10 to twist or writhe in anxious longing, i.e., to wait with extreme anxiety (1·5) 296

יוֹנָה dove (5·35) 401

תֵּבָה ark (26·28) 1061

יוֹנָה 11 dove (5·35) 401

עָלֶה leaf (2·17) 750

זַיִת olive tree (1·38) 268

טָרָף fresh plucked (1·2) 383

נוחל 12 to wait (1·2·42) 403

יוֹנָה dove (5·35) 401

חרב 13 to be dry (2·17·37[?]) 351

מִכְסֶה covering (1·16) 492

תֵּבָה ark (26·28) 1061

תֵּבָה 16 ark (26·28) 1061

4

רֶמֶשׂ 17 creeping thing (9·16) 943

רמשׂ   to creep (10·16·16) 942

שָׁרַץ   to swarm (5·14·14) 1056

פרה   to be fruitful (10·22·29) 826

רֶמֶשׂ 19 creeping thing (9·16) 943

רמשׂ   to move about (10·16·16) 942

תֵּבָה   ark (26·28) 1061

הריח 21 to smell (2·11·14) 926

נִיחוֹחַ   soothing, tranquillizing (1·43) 629

בַּעֲבוּר   for the sake of (15·46) 721

יֵצֶר   imagination (2·9) 428

נְעוּרִים   youth (2·46) 655

קָצִיר 22 crop, harvest (3·49) 894

קֹר   cold (1·1) 903

חֹם   heat (1·4) 328

קַיִץ   summer (1·20) 884

חֹרֶף   autumn (1·7) 358

Chapter 9

פרה 1 to be fruitful (10·22·29) 826

מוֹרָא 2 fear (1·12) 432

חַת   terror, fear (1·4) 369

רמשׂ   to creep (10·16·16) 942

דָּג   fish (1·19) 185

רֶמֶשׂ 3 moving things (9·16) 943

אָכְלָה   food (4·18) 38

יֶרֶק   green (2·8) 438

עֵשֶׂב   herb (7·33) 793

צֶלֶם 6 image (5·17) 853

פרה 7 to be fruitful (10·22·29) 826

שָׁרַץ   to swarm (5·14·14) 1056

תֵּבָה 10 ark (26·28) 1061

מַבּוּל 11 flood (12·13) 550

ענן 14 to bring clouds (1·1·11) 778

מַבּוּל 15 flood (12·13) 550

תֵּבָה 18 ark (26·28) 1061

נָפַץ 19 to be scattered
(1·5·21[?]) 659

שׁכר 21 to become drunk (2·9·20) 1016

שִׂמְלָה 23 garment (7·29) 971

שְׁכֶם   shoulder (6·22) 1014

אֲחֹרַנִּית   backwards (2·7) 30

יקץ 24 to awake (5·11·11) 429

קָטָן   young (6·47) 881

פתה 27 to make wide (1·1·1) 834

מַבּוּל 28 flood (12·13) 550

Chapter 10

תּוֹלְדוֹת 1 generations (13·39) 410

מַבּוּל   flood (12·13) 550

נפרד 5 to divide (7·12·26) 825

אִי   coast, region (1·36) 15

צַיִד 9 hunting, game (12·14) 844

נפלג 25 to divide (1·2·4) 811

מוֹשָׁב 30 dwelling place (3·43) 444

תּוֹלְדוֹת 32 generations (13·39) 410

נפרד   to divide (7·12·26) 825

מַבּוּל   flood (12·13) 550

Chapter 11

בִּקְעָה 2 plain, broad valley (1·19) 132

יהב 3 to come now (8·27·27) 396

לבן   to make brick (1·3·3) 527

לְבֵנָה   brick (2·12) 527

שְׂרֵפָה   [place of] burning (1·13) 977

חֵמָר   asphalt (2·3) 330

חֹמֶר   mortar, cement (1·17) 330

יהב 4 to come now (8·27·27) 396

מִגְדָּל   tower (2·49) 154

מִגְדָּל 5 tower (2·49) 154

נבצר 6 to be withheld (1·2·4) 130

זָמַם   to purpose, divise (1·13·13) 273

יהב 7 to come now (8·27·27) 396

בָּלַל   to confuse, confound (2·41·42) 117

בָּלַל 9 to confuse, confound (2·41·42) 117

תּוֹלְדוֹת 10 generations (13·39) 410

5

מַבּוּל flood (12·13) 550

תּוֹלֵדוֹת 27 generations (13·39) 410

מוֹלֶדֶת 28 kindred (9·22) 409

עָקָר 30 barren (3·11) 785

וָלָד offspring, child (1·1) 409

כַּלָּה 31 daughter-in-law (4·34) 483

Chapter 12

מוֹלֶדֶת 1 kindred (9·22) 409

רְכוּשׁ 5 property (11·28) 940

רָכַשׁ to gather [property], acquire (5·5·5) 940

אֵלוֹן 6 terebinth, tall tree (4·10) 18

הַעְתִּיק 8 to move forward (2·5·9) 801

כָּבֵד 10 grievous (9·39) 458

יָפֶה 11 beautiful (9·40) 421

בַּעֲבוּר 13 on account of (15·46) 721

בִּגְלַל on account of, for the sake of (3·10) 164

יָפֶה 14 beautiful (9·40) 421

בַּעֲבוּר 16 for the sake of (15·46) 721

אָתוֹן she-ass (4·35) 87

Chapter 13

כָּבֵד 2 rich (9·39) 458

מַסַּע 3 journey (1·12) 652

תְּחִלָּה beginning (4·22) 321

רְכוּשׁ 6 property (11·28) 940

מְרִיבָה 8 strife, contention (1·2) 937

נִפְרָד 9 to divide, separate (7·12·26) 825

הֵימִין to go to the right (1·5·5) 412

הִשְׂמְאִיל to go to the left (1·5·5) 970

מַשְׁקֶה 10 well-irrigated (11[?]·19[?]) 1052

גַּן garden (14·41) 171

נִפְרָד 11 to divide, separate (7·12·26) 825

אֹהֶל 12 to pitch one's tent (2·2·3) 14

חַטָּא 13 sinner, sinful (1·19) 308

נִפְרָד 14 to divide, separate (7·12·26) 825

קֶדֶם eastward (3·26) 870

מנה 16 to count (1·12·28) 584

נמנה to be counted (1·6·28) 584

אהל 18 to move one's tent (2·2·3) 14

אֵלוֹן terebinth, tall tree (4·10) 18

Chapter 14

חבר 3 to come as allies, unite (1·11·28) 287

מֶלַח salt (2·28) 571

מרד 4 to rebel (1·25·25) 597

שָׁוֵה 5 plain (1·1) 1001

בְּאֵר 10 pit (24·38) 91

חֵמָר asphalt (2·3) 330

רְכוּשׁ 11 property (11·28) 940

אֹכֶל food (16·44) 38

רְכוּשׁ 12 property (11·28) 940

פָּלִיט 13 fugitive (1·19) 812

אֵלוֹן terebinth, tall tree (4·10) 18

נִשְׁבָּה 14 to be taken captive (1·8·37) 985

הֵרִיק to lead forth, i.e., muster (2·17·19) 937

חָנִיךְ trained, experienced (1·1) 335

יָלִיד born (4·12) 409

רְכוּשׁ 16 property (11·28) 940

קָנָה 19 to get, acquire, i.e., to create (2·5·5[?]) 888

מִגֵּן 20 to deliver (1·3·3) 171

מַעֲשֵׂר tithe (1·31) 78

רְכוּשׁ 21 property (11·28) 940

קָנָה 22 to get, acquire, i.e., to create (2·5·5[?]) 888

חוּט 23 thread, cord (1·7) 296

שְׂרוֹךְ thong (1·2) 976

נַעַל sandal (1·22) 653

הֶעֱשִׁיר 23 to make rich (1·14·17) 799

בִּלְעָדֵי 24 not to me!, i.e., not at all! (3·5) 116

Chapter 15

מַחֲזֶה	1 vision (1·4)	303
שָׂכָר	reward (7·28)	969
עֲרִירִי	2 childless (1·4)	792
מֶשֶׁק	acquisition (1·1)	606
מֵעֶה	4 inward parts (2·31)	588
כּוֹכָב	5 star (5·37)	456
בַּמָּה	8 whereby (1·29)	552
עֶגְלָה	9 heifer (1·12)	722
שָׁלַשׁ	to divide into three parts; here = three-years old (3·5·9·)	1026
תֹּר	turtledove (1·14)	1076
גּוֹזָל	young [of a bird] (1·2)	160
בָּתַר	10 to cut in two (1·1·2)	144
בֶּתֶר	half, piece (1·3)	144
צִפּוֹר	bird[s] (2·4)	861
בָּתַר	to cut in two (1·1·2)	144
עַיִט	11 birds of prey (1·8)	743
פֶּגֶר	corpse (1·22)	803
הַנְשֵׁב	to drive away (1·2·3)	674
תַּרְדֵּמָה	12 deep sleep (2·7)	922
אֵימָה	terror, dread (1·17)	33
חֲשֵׁכָה	darkness (1·6)	365
דִּין	14 to judge (4·23·24)	192
רְכוּשׁ	property (11·28)	940
שֵׂיבָה	15 old age (5·20[?])	966
הֵנָּה	16 hither (8·49)	244
שָׁלֵם	full (3·28)	1023
עֲלָטָה	17 thick darkness (1·4)	759
תַּנּוּר	firepot (1·15)	1072
עָשָׁן	smoke (1·25)	798
לַפִּיד	torch (1·13)	542
גֶּזֶר	half, part (1·2)	160

Chapter 16

עָצַר	2 to restrain (3·36·46)	783
אוּלַי	perhaps (12·45)	19

הָרָה	4 to conceive (20·38·40)	247
גְּבֶרֶת	mistress (3·15)	150
חֵיק	5 bosom (1·38)	300
הָרָה	to conceive (20·38·40)	247
אֵי	8 where? (3·29)	32
אָנָה	whither? where? (3·39)	33
גְּבֶרֶת	mistress (3·15)	150
גְּבֶרֶת	9 mistress (3·15)	150
הָרָה	11 to conceive (20·38·40)	247
עֳנִי	affliction (4·36)	777
פֶּרֶא	12 wild ass (1·10)	825
רְאִי	13 seeing (1·4)	909
הֲלֹם	here (1·11)	240
בְּאֵר	14 well, pit (24·38)	91

Chapter 17

שַׁדַּי	1 Almighty (6·48)	994
הפרה	6 to make fruitful (5·7·29)	826
מְגוּרִים	8 sojourning (6·11)	158
נָמוֹל	10 to be circumcised (13·17·29)	557
מלל	11 to be circumcised (1·3[?]·4[?])	576
עָרְלָה	foreskin (6·16)	790
נָמוֹל	12 to be circumcised (13·17·29)	557
יָלִיד	born (4·12)	409
מִקְנָה	possession (5·15)	889
נֵכָר	that which is foreign, foreigner (4·36)	648
נָמוֹל	13 to be circumcised (13·17·29)	557
יָלִיד	born (4·12)	409
מִקְנָה	possession (5·15)	889
עָרֵל	14 uncircumcised (1·35)	790
נָמוֹל	to be circumcised (13·17·29)	557
עָרְלָה	foreskin (6·16)	790
עַם	kinsman (6·34)	769
הֵפֵר	to break (1·41·44)	830
צָחַק	17 to laugh (6·6·13)	850
לוּ	18 if only (4·19)	530
אֲבָל	19 nay, but (2·11)	6

7

הִפְרָה 20 to make fruitful (5·7·29) 826

יָלִיד 23 born (4·12) 409

מִקְנָה possession (5·15) 889

מוּל to circumcise (2·12·29) 557

עָרְלָה foreskin (6·16) 790

נִמּוֹל 24 to be circumcised (13·17·29) 557

עָרְלָה foreskin (6·16) 790

נִמּוֹל 25 to be circumcised (13·17·29) 557

עָרְלָה foreskin (6·16) 790

נִמּוֹל 26 to be circumcised (13·17·29) 557

יָלִיד 27 born (4·12) 409

מִקְנָה possession (5·15) 889

נֵכָר that which is foreign = foreigner (4·36) 648

נִמּוֹל to be circumcised (13·17·29) 557

Chapter 18

אֵלוֹן 1 terebinth, tall tree (4·10) 18

חֹם heat (1·1[?]) 328

נִשְׁעַן 4 to support oneself (1·22·22) 1043

פַּת 5 bit (1·14) 837

סָעַד to sustain (1·12·12) 703

סְאָה 6 measure of grain (1·9) 684

קֶמַח flour (1·14) 887

לוּשׁ to knead (1·5·5) 534

עֻגָה bread cake (1·7) 728

רַךְ 7 tender (3·16) 940

חֶמְאָה 8 curd (1·10) 326

חָלָב milk (2·44) 316

אַיֵּה 9 where? (4·44) 32

צָחַק 12 to laugh (6·6·13) 850

בָּלָה to become old and worn out (1·11·16) 115

עֶדְנָה delight (1·1) 726

זָקֵן to be old (6·25·27) 278

צָחַק 13 to laugh (6·6·13) 850

אָמְנָם truly, verily, indeed (1·5) 53

זָקֵן to be old (6·25·27) 278

נִפְלָא 14 to be beyond one's power (1·13·24) 810

כָּחַשׁ 15 to deceive (1·19·22) 471

צָחַק to laugh (6·6·13) 850

הִשְׁקִיף 16 to look down (3·12·22) 1054

עָצוּם 18 mighty (1·31) 783

זַעֲקָה 20 outcry against (1·18) 277

רַבַב to be great (2·23·24) 912

צְעָקָה 21 outcry (3·21) 858

כָּלָה completely, altogether (1·22) 478

סָפָה 23 to sweep away (2·8·18) 705

אוּלַי 24 if perhaps (12·45) 19

סָפָה to sweep away (2·8·18) 705

חָלִילָה 25 far be it (4·21) 321

בַּעֲבוּר 26 on account of (15·46) 721

הוֹאֵל 27 to undertake to do (2·18·18) 383

אֵפֶר ashes (1·22) 68

אוּלַי 28 if perhaps (12·45) 19

חָסֵר to lack, be lacking (3·20·24) 341

אוּלַי 29 if perhaps (12·45) 19

בַּעֲבוּ on account of (15·46) 721

אוּלַי 30 if perhaps (12·45) 19

הוֹאֵל 31 to undertake to do (2·18·18) 383

אוּלַי if perhaps (12·45) 19

בַּעֲבוּר on account of (15·46) 721

אוּלַי 32 if perhaps (12·45) 19

בַּעֲבוּר on account of (15·46) 721

Chapter 19

רְחוֹב 2 broad open place, plaza (1·43) 932

פָצַר 3 to urge (3·6·7) 823

מִשְׁתֶּה feast (5·45) 1059

אָפָה to bake (1·9·12) 66

טֶרֶם 4 not yet (5·16) 382

אַיֵּה 5 where? (4·44) 32

אֵל 8 these (4·10[?]) 41

קוֹרָה roof (1·5) 900

הָלְאָה 9 out there, onward (1·13) 229

פָּצַר to press (3·6·7) 823

סַנְוֵרִים 11 sudden blindness (1·3) 703

לָאָה to be weary (1·3·19) 521

פֹּה 12 here (3·44) 805

חָתָן son-in-law (3·20) 368

צְעָקָה 13 outcry (3·21) 858

חָתָן 14 son-in-law (3·20) 368

צָחַק to jest (5·7·13) 850

שַׁחַר 15 dawn (3·23) 1007

הָאוּץ to hasten (1·2·10) 21

נספה to be swept away (2·9·18) 705

הִתְמַהּ 16 to linger (2·9·9) 554

חֶמְלָה compassion, mercy (1·2) 328

נספה 17 to be swept away (2·9·18) 705

מִצְעָר 20 small thing (2·6) 859

הִמְטִיר 24 to rain (3·16·17) 565

גָּפְרִית brimstone (1·7) 172

אֵל 25 these (4·10) 41

צֶמַח growth (1·12) 855

נְצִיב 26 pillar (1·11) 662

מֶלַח salt (2·28) 571

הִשְׁקִיף 28 to look down (3·12·22) 1054

קִיטוֹר thick smoke (2·4) 882

כִּבְשָׁן kiln (1·4) 461

מְעָרָה 30 cave (11·40) 792

בְּכִירָה 31 firstborn (5·6) 114

צָעִיר young (8·22) 859

זָקֵן to be old (6·25·27) 278

בְּכִירָה 33 firstborn (5·6) 114

מָחֳרָת 34 the morrow (1·32) 564

בְּכִירָה firstborn (5·6) 114

צָעִיר young (8·22) 859

אֶמֶשׁ yesterday (3·5) 57

צָעִיר 35 young (8·22) 859

הָרָה 36 to conceive (20·28·40) 247

בְּכִירָה 37 firstborn (5·6) 114

צָעִיר 38 young (8·22) 859

Chapter 20

בָּעַל 3 to marry (1·1·13) 127

תֹּם 5 integrity (2·23) 1070

נִקָּיוֹן innocency (1·5) 667

תֹּם 6 integrity (2·23) 1070

חָשַׂךְ to withhold (4·26·28) 362

יִרְאָה 11 fear, reverence (1·45) 432

אָמְנָה 12 truly, indeed (1·2[?]) 53

הִתְעָה 13 to cause to wander about (1·21·49) 1073

כְּסוּת 16 covering (1·8) 492

עָצַר 18 to shut up (3·36·46) 783

רֶחֶם womb (4·33) 933

Chapter 21

הָרָה 2 to conceive (20·38·40) 247

זְקֻנִים old age (4·4) 279

מוֹל 4 to circumcise (2·12·29) 557

צְחֹק 6 laughter (1·2) 850

צָחַק to laugh (6·6·13) 850

מִלֵּל 7 to speak (1·4·5[?]) 576

הֵינִיק to nurse (2·10·18) 413

זְקֻנִים old age (4·4) 279

נִגְמַל 8 to be weaned (2·3·37) 168

מִשְׁתֶּה feast (5·45) 1059

צָחַק 9 to play, sport (5·7·13) 850

גֵּרֵשׁ 10 to drive out (3·35·48) 176

אוֹדֹת 11 cause; עַל־אֹ=because of (3·11) 15

חֵמֶת 14 waterskin (3·3) 332

שְׁכֶם shoulder (6·22) 1014

תָּעָה to wander about (2·26·49) 1073

חֵמֶת 15 waterskin (3·3) 332

שִׂיחַ bush (2·4) 967

מִנֶּגֶד 16 opposite (2·26) 617

טָחָה to shoot (1·1) 377

בַּאֲשֶׁר 17 in where (3·19) 84

פָּקַח 19 to open (1·17·20) 824

בְּאֵר well, pit (24·38) 91
חֵמֶת waterskin (3·3) 332
רבה 20 to shoot, ptc.=a shooter (1·1·1) 916
קַשָּׁת bowman (1·1) 906
הֵנָּה 23 here (8·49) 244
שׁקר to do falsely (1·1·6) 1055
נִין offspring (1·4) 630
נֶכֶד posterity (1·3) 645
אֹדֹת 25 cause; על־א׳=because of (3·11) 15
בְּאֵר well, pit (24·38) 91
גָּזַל to seize (2·29·30) 159
בִּלְתִּי 26 except (4·24) 116
כִּבְשָׂה 28 ewe lamb (3·8) 461
כִּבְשָׂה 29 ewe lamb (3·8) 461
כִּבְשָׂה 30 ewe lamb (3·8) 461
בַּעֲבוּר in order that (15·46) 721
עֵדָה witness (2·3) 729
חָפַר to dig (7·22·22) 343
בְּאֵר well, pit (24·38) 91
אֵשֶׁל 33 tamarisk tree (1·3) 79

Chapter 22

נִסָּה 1 to test (9·36·36) 650
יָחִיד 2 only (3·12) 402
חבש 3 to bind, bind on, i.e., to saddle (1·27·31) 289
פֹּה 5 here (3·44) 805
מַאֲכֶלֶת 6 knife (2·4) 38
אַיֵּה 7 where? (4·44) 32
שֶׂה a sheep (4·44) 961
שֶׂה 8 a sheep (4·44) 961
עקד 9 to bind (1·1·1) 785
מִמַּעַל on top of (1·29) 751
מַאֲכֶלֶת 10 knife (2·4) 38
מְאוּמָה 12 anything (6·32) 548
יָרֵא fearing (1·46) 431
חָשַׂךְ to withhold (4·26·28) 362
יָחִיד only (3·12) 402

סְבַךְ 13 thicket (1·3) 687
חָשַׂךְ 16 to withhold (4·26·28) 362
יָחִיד only (3·12) 402
כּוֹכָב 17 star (5·37) 456
חוֹל sand (3·22) 297
עֵקֶב 18 because (2·15) 784
פִּילֶגֶשׁ 24 concubine (4·37) 811

Chapter 23

ספד 2 to lament (2·27·29) 704
תּוֹשָׁב 4 sojourner (1·14) 444
מִבְחָר 6 choicest (1·12) 104
פָּגַע 8 to entreat (3·40·46) 803
מְעָרָה 9 cave (11·40) 792
מְעָרָה 11 cave (11·40) 792
לוּ 13 if only (4·19) 530
שָׁקַל 16 to weigh out (1·19·22) 1053
סֹחֵר trader, merchant (2·16[?]) 695
מְעָרָה 17 cave (11·40) 792
מִקְנָה 18 possession (5·15) 889
מְעָרָה 19 cave (11·40) 792
מְעָרָה 20 cave (11·40) 792

Chapter 24

זָקֵן 1 to be old (6·25·27) 278
יָרֵךְ 2 thigh, loins (9·34) 437
מוֹלֶדֶת 4 kindred (9·22) 409
אוּלַי 5 perhaps (12·45) 19
מוֹלֶדֶת 7 kindred (9·22) 409
נקה 8 to be free (2·23·36) 667
שְׁבוּעָה oath (2·30) 989
יָרֵךְ 9 thigh, loins (9·34) 437
טוּב 10 goods (4·32) 375
הברך 11 to cause to kneel (1·1·3) 138
בְּאֵר well (24·38) 91
שֹׁאֵב water drawer (1·5) 980
הִקְרָה 12 to cause to occur, i.e., grant success (2·3·27) 899

שָׁאַב	13 to draw (7·14·14) 980	
כַּד	14 jar (9·18) 461	
טֶרֶם	15 not yet (5·16) 382	
כַּד	jar (9·18) 461	
שְׁכֶם	shoulder (6·22) 1014	
בְּתוּלָה	16 virgin (1·50) 143	
כַּד	jar (9·18) 461	
הִגְמִיא	17 to let [one] drink (1·1·2) 167	
כַּד	jar (9·18) 461	
כַּד	18 jar (9·18) 461	
שָׁאַב	19 to draw (7·14·14) 980	
עָרָה	20 to empty (1·8·14) 788	
כַּד	jar (9·18) 461	
שֹׁקֶת	watering trough (2·2) 1052	
בְּאֵר	well (24·38) 91	
שָׁאַב	to draw (7·14·14) 980	
הִשְׁתָּאֵה	21 to gaze (1·1·1) 981	
הֶחֱרִישׁ	to be silent (2·38·46) 361	
נֶזֶם	22 ring (4·17) 633	
בֶּקַע	half [shekel] (1·2) 132	
מִשְׁקָל	weight (3·48) 1054	
צָמִיד	bracelet (3·6) 855	
תֶּבֶן	25 straw (2·17) 1061	
מִסְפּוֹא	fodder (4·5) 704	
קָדַד	26 to bow down (3·15·15) 869	
נחה	27 to lead (1·14·40) 634	
נֶזֶם	30 ring (4·17) 633	
צָמִיד	bracelet (3·6) 855	
תֶּבֶן	32 straw (2·17) 1061	
מִסְפּוֹא	fodder (4·5) 704	
זִקְנָה	36 old age (1·6) 279	
אוּלַי	39 perhaps (12·45) 19	
נָקָה	41 to be free (2·23·36) 667	
אָלָה	oath (3·36) 46	
נָקִי	free from (2·43) 667	
עַלְמָה	43 young woman (1·9) 761	
שָׁאַב	to draw (7·14·14) 980	
כַּד	jar (9·18) 461	

שָׁאַב	44 to draw (7·14·14) 980	
טֶרֶם	45 not yet (5·16) 382	
כַּד	jar (9·18) 461	
שְׁכֶם	shoulder (6·22) 1014	
שָׁאַב	to draw (7·14·14) 980	
כַּד	46 jar (9·18) 461	
נֶזֶם	47 ring (4·17) 633	
צָמִיד	bracelet (3·6) 855	
קָדַד	48 to bow down (3·15·15) 869	
הנחה	to lead (1·26·40) 634	
מִגְדָּנָה	53 choice thing (1·4) 550	
עָשׂוֹר	55 period of ten days (1·15) 797	
אחר	56 to keep back (2·15·17) 29	
מֵינֶקֶת	59 nurse (2·5[?]) 413	
רְבָבָה	60 myriad (1·16) 914	
שֹׂנֵא	enemy (1·41) 971	
שׂוּחַ	63 to rove about (1·1·1) 962	
הַלָּזֶה	65 this (2·3) 229	
צָעִיף	veil (3·3) 858	

Chapter 25

פִּילֶגֶשׁ	6 concubine (4·37) 811	
מַתָּנֹת	gifts (1·17) 682	
בְּעוֹד	while yet (4·20) 728	
קֶדֶם	eastward (3·26) 870	
גָּוַע	8 to expire, die (6·24·24) 157	
שֵׂיבָה	old age (5·20[?]) 966	
עַם	kinsman (6·34) 769	
מְעָרָה	9 cave (11·40) 792	
תּוֹלְדֹת	12 generations (13·39) 410	
תּוֹלְדֹת	13 generations (13·39) 410	
טִירָה	16 encampment (1·7) 377	
אֻמָּה	tribe (1·3) 52	
גָּוַע	17 to expire, die (6·24·24) 157	
עַם	kinsman (6·34) 769	
תּוֹלְדֹת	19 generations (13·39) 410	
עתר	21 to pray (1·5·20) 801	
לְנֹכַח	on behalf of (2·3) 647	

11

עָקָר	barren (3·11) 785		עֵקֶב	5 because (2·15) 784
נֶעְתַּר	to be moved by entreaties (1·8·20) 801		אָרֵךְ	8 to be long (1·3·34) 73
הָרָה	to conceive (20·38·40) 247		הִשְׁקִיף	to look down (3·12·22) 1054
הִתְרֹצֵץ	22 to crush one another (1·1·19) 954		חַלּוֹן	window (2·30) 319
לְאֹם	23 people (4·35) 522		צִחֵק	to toy with, to caress (5·7·13) 850
מֵעֶה	womb (2·31) 588		אָשָׁם	10 guilt (1·46) 79
נִפְרָד	to divide (7·12·26) 825		שַׁעַר	12 measure (1·1) 1045
אמץ	to be strong (1·16·41) 54		עֲבֻדָּה	14 service [referring to body of household servants] (1·2) 850
צָעִיר	young (8·22) 859		קִנֵּא	to be envious of (3·30·34) 888
תוֹמִם	24 twins (2·6) 1060		בְּאֵר	15 well (24·38) 91
אַדְמוֹנִי	25 red, ruddy (1·3) 10		חָפַר	to dig (8·23·23) 343
אַדֶּרֶת	cloak (1·12) 12		סָתַם	to stop up (2·2·13) 711
שֵׂעָר	hair (1·28) 972		עָצַם	16 to be mighty (1·16·18) 782
עָקֵב	26 heel (3·14) 784		חָפַר	18 to dig (8·23·23) 343
צַיִד	27 hunting (12·14) 844		בְּאֵר	well (24·38) 91
תָּם	wholesome (1·15) 1070		סָתַם	to stop up (2·2·13) 711
צַיִד	28 game (12·14) 844		חָפַר	19 to dig (8·23·23) 343
הֵזִיד	29 to boil (1·8·10) 267		בְּאֵר	well (24·38) 91
נָזִיד	boiled leguminous food (2·6) 268		בְּאֵר	20 well (24·38) 91
עָיֵף	weary (2·17) 746		הִתְעַשֵּׂק	to contend (1·1·1) 796
הִלְעִיט	30 to swallow (1·1·1) 542		חָפַר	21 to dig (8·23·23) 343
אָדֹם	red (2·9) 10		בְּאֵר	well (24·38) 91
עָיֵף	weary (2·17) 746		הֶעְתִּיק	22 to move forward (2·5·9) 801
בְּכֹרָה	31 right of first born (6·10) 114		חָפַר	to dig (8·23·23) 343
בְּכֹרָה	32 right of first born (6·10) 114		בְּאֵר	well (24·38) 91
בְּכֹרָה	33 right of first born (6·10) 114		הִרְחִיב	to enlarge (1·21·25) 931
נָזִיד	34 boiled leguminous food (2·6) 268		פרה	to be fruitful (10·22·29) 826
עֲדָשָׁה	lentile (1·4) 727		בַּעֲבוּר	24 for the sake of (15·46) 721
בזה	to despise (1·31·42) 102		כָּרָה	25 to dig (2·13·14) 500
בְּכֹרָה	right of first born (6·10) 114		בְּאֵר	well (24·38) 91

Chapter 26

מִלְּבַד	1 besides (2·33) 94		מֵרֵעַ	26 companion (1·7) 946
אֵל	3 these (4·10[?]) 41		אָלָה	28 oath (3·36) 46
שְׁבוּעָה	oath (2·30) 989		מִשְׁתֶּה	30 feast (5·45) 1059
כּוֹכָב	4 star (5·37) 456		אֹדוֹת	32 cause; עַל־אֹ=because of (3·11) 15
אֵל	these (4·10[?]) 41		בְּאֵר	well (24·38) 91
			חָפַר	to dig (8·23·23) 343
			מֹרָה	35 bitterness (1·2[?]) 601

Chapter 27

זָקֵן 1 to be old (6·25·27) 278

כהה to grow dim (1·5·8) 462

זָקֵן 2 to be old (6·25·27) 278

תְּלִי 3 quiver (1·1) 1068

צוד to hunt (3·12·16) 844

צַיִד game (12·14) 844

מַטְעַמִּים 4 savory food (6·8) 381

בַּעֲבוּר in order that (15·46) 721

בְּטֶרֶם before (5·39) 382

צוד 5 to hunt (3·12·16) 844

צַיִד game (12·14) 844

צַיִד 7 game (12·14) 844

מַטְעַמִּים savory food (6·8) 381

לַאֲשֶׁר 8 to that which (4·38) 81

גְּדִי 9 kid (5·16) 152

מַטְעַמִּים savory food (6·8) 381

בַּעֲבוּר 10 in order that (15·46) 721

שָׂעִר 11 hairy (2·2) 972

חָלָק smooth (1·12) 325

אוּלַי 12 perhaps (12·45) 19

משׁשׁ to feel (2·2·8) 606

מְתַעְתֵּעַ ptc. of תעע, a mocker (1·1·2) 1073

קְלָלָה curse (2·33) 887

קְלָלָה 13 curse (2·33) 887

מַטְעַמִּים 14 savory food (6·8) 381

חֲמוּדָה 15 desirable choice (1·9) 326

קָטָן young (6·47) 881

גְּדִי 16 kid (5·16) 152

חֶלְקָה smooth part (1·2) 325

צַוָּאר neck (8·41) 848

מַטְעַמִּים 17 savory food (6·8) 381

צַיִד 19 game (12·14) 844

בַּעֲבוּר in order that (15·46) 721

הִקְרָה 20 to cause to occur (2·3·27) 899

מוש 21 to feel (1–1·4[?]) 559

משׁשׁ 22 to feel (2·6·8) 606

הִכִּיר 23 to recognize (6·37·40) 647

שָׂעִר hairy (2·2) 972

צַיִד 25 game (12·14) 844

נשׁק 26 to kiss (7·26·32) 676

נשׁק 27 to kiss (7·26·32) 676

הֵרִיחַ to smell (2·11·14) 926

טַל 28 dew (2·31) 378

שָׁמָן fat, fertile place (2·2) 1032

דָּגָן grain (2·40) 186

תִּירוֹשׁ new wine (2·38) 440

לְאֹם 29 people (4·35) 522

גְּבִיר lord (2·2) 150

צַיִד 30 hunting (12·14) 844

מַטְעַמִּים 31 savory food (6·8) 381

צַיִד game (12·14) 844

בַּעֲבוּר in order that (15·46) 721

חָרַד 33 to tremble (2·23·39) 353

חֲרָדָה trembling, fear (1·9[?]) 353

אֵפוֹא then (3·15) 66

צוד to hunt (3·12·16) 844

צַיִד game (12·14) 844

בְּטֶרֶם before (5·39) 382

צְעָקָה 34 cry of distress (3·21) 858

מַר bitter (1·38) 600

מִרְמָה 35 deceit (2·39) 941

עָקַב 36 to overreach, i.e., to supplant (1·3·3) 784

בְּכֹרָה right of firstborn (6·10) 114

אצל to reserve, withdraw (1·4·5) 69

גְּבִיר 37 lord (2·2) 150

דָּגָן grain (2·40) 186

תִּירוֹשׁ new wine (2·38) 440

סָמַךְ to support, sustain (1·41·48) 701

אֵפוֹא then (3·15) 66

שָׁמָן 39 fat, fertile place (2·2) 1032

מוֹשָׁב dwelling place (3·43) 444

טַל dew (2·31) 378

עַל above (2·7) 752

הֵרִיד 40 to show restlessness (1·2·4) 923

13

פרק	to tear away (1·4·10) 830
עֹל	yoke (1·40) 760
צַוָּאר	neck (8·41) 848
שׂטם	41 to bear a grudge against (3·6) 966
אֵבֶל	mourning (4·24) 5
קָטָן	42 young (6·47) 881
שׁכל	45 to be bereaved (3·4·24) 1013
קוץ	46 to feel a loathing (1·8·8) 880

Chapter 28

שַׁדַּי	3 Almighty (6·48) 994
הפרה	to make fruitful (5·7·29) 826
פָּגַע	11 to meet, light upon (3·40·46) 803
מְרַאֲשׁוֹת	head place (2·10) 912
חלם	12 to dream (14·26·28) 321
סֻלָּם	ladder (1·1) 700
פָּרַץ	14 to break over, increase (4·46·49) 829
קֶדֶם	eastward (3·26) 870
יקץ	16 to awake (5·11·11) 429
שֵׁנָה	sleep (2·23) 446
אָכֵן	surely, truly (1·18) 38
נוֹרָא	17 awe-inspiring (1·44) 431
מְרַאֲשׁוֹת	18 head place (2·10) 912
מַצֵּבָה	pillar (10·35) 663
אוּלָם	19 but (2·19) 19
נָדַר	20 to vow (2·30·30) 623
מַצֵּבָה	22 pillar (10·35) 663
עשׂר	to give tithe (2·5·9) 797

Chapter 29

בְּאֵר	2 well (24·38) 91
עֵדֶר	flock (10·39) 727
רָבַץ	to lie down (5·24·30) 918
עֵדֶר	3 flock (10·39) 727
גלל	to roll away (3·10·17) 164
בְּאֵר	well (24·38) 91
מֵאַיִן	4 where? whence? (2·48) 32

עֵדֶר	8 flock (10·39) 727
גלל	to roll away (3·10·17) 164
בְּאֵר	well (24·38) 91
גלל	10 to roll away (3·10·17) 164
בְּאֵר	well (24·38) 91
נָשַׁק	11 to kiss (7·26·32) 676
שֵׁמַע	13 report (1·17) 1034
חבק	to embrace (3·10·13) 287
נָשַׁק	to kiss (4·5·32) 676
חִנָּם	15 gratuitously, for nothing (1·32) 336
מַשְׂכֹּרֶת	wages (3·4) 969
קָטָן	16 young (6·47) 881
רַךְ	17 weak (3·16) 940
יָפֶה	beautiful (9·40) 421
תֹּאַר	form (4·15) 1061
קָטָן	18 young (6·47) 881
יהב	21 to give (8·27·27) 396
מִשְׁתֶּה	22 feast (5·45) 1059
רָמָה	25 to deceive (1·8·8) 941
צָעִיר	26 young (8·22) 859
בְּכִירָה	firstborn (5·6) 114
שָׁבוּעַ	27 week (2·20) 988
שָׁבוּעַ	28 week (2·20) 988
רֶחֶם	31 womb (4·33) 933
עָקָר	barren (3·11) 785
הָרָה	32 to conceive (20·38·40) 247
עֳנִי	affliction (4·36) 777
הָרָה	33 to conceive (20·38·40) 247
הָרָה	34 to conceive (20·38·40) 247
נִלְוָה	to be joined (1·11·12) 530
הָרָה	35 to conceive (20·38·40) 247

Chapter 30

קִנֵּא	1 to be envious of (3·30·34) 888
יהב	to give (8·27·27) 396
מָנַע	2 to withhold (1·25·29) 586
בֶּרֶךְ	3 knee (3·25) 139
הָרָה	5 to conceive (20·38·40) 247

דִּין	6 to execute vindication (4·23·24[?]) 192	
הָרָה	7 to conceive (20·38·40) 247	
נַפְתּוּלִים	8 wrestlings (1·1) 836	
נפתל	to wrestle (1·3·5) 836	
גָּד	11 good fortune (1·2) 151	
אֹשֶׁר	13 happiness (1·1) 81	
אשר	to call blessed (1·7·9) 80	
קָצִיר	14 time of harvest (3·49) 894	
חִטָּה	wheat (1·30) 334	
דּוּדַי	mandrake (5·6) 188	
דּוּדַי	15 mandrake (5·6) 188	
שָׂכַר	16 to hire (2·17·20) 968	
דּוּדַי	mandrake (5·6) 188	
הָרָה	17 to conceive (20·38·40) 247	
שָׂכָר	18 wages (7·28) 969	
הָרָה	19 to conceive (20·38·40) 247	
זבד	20 to endow (1·1·1) 256	
זֶבֶד	gift (1·1) 256	
זבל	prob. to exalt, honor (1·1·1) 259	
רֶחֶם	22 womb (4·33) 933	
הָרָה	23 to conceive (20·38·40) 247	
נָחֵשׁ	27 to observe signs (3·9·9) 638	
בִּגְלַל	on account of (3·10) 164	
נקב	28 to designate (1·13·19[?]) 666	
שָׂכָר	wages (7·28) 969	
פָּרַץ	30 to break over, increase (4·46·49) 829	
מָתַי	when? (1·42) 607	
מְאוּמָה	31 anything (6·32) 548	
שֶׂה	32 a sheep (4·44) 961	
נָקֹד	speckled (8·8) 666	
טָלוּא	spotted (6·7) 378	
חוּם	dark brown, black (4·4) 299	
כֶּשֶׂב	lamb (4·13) 461	
שָׂכָר	wages (7·28) 969	
שָׂכָר	33 wages (7·28) 969	
נָקֹד	speckled (8·8) 666	

טָלוּא	spotted (6·7) 378	
חוּם	dark brown, black (4·4) 299	
כֶּשֶׂב	lamb (4·13) 461	
גנב	to steal (9·30·38) 170	
לוּ	34 if only (4·19) 530	
תַּיִשׁ	35 he-goat (2·4) 1066	
עָקֹד	striped (7·7) 758	
טָלוּא	spotted (6·7) 378	
נָקֹד	speckled (8·8) 666	
לָבָן	white (3·28) 526	
חוּם	dark brown, black (4·4) 299	
כֶּשֶׂב	lamb (4·13) 461	
מַקֵּל	37 rod (7·18) 596	
לִבְנֶה	poplar (1·2) 527	
לַח	fresh (1·6) 535	
לוּז	almond wood (1·1) 531	
עַרְמוֹן	plane-tree (1·2) 790	
פָּצֵל	to peel (2·2·2) 822	
פְּצָלוֹת	peeled spot, stripe (1·1) 822	
לָבָן	white (3·28) 526	
מַחְשֹׂף	a laying-bare (1·1) 362	
הִצִּיג	38 to set (4·15·16) 426	
מַקֵּל	rod (7·18) 596	
פָּצֵל	to peel (2·2·2) 822	
רַהַט	trough (2·4) 923	
שֹׁקֶת	watering trough (2·2) 1052	
לְנֹכַח	in front of (2·3) 647	
יחם	to be ruttish (2·2·6) 404	
יחם	39 to be ruttish (2·2·6) 404	
מַקֵּל	rod (7·18) 596	
עָקֹד	striped (7·7) 758	
נָקֹד	speckled (8·8) 666	
טָלוּא	spotted (6·7) 378	
כֶּשֶׂב	40 lamb (4·13) 461	
הִפְרִיד	to divide (1·7·26) 825	
עָקֹד	striped (7·7) 758	
חוּם	dark brown, black (4·4) 299	
עֵדֶר	flock (10·39) 727	

יחם 41 to be ruttish (3·4·6) 404

מְקֻשָּׁרוֹת Pu. ptc. of קשׁר, vigorous (1·1·44) 905

מַקֵּל rod (7·18) 596

רַהַט trough (2·4) 923

יחם to be ruttish (3·4·6) 404

הַעֲטִיף 42 to show feebleness (1·1·11) 742

עֲטוּף feeble (1·2) 742

קָשׁוּר vigorous (1·1[?]) 905

פָּרַץ 43 to increase (4·46·49) 829

Chapter 31

מֵאֲשֶׁר 1 from that which (1·17) 84

תְּמוֹל 2 yesterday; ת׳=שׁלשׁום =formerly (2·22) 1069

שִׁלְשׁוֹם three days ago (2·25) 1026

מוֹלֶדֶת 3 kindred (9·22) 409

תְּמֹל 5 yesterday; ת׳=שׁלשׁום =formerly (2·22) 1069

שִׁלְשׁוֹם three days ago (2·25) 1026

הָתֶל 7 to mock, trifle with (1·7·8) 1068

הֶחֱלִיף to change (1·2·26) 322

מַשְׂכֹּרֶת wages (3·4) 969

מֹנֶה time, counted number (2·2) 584

נָקֹד 8 speckled (8·8) 666

שָׂכָר wages (7·28) 969

עָקֹד striped (7·7) 758

יחם 10 to be ruttish (3·4·6) 404

עַתּוּד he-goat (2·29) 800

עָקֹד striped (7·7) 758

נָקֹד speckled (8·8) 666

בָּרֹד spotted (2·4) 136

עַתּוּד 12 he-goat (2·29) 800

עָקֹד striped (7·7) 758

נָקֹד speckled (8·8) 666

בָּרֹד spotted (2·4) 136

מַצֵּבָה 13 pillar (10·35) 663

נָדַר to vow (2·30·30) 623

מוֹלֶדֶת kindred (9·22) 409

נָכְרִי 15 foreign (1·45) 648

עשֶׁר 16 riches (1·37) 799

נָהַג 18 to drive (1·20·30) 624

רְכוּשׁ property (11·28) 940

רָכַשׁ to gather [property] (5·5·5) 940

קִנְיָן thing acquired (3·9) 889

גזז 19 to shear (3·14·15) 159

גנב to steal (9·30·38) 170

תְּרָפִים idols (3·15) 1076

גנב 20 to steal (9·30·38) 170

בְּלִי not (1·23) 115

הִשִּׂיג 25 to overtake (4·49·49) 673

גנב 26 to steal (9·30·38) 170

נָהַג to drive away (1·10·30) 624

שָׁבָה to take captive (2·29·37) 985

נֶחְבָּא 27 to be hidden (2·16·34) 285

גנב to steal (9·30·38) 170

תֹּף timbrel (1·17) 1074

כִּנּוֹר lyre (2·41) 490

נָטַשׁ 28 to let (1·33·40) 643

נשׁק to kiss (4·5·32) 676

הִשְׂכִּיל to do foolishly (1·2·8) 698

אֵל 29 power (1·5) 43

אֶמֶשׁ yesterday (3·5) 57

נכסף 30 to long for (2·4·6) 493

גנב to steal (9·30·38) 170

גָּזַל 31 to seize, rob (2·29·30) 159

הִכִּיר 32 to identify (8·37·40) 647

גנב to steal (9·30·38) 170

תְּרָפִים 34 idols (3·15) 1076

כַּר basket saddle (1·1) 468

משׁשׁ to feel (2·6·8[?]) 606

חפשׁ 35 to search (2·8·23) 344

תְּרָפִים idols (3·15) 1076

דלק 36 to hotly pursue (1·7·9) 196

משש	37 to feel (2·6·8[?]) 606	
רָחֵל	38 ewe (2·4) 932	
שכל	to miscarry (2·18·24) 1013	
טְרֵפָה	39 animal torn (1·9) 383	
גנב	to steal (9·30·38) 170	
חֹרֶב	40 parching heat (1·16) 351	
קֶרַח	frost (1·7) 901	
נדד	to flee (1·20·24) 622	
שֵׁנָה	sleep (2·23) 446	
הֶחֱלִיף	41 to change (1·2·26) 322	
מַשְׂכֹּרֶת	wages (3·4) 969	
מֹנֶה	time, counted number (2·2) 584	
לוּלֵי	42 unless (1·10) 530	
פַּחַד	dread (2·49) 808	
רֵיקָם	empty [handed] (1·16) 938	
עֳנִי	affliction (4·36) 777	
יְגִיעַ	toil (1·16) 388	
אֶמֶשׁ	yesterday (3·5) 57	
מַצֵּבָה	45 pillar (10·35) 663	
לקט	46 to gather (1·14·36) 544	
גַּל	heap (9·20) 164	
יְגַר	47 Aram. [stone] heap (1·1) 1094	
שָׂהֲדוּ	Aram. testimony (1·1) 1113	
גַּל, גַּלְעֵד	heap; גַּלְעֵד=heap of witness (9·20) 164	
גַּל	48 heap (9·20) 164	
צפה	49 to keep watch (1·9·18) 859	
גַּל	51 heap (9·20) 164	
מַצֵּבָה	pillar (10·35) 663	
גַּל	52 heap (9·20) 164	
עֵדָה	witness (2·3) 729	
מַצֵּבָה	pillar (10·35) 663	
פַּחַד	53 dread (2·49) 808	

Chapter 32

נשק	1 to kiss (4·5·32) 676
פָּגַע	2 to meet (3·40·46) 803
אחר	5 to tarry (1·1·17) 29

חצה	8 to divide (2·11·15) 345
פְּלֵיטָה	9 escaped remnant (2·28) 812
מוֹלֶדֶת	10 kindred (9·22) 409
קטן	11 to be insignificant (1·3·4) 881
מַקֵּל	staff (7·11) 596
חוֹל	13 sand (3·22) 297
תַּיִשׁ	15 he-goat (2·4) 1066
רָחֵל	ewe (2·4) 932
הֵינִיק	16 to give suck to (2·10·18) 413
פָּרָה	cow (12·26) 831
אָתוֹן	she-ass (4·35) 87
עַיִר	male ass (2·9) 747
עֵדֶר	17 herd (10·39) 727
רֶוַח	space, interval (1·2) 926
פגש	18 to meet (2·10·14) 803
לְמִי	to whom, whose (3·20) 566
אָנָה	whither? where? (3·39) 33
עֵדֶר	20 herd (10·39) 727
אוּלַי	21 perhaps (12·45) 19
מַעֲבַר	23 ford (1·3) 721
נאבק	25 to wrestle (2·2·2) 7
שַׁחַר	dawn (3·23) 1007
יָרֵךְ	26 thigh (9·34) 437
יקע	to be dislocated (1·4·8) 429
נאבק	to wrestle (2·2·2) 7
שַׁחַר	27 dawn (3·23) 1007
שָׂרָה	29 to persist, exert onesel (1·2) 975
זרח	32 to rise, come forth (1·18·18) 280
צלע	to limp (1·4) 854
יָרֵךְ	thigh (9·34) 437
גִּיד	33 sinew (2·7) 161
נָשֶׁה	thigh-vein (2·2) 674
יָרֵךְ	thigh (9·34) 437

Chapter 33

חצה	1 to divide (2·11·15) 345
חבק	4 to embrace (3·10·13) 287
צַוָּאר	neck (8·41) 848

נָשַׁק to kiss (7·26·32) 676

פָּגַשׁ 8 to meet (2·10·14) 803

פָּצַר 11 to urge (3·6·7) 823

לְנֶגֶד 12 before (1·32) 617

רַךְ 13 tender (3·16) 940

עוּל to nurse (1·5·5) 732

דָּפַק to beat (1·2·3) 200

הִתְנַהֵל 14 to journey by stages (1·1·10) 624

אַט gently (1·5) 31

הִצִּיג 15 to place (4·15·16) 426

סֻכָּה 17 booth (1·31) 697

שָׁלֵם 18 safe (3·28) 1023

חֶלְקָה 19 portion [of ground] (1·24) 324

קְשִׂיטָה unit of weight [dub.] (1·3) 903

Chapter 34

הֶחֱרִישׁ 5 to be silent (2·38·46) 361

הִתְעַצֵּב 7 to be vexed, grieved (2·2·15) 780

נְבָלָה disgraceful folly (1·13) 615

חָשַׁק 8 to love (1·8·11) 365

הִתְחַתֵּן 9 to form a marriage alliance with (1·11·11) 368

רחס 10 to go about (3·4·5) 695

מֹהַר 12 purchase price (1·3) 555

מַתָּן gift[s] (1·5) 682

מִרְמָה 13 deceit (2·39) 941

עָרְלָה 14 foreskin (6·16) 790

בְּזֹאת 15 with this = on these conditions (4·15) 260

נֵאוֹת to consent (3·4·4) 22

נִמּוֹל to be circumcised (13·17·29) 557

נִמּוֹל 17 to be circumcised (13·17·29) 557

אַחַר 19 to delay, tarry (2·15·17) 29

שָׁלֵם 21 at peace (3·28) 1023

סָחַר to go about (3·4·5) 695

רָחָב wide, broad (1·21) 932

בְּזֹאת 22 with this = on these conditions (4·15) 260

נֵאוֹת to consent (3·4·4) 22

נִמּוֹל to be circumcised (13·17·29) 557

קִנְיָן 23 acquired thing (3·9) 889

נֵאוֹת to consent (3·4·4) 22

נִמּוֹל 24 to be circumcised (13·17·29) 557

כָּאַב 25 to be in pain (1·4·8) 456

בֶּטַח securely (1·43) 105

בזז 27 to plunder (2·37·40) 102

טַף 29 children (8·41) 381

שָׁבָה to take captive (2·29·37) 985

בזז to plunder (2·37·40) 102

עָכַר 30 to trouble (1·12·14) 747

הִבְאִישׁ to cause to stink (1·7·16) 92

מַת man (1·21) 607

זוֹנָה 31 harlot (2·33[?]) 275

Chapter 35

נֵכָר 2 foreignness (4·36) 648

הֶחֱלִיף to change (1·2·26) 322

שִׂמְלָה mantle, garment (7·29) 971

נֵכָר 4 foreignness (4·36) 648

נֶזֶם ring (4·17) 633

טָמַן to hide (i·28·31) 380

אֵלָה terebinth [tree] (1·17) 18

חִתָּה 5 terror (1·1) 369

מֵינֶקֶת 8 nurse (2·5) 413

אַלּוֹן oak [tree] (2·9) 47

בָּכוּת weeping (1·1) 113

שַׁדַּי 11 Almighty (6·48) 994

פרה to be fruitful (10·22·29) 826

חָלָץ loins (1·10) 323

מַצֵּבָה 14 pillar (10·35) 663

הִסִּיךְ to pour out (1·13·24) 650

כִּבְרָה 16 distance (2·3) 460

קָשָׁה	to make hard, severe (1 · 1 · 28) 904
הִקְשָׁה	17 to make difficult (1 · 21 · 28) 904
מְיַלֶּדֶת	midwife (2 · 9) 408
מַצֵּבָה	20 pillar (10 · 35) 663
קְבוּרָה	grave (3 · 14) 869
מֵהָלְאָה	21 beyond (1 · 3) 229
פִּילֶגֶשׁ	22 concubine (4 · 37) 811
גָּוַע	29 to die, expire (6 · 24 · 24) 157
עַם	kinsman (6 · 34) 769
שָׂבֵעַ	satisified (2 · 10) 960

Chapter 36

תּוֹלְדוֹת	1 generations (13 · 39) 410
קִנְיָן	6 acquired thing (3 · 9) 889
רָכַשׁ	to gather [property] (5 · 5 · 5) 940
רְכוּשׁ	7 property (11 · 28) 940
תּוֹלְדוֹת	9 generations (13 · 39) 410
פִּילֶגֶשׁ	12 concubine (4 · 37) 811
יֵמִם	24 hot springs (1 · 1) 411
מוֹשָׁב	43 dwelling place (3 · 44) 444

Chapter 37

מְגוּרִים	1 sojourning (6 · 11) 158
תּוֹלְדוֹת	2 generations (13 · 39) 410
דִּבָּה	evil report (1 · 9) 179
זְקֻנִים	3 old age (4 · 4) 279
כְּתֹנֶת	tunic (9 · 30) 509
פַּס	flat of hand or foot; כְּתֹנֶת פַּסִּים = floor length, long sleeved tunic (3 · 5) 821
חָלַם	5 to dream (14 · 26 · 28[?]) 321
חָלַם	6 to dream (14 · 26 · 28[?]) 321
אָלַם	7 to bind (1 · 1 · 9) 47
אֲלֻמָּה	sheaf (4 · 5) 48
חָלַם	9 to dream (14 · 26 · 28[?]) 321
יָרֵחַ	moon (1 · 27) 437
כּוֹכָב	star (5 · 37) 456
גָעַר	10 to rebuke (1 · 14 · 14) 172

חָלַם	to dream (14 · 26 · 28[?]) 321
קָנָא	11 to be envious of (3 · 30 · 34) 888
תָּעָה	15 to wander about (2 · 26 · 49) 1073
אֵיפֹה	16 where? (1 · 10) 33
בְּטֶרֶם	18 before (5 · 39) 382
הִתְנַכֵּל	to deal knavishly (1 · 2 · 4) 647
הַלָּזֶה	19 this (2 · 3) 229
הִפְשִׁיט	23 to strip (1 · 15 · 43) 832
כְּתֹנֶת	tunic (9 · 30) 509
פַּס	flat of hand or foot, cf. v.3 (3 · 5) 821
רֵיק	24 empty (2 · 14) 938
אֹרְחָה	25 caravan (1 · 3[?]) 73
נְכֹאת	spice (2 · 2) 644
צְרִי	a kind of balsam (2 · 6) 863
לֹט	myrrh (2 · 2) 538
בֶּצַע	26 [selfish] profit (1 · 23) 130
סֹחֵר	28 trader (2 · 16) 695
מָשַׁךְ	to draw out (1 · 30 · 36) 604
אָנָה	30 whither? where? (3 · 39) 33
כְּתֹנֶת	31 tunic (9 · 30) 509
טָבַל	to dip (1 · 15 · 16) 371
כְּתֹנֶת	32 tunic (9 · 30) 509
פַּס	flat of hand or foot, cf. v.3 (3 · 5) 821
הִכִּיר	to observe (8 · 37 · 40) 647
הִכִּיר	33 to observe (8 · 37 · 40) 647
כְּתֹנֶת	tunic (9 · 30) 509
טָרַף	to tear (3 · 13 · 24) 382
טֹרֵף	to be torn (2 · 2 · 24) 382
שִׂמְלָה	34 clothes (7 · 29) 971
שַׂק	sack cloth (5 · 48) 974
מָתְנַיִם	loins (1 · 50) 608
הִתְאַבֵּל	to mourn (1 · 19 · 38) 5
מֵאֵן	35 to refuse (3 · 45 · 45) 549
אָבֵל	mourning (1 · 8) 5
סָרִיס	36 eunuch (4 · 45) 710
טַבָּח	guardsman (6 · 32) 371

Chapter 38

הָרָה	3	to conceive (20·38·40) 247
הָרָה	4	to conceive (20·38·40) 247
יבם	8	to do the duty of a husband's brother (2·3·3) 386
כַּלָּה	11	daughter-in-law (4·34) 483
גזז	12	to shear (3·14·15) 159
חָם	13	father-in-law (2·4) 327
גזז		to shear (3·14·15) 159
אַלְמָנוּת	14	widowhood (2·4) 48
צָעִיף		shawl, veil (3·3) 858
הִתְעַלֵּף		to enwrap oneself (1·3·5) 763
זוֹנָה	15	harlot (2·33[?]) 275
יהב	16	to come now (8·23·27) 396
כַּלָּה		daughter-in-law (4·34) 483
גְּדִי	17	kid (5·16) 152
עֵרָבוֹן		pledge (3·3) 786
עֵרָבוֹן	18	pledge (3·3) 786
חֹתָם		signet ring (1·13) 368
פָּתִיל		cord (2·11) 836
הָרָה		to conceive (20·38·40) 247
צָעִיף	19	wrapper, veil (3·3) 858
אַלְמָנוּת		widowhood (2·4) 48
גְּדִי	20	kid (5·16) 152
עֵרָבוֹן		pledge (3·3) 786
אַיֵּה	21	where? (4·44) 32
קָדֵשׁ		temple prostitute (3·11) 873
בָּזֶה		in this [place], here (3·19) 260
בָּזֶה	22	in this [place], here (3·19) 260
קָדֵשׁ		temple prostitute (3·11) 873
בּוּז	23	object of contempt (1·11) 100
גְּדִי		kid (5·16) 152
כַּלָּה	24	daughter-in-law (4·34) 483
הָרָה		to conceive (20·38·40) 247
זְנוּנִים		fornication (1·11) 276
חָם	25	father-in-law (2·4) 327
הָרָה		to conceive (20·38·40) 247

הִכִּיר		to regard, observe (8·37·40) 647
לְמִי		to whom, whose (3·20) 566
חֹתֶמֶת		signet ring (1·1) 368
פָּתִיל		cord (2·11) 836
הִכִּיר	26	to regard, observe (8·37·40) 647
צדק		to be in the right (1·22·41) 842
תְּאוֹמִים	27	twins (2·6) 1060
מְיַלֶּדֶת	28	midwife (2·9) 408
קָשַׁר		to bind (3·35·44) 905
שָׁנִי		scarlet [thread] (2·42) 1040
פָּרַץ	29	to break out (4·46·49) 829
פֶּרֶץ		a bursting forth (1·18) 829
שָׁנִי	30	scarlet [thread] (2·42) 1040

Chapter 39

סָרִיס	1	eunuch (4·45) 710
טַבָּח		guardsman (6·32) 371
מֵאָז	5	since (1·18) 23
בִּגְלַל		on account of (3·10) 164
מְאוּמָה	6	anything (6·32) 548
יָפֶה		beautiful (9·40) 421
תֹּאַר		form (4·15) 1061
מאן	8	to refuse (3·45·45) 549
חָשַׂךְ	9	to withhold (4·26·28) 362
מְאוּמָה		anything (6·32) 548
בַּאֲשֶׁר		inasmuch as (3·19) 84
צחק	14	to make a toy of (5·7·13) 850
צחק	17	to make a toy of (5·7·13) 850
סֹהַר	20	roundness (8·8) 690
אָסִיר		prisoner (3·18) 64
סֹהַר	21	roundness (8·8) 690
סֹהַר	22	roundness (8·8) 690
אָסִיר		prisoner (3·18) 64
סֹהַר	23	roundness (8·8) 690
מְאוּמָה		anything (6·32) 548
בַּאֲשֶׁר		inasmuch as (3·19) 84

20

Chapter 40

מַשְׁקֶ	1 cupbearer (11[?]·19[?]) 1052
אֹפֶה	baker (8·12[?]) 66
קָצַף	2 to be wroth (2·28·34) 893
סָרִיס	eunuch (4·45) 710
מַשְׁקֶ	cupbearer (11[?]·19[?]) 1052
אֹפֶה	baker (8·12[?]) 66
מִשְׁמָ	3 prison (6·20) 1038
טַבָּח	guardsman (6·32) 371
סֹהַר	roundness (8·8) 690
טַבָּח	4 guardsman (6·32) 371
מִשְׁמָ	prison (6·20) 1038
חָלַם	5 to dream (14·26·28[?]) 321
פִּתְרֹ	interpretation (5·5) 837
מַשְׁקֶ	cupbearer (11[?]·19[?]) 1052
אֹפֶה	baker (8·12[?]) 66
סֹהַר	roundness (8·8) 690
זָעַף	6 to be out of humor (1·1·4) 277
סָרִיס	7 eunuch (4·45) 710
מִשְׁמָ	prison (6·20) 1038
חָלַם	8 to dream (14·26·28[?]) 321
פָּתַר	to interpret (9·9·9) 837
פִּתְרֹ	interpretation (5·5) 837
מַשְׁקֶ	9 cupbearer (11[?]·19[?]) 1052
שָׂרִי	10 twig (2·3) 974
פָּרַח	to bud (1·29·34) 827
נִצָּה	blossom (1·4) 665
הִבְשִׁ	to be ripened (1·1·27) 143
אֶשְׁכֹּ	cluster (1·9) 79
עֵנָב	grape[s] (3·19) 772
כּוֹס	11 cup (5·31) 468
עֵנָב	grape[s] (3·19) 772
שָׂחַט	to squeeze out (1·1·1) 965
פִּתְרֹ	12 interpretation (5·5) 837
שָׂרִי	twig (2·3) 974
בְּעוֹד	13 within yet (4·20) 728
כֵּן	office (2·7) 487

כּוֹס	cup (5·31) 468
מַשְׁקֶה	cupbearer (11[?]·19[?]) 1052
גָּנַב	15 to be stolen away (2·4·39) 170
פֹּה	here, hither (3·44) 805
מְאוּמָה	anything (6·32) 548
אֹפֶה	16 baker (8·12[?]) 66
פָּתַר	to interpret (9·9·9) 837
סַל	basket (4·15) 700
חֹרִי	white bread (1·1) 301
סַל	17 basket (4·15) 700
מַאֲכָל	food (4·30) 38
אֹפֶה	baker (8·12[?]) 66
פִּתְרוֹן	18 interpretation (5·5) 837
סַל	basket (4·15) 700
בְּעוֹד	19 within yet (4·20) 728
תָּלָה	to hang (3·23·27) 1067
מִשְׁתֶּה	20 feast (5·45) 1059
מַשְׁקֶה	cupbearer (11[?]·19[?]) 1052
אֹפֶה	baker (8·12[?]) 66
מַשְׁקֶה	21 cupbearer (11[?]·19[?]) 1052
כּוֹס	cup (5·31) 468
אֹפֶה	22 baker (8·12[?]) 66
תָּלָה	to hang (3·23·27) 1067
פָּתַר	to interpret (9·9·9) 837
מַשְׁקֶה	23 cupbearer (11[?]·19[?]) 1052

Chapter 41

חָלַם	1 to dream (14·26·28) 321
פָּרָה	2 cow (12·26) 831
יָפֶה	fair (9·40) 421
בָּרִיא	fat (6·14) 135
אָחוּ	reeds (2·3) 28
פָּרָה	3 cow (12·26) 831
דַּק	thin (6·14) 201
פָּרָה	4 cow (12·26) 831
דַּק	thin (6·14) 201
יָפֶה	fair (9·40) 421
בָּרִיא	fat (6·14) 135

Gen 41:4–41:35

יקץ	to awake (5·11·11) 429	תֹּאַר	form (4·15) 1061
ישן	5 to sleep (2·24·25) 445	אָחוּ	reeds (2·3) 28
חָלַם	to dream (14·26·28) 321	פָּרָה	19 cow (12·26) 831
שִׁבֹּלֶת	ear of grain (10·20[?]) 987	דַּל	weak, thin (1·48) 195
בָּרִיא	fat (6·14) 135	תֹּאַר	form (4·15) 1061
שִׁבֹּלֶת	6 ear of grain (10·20[?]) 987	רַק	thin (3·3) 956
דַּק	thin (6·14) 201	רֹעַ	badness (1·19) 947
שָׁדַף	to scorch (3·3·3) 995	פָּרָה	20 cow (12·26) 831
צָמַח	to sprout (3·15·33) 855	רַק	thin (3·3) 956
שִׁבֹּלֶת	7 ear of grain (10·20[?]) 987	בָּרִיא	fat (6·14) 135
דַּק	thin (6·14) 201	תְּחִלָּה	21 beginning (4·22) 321
בָּרִיא	fat (6·14) 135	יקץ	to awake (5·11·11) 429
יקץ	to awake (5·11·11) 429	שִׁבֹּלֶת	22 ear of grain (10·20[?]) 987
נפעם	8 to be disturbed (1·3·5) 821	שִׁבֹּלֶת	23 ear of grain (10·20[?]) 987
חַרְטֹם	magician (2·11) 355	צְנֻמוֹת	Qal ptc. pass. = dried up, hardened
פָּתַר	to interpret (9·9·9) 837		(1·1·1) 856
מַשְׁקֶה	9 cupbearer (11[?]·19[?]) 1052	דַּק	thin (6·14) 201
חֵטְא	sin (1·33) 307	שָׁדַף	to scorch (3·3·3) 995
קָצַף	10 to be wroth (2·28·34) 893	צָמַח	to sprout (3·15·33) 855
מִשְׁמָר	prison (6·20) 1038	שִׁבֹּלֶת	24 ear of grain (10·20[?]) 987
טַבָּח	guardsman (6·32) 371	דַּק	thin (6·14) 201
אֹפֶה	baker (8·12[?]) 66	חַרְטֹם	magician (2·11) 355
חָלַם	11 to dream (14·26·28) 321	פָּרָה	26 cow (12·26) 831
פִּתְרוֹן	interpretation (5·5) 837	שִׁבֹּלֶת	ear of grain (10·20[?]) 987
טַבָּח	12 guardsman (6·32) 371	פָּרָה	27 cow (12·26) 831
פָּתַר	to interpret (9·9·9) 837	רַק	thin (3·3) 956
פָּתַר	13 to interpret (9·9·9) 837	שִׁבֹּלֶת	ear of grain (10·20[?]) 987
כֵּן	office (2·7) 487	רֵיק	empty (2·14) 938
תָּלָה	to hang (3·23·27) 1067	שָׁדַף	to scorch (3·3·3) 995
גלח	14 to shave oneself (1·18·23) 164	שָׂבָע	29 plenty (6·8) 960
חלף	to change (1·2·26) 322	שָׂבָע	30 plenty (6·8) 960
שִׂמְלָה	clothes (7·29) 971	שָׂבָע	31 plenty (6·8) 960
חָלַם	15 to dream (14·26·28) 321	כָּבֵד	grievous (9·39) 458
פָּתַר	to interpret (9·9·9) 837	נשנה	32 to be repeated (1·1·26[?]) 1040
בִּלְעָדַי	16 not to me! i.e., not at all! (3·5) 116	פָּקִיד	34 overseer (1·13) 824
פָּרָה	18 cow (12·26) 831	חמש	to take a fifth part of (1·1·5[?]) 332
בָּרִיא	fat (6·14) 135	שָׂבָע	plenty (6·8) 960
יָפֶה	fair, beautiful (9·40) 421	אֹכֶל	35 food (16·44) 38

22

צָבַר — to heap up (2·7·7) 840

בַּר — grain (5·14) 141

אֹכֶל — 36 food (16·44) 38

פִּקָּדוֹן — store (1·2) 824

כָּזֶה — 38 such (1·6) 262

נָשַׁק — 40 to kiss (7·26·32) 676

טַבַּעַת — 42 signet ring (1·44) 371

שֵׁשׁ — linen (1·38) 1058

רָבִיד — ornament for neck, necklace (1·2) 914

צַוָּאר — neck (8·41) 848

מֶרְכָּבָה — 43 chariot (2·44) 939

מִשְׁנֶה — second (3·35) 1041

אַבְרֵךְ — prostrate yourself! bow down! [dub.] (1·1) 7

בִּלְעֲדֵי — 44 apart from, without (3·5) 116

שָׂבָע — 47 plenty (6·8) 960

קֹמֶץ — handfuls (1·4) 888

אֹכֶל — 48 food (16·44) 38

צָבַר — 49 to heap up (2·7·7) 840

בַּר — grain (5·14) 141

חוֹל — sand (3·22) 292

בְּטֶרֶם — 50 before (5·39) 382

נשׁה — 51 to make to forget (1·1·5) 674

הפרה — 52 to make fruitful (5·7·29) 826

עֳנִי — affliction (4·36) 777

שָׂבָע — 53 plenty (6·8) 960

רָעֵב — 55 to be hungry (1·12·14) 944

שׁבר — 56 to buy grain (13·16·21) 991

שׁבר — 57 to buy grain (13·16·21) 991

Chapter 42

שֶׁבֶר — 1 grain (7·9) 991

שֶׁבֶר — 2 grain (7·9) 991

שׁבר — to buy grain (13·16·21) 991

שׁבר — 3 to buy grain (13·16·21) 991

בַּר — grain (5·14) 141

אָסוֹן — 4 mischief, evil (3·5) 62

שׁבר — 5 to buy grain (13·16·21) 991

שַׁלִּיט — 6 ruler (1·4) 1020

השׁבר — to sell grain (1·5·21) 991

הִכִּיר — 7 to recognize (8·37·40) 647

התנכר — to disguise oneself (1·2·40) 647

קָשֶׁה — hard, severe (2·36) 904

מֵאַיִן — where? whence? (2·48) 32

שׁבר — to buy grain (13·16·21) 991

אֹכֶל — food (16·44) 38

הִכִּיר — 8 to recognize (8·37·40) 647

חָלַם — 9 to dream (14·26·28) 321

מְרַגְּלִים — spies (6·10) 920

שׁבר — 10 to buy grain (13·16·21) 991

אֹכֶל — food (16·44) 38

כֵּן — 11 honest (5·23) 467

מְרַגְּלִים — spies (6·10) 920

מְרַגְּלִים — 14 spies (6·10) 920

בְּזֹאת — 15 by, through this (4·15) 260

נבחן — to be tried, proved (2·3·28) 103

הֵנָּה — hither (8·49) 244

נבחן — 16 to be tried, proved (2·3·28) 103

מְרַגְּלִים — spies (6·10) 920

מִשְׁמָר — 17 prison (6·20) 1038

כֵּן — 19 honest (5·23) 467

מִשְׁמָר — prison (6·20) 1038

שֶׁבֶר — grain (7·9) 991

רְעָבוֹן — famine (2·3) 944

אֲבָל — 21 of a truth, verily (2·11) 6

אָשֵׁם — guilty (1·3) 79

הליץ — 23 ptc.=interpreter (1·9·12) 539

בַּר — 25 grain (5·14) 141

שַׂק — sack (5·48) 974

צֵידָה — provision (2·9) 845

שֶׁבֶר — 26 grain (7·9) 991

שַׂק — 27 sack (5·48) 974

מִסְפּוֹא — fodder (4·5) 704

מָלוֹן — lodging-place (2·8) 533

אַמְתַּחַת — sack (15·15) 607

23

אַמְתַּחַת 28 sack (15·15) 607

חָרַד to tremble (2·23·39) 353

קָרָה 29 to befall (2·13·27) 899

קָשֶׁה 30 hard, severe (2·36) 904

רגל to go about as a spy (1·14·16) 920

כֵּן 31 honest (5·23) 467

מְרַגְּלִים spies (6·10) 920

בְּזֹאת 33 by, through this (4·15) 260

כֵּן honest (5·23) 467

רְעָבוֹן famine (2·3) 944

מְרַגְּלִים 34 spies (6·10) 920

כֵּן honest (5·23) 467

סחר to go about (3·4·5) 695

הריק 35 to empty out (2·17·19) 937

שַׂק sack (5·48) 974

צְרוֹר bundle (2·7) 865

שׁכל 36 to make childless (2·18·24) 1013

אָסוֹן 38 mischief, evil (3·5) 62

שֵׂיבָה grey hair (5·20[?]) 966

יָגוֹן sorrow (2·14) 387

Chapter 43

כָּבֵד 1 grievous (9·39) 458

שֶׁבֶר 2 grain (7·9) 991

שׁבר to buy grain (13·16·21) 991

אֹכֶל food (16·44) 38

הֵעִיד 3 to warn (2·40·45) 729

בִּלְתִּי except (4·24) 116

שׁבר 4 to buy grain (13·16·21) 991

אֹכֶל food (16·44) 38

בִּלְתִּי 5 except (4·24) 116

מוֹלֶדֶת 7 kindred (9·22) 409

טַף 8 children (8·41) 381

ערב 9 to be surety (2·15·17) 786

הִצִּיג to set (4·15·16) 426

לוּלֵא 10 unless (1·4) 530

הִתְמַהְמֵהַּ to linger (2·9·9) 554

אֵפוֹא 11 then (3·15) 66

זִמְרָה choice products (1·4[?]) 275

צֳרִי a kind of balsam (2·6) 863

נְכֹאת a spice (2·2) 644

לֹט myrrh (2·2) 538

בָּטְנִים pistachio nuts (1·1) 106

שָׁקֵד almond (1·4) 1052

מִשְׁנֶה 12 double (3·35) 1041

אַמְתַּחַת sack (15·15) 607

אוּלַי perhaps (12·45) 19

מִשְׁגֶּה mistake (1·1) 993

שַׁדַּי 14 Almighty (6·48) 994

רַחֲמִים compassion (2·38) 933

שכל to be bereaved (3·4·24) 1013

מִשְׁנֶה 15 double (3·35) 1041

לַאֲשֶׁר 16 to him who (4·38) 81

טבח to slaughter (1·11·11) 370

טֶבַח slaughter (1·12) 370

צָהֳרַיִם midday, noon (2·23) 843

אַמְתַּחַת 18 sack (15·15) 607

תְּחִלָּה beginning (4·22) 321

הִתְגַּלְגֵּל to roll oneself (1·2·17) 164

בִּי 20 I pray, excuse me (2·12) 106

תְּחִלָּה beginning (4·22) 321

שׁבר to buy grain (13·16·21) 991

אֹכֶל food (16·44) 38

מָלוֹן 21 lodging-place (2·8) 533

אַמְתַּחַת sack (15·15) 607

מִשְׁקָל weight (3·49) 1054

שׁבר 22 to buy grain (13·16·21) 991

אֹכֶל food (16·44) 38

אַמְתַּחַת sack (15·15) 607

מַטְמוֹן 23 treasure (1·5) 380

אַמְתַּחַת sack (15·15) 607

מִסְפּוֹא 24 fodder (4·5) 704

צָהֳרַיִם 25 midday, noon (2·23) 843

קדד 28 to bow down (3·15·15) 869

נכמר 30 to grow tender (1·4·4) 485

רַחֲמִים compassion (2·38) 933

חֶדֶר chamber, room (1·34) 293

הִתְאַפֵּק 31 to restrain oneself (2·7·7) 67

בְּכֹרָה 33 right of first-born (6·10) 114

צָעִיר young (8·22) 859

צְעִירָה youth (1·2) 859

תמה to look in astonishment (1·8·9) 1069

מַשְׂאֵת 34 portion (3·16) 673

שכר to become drunken (2·9·20) 1016

Chapter 44

אַמְתַּחַת 1 sack (15·15) 607

אֹכֶל food (16·44) 38

גָּבִיעַ 2 cup (5·14) 149

אַמְתַּחַת sack (15·15) 607

שֶׁבֶר grain (7·9) 991

לַאֲשֶׁר 4 to him who (4·38) 81

הִשִּׂיג to overtake (4·49·49) 673

נִחֵשׁ 5 to practice divination (3·9·9) 638

הִשִּׂיג 6 to overtake (4·49·49) 673

חָלִיל 7 far be it [for] (4·21) 321

אַמְתַּחַת 8 sack (15·15) 607

גנב to steal (9·30·39) 170

נָקִי 10 free from, exempt (2·43) 667

אַמְתַּח 11 sack (15·15) 607

חפשׂ 12 to search for (2·8·23) 344

גָּבִיעַ cup (5·14) 149

אַמְתַּחַת sack (15·15) 607

שִׂמְלָה 13 clothes (7·29) 971

עמס to load (1·7·9) 770

נִחֵשׁ 15 to practice divination (3·9·9) 638

נִצְטַדָּק 16 Hithp. צדק, to justify oneself (1·1·41) 842

גָּבִיעַ cup (5·14) 149

חָלִיל 17 far be it [for] (4·21) 321

גָּבִיעַ cup (5·14) 149

בִּי 18 I pray, excuse me (2·12) 106

זְקֻנִים 20 old age (4·4) 279

קָטָן young (6·47) 881

שׁבר 25 to buy grain (13·16·21) 991

אֹכֶל food (16·44) 38

טָרַף 28 to tear (3·13·24) 382

טרף to be torn (2·2·24) 382

הֵנָּה hither (8·49) 244

קרה 29 to befall (2·13·27) 899

אָסוֹן mischief, evil (3·5) 62

שֵׂיבָה gray hair (5·20[?]) 966

קָשַׁר 30 to bind (2·35·43) 905

שֵׂיבָה 31 gray hair (5·20[?]) 966

יָגוֹן sorrow (2·14) 387

עָרַב 32 to be surety (2·15·17) 786

Chapter 45

הִתְאַפֵּק 1 to restrain oneself (2·7·7) 67

בְּכִי 2 weeping (1·30) 113

נִבְהַל 3 to be disturbed, dismayed (1·24·39) 96

נֶעֱצַב 5 to be grieved (1·7·15) 780

הֵנָּה hither (8·49) 244

מִחְיָה preservation of life (1·8) 313

חָרִישׁ 6 ploughing (1·3) 361

קָצִיר harvesting (3·49) 894

פְּלֵיטָה 7 escape, deliverance (2·28) 812

הֵנָּה 8 hither (8·49) 244

מֹשֵׁל ruler (2·24) 605

כִּלְכֵּל 11 to sustain (3·23·36) 465

הֵנָּה 13 hither (8·49) 244

צַוָּאר 14 neck (8·41) 848

נשׁק 15 to kiss (4·5·32) 676

טען 17 to load (1·1·1) 381

בְּעִיר beast (1·6) 129

טוּב 18 good things (4·32) 375

עֲגָלָה 19 cart (4·25) 722

טַף children (8·41) 381

חוּס 20 to pity (1·24·24) 299

טוּב good things (4·32) 375

עֲגָלָה 21 cart (4·25) 722

צֵידָה provision (2·9) 845

חֲלִיפָה 22 change |of raiment| (2·12) 322

שִׂמְלָה garment (7·29) 971

כָּזֹאת 23 the like of this = as follows (1·1) 260

טוּב good things (4·32) 375

אָתוֹן she-ass (4·35) 87

בָּר grain (5·14) 141

מָזוֹן sustenance (1·2) 266

רָגַז 24 to quarrel (1·30·41) 919

מֹשֵׁל 26 ruler (2·24) 605

פוּג to grow numb (1·3·4) 806

עֲגָלָה 27 cart (4·25) 722

בְּטֶרֶם 28 before (5·39) 382

Chapter 46

מַרְאָה 2 vision (1·12) 909

טַף 5 children (8·41) 381

עֲגָלָה cart (4·25) 722

רְכוּש 6 property (11·28) 940

רכש to gather |property| (5·5·5) 940

יָרֵךְ 26 thigh, loins (9·34) 437

מִלְּבַד besides (2·33) 94

הורה 28 to teach (1·45[?]·45[?]) 434

מֶרְכָּבָה 29 chariot (2·44) 939

צַוָּאר neck (8·41) 848

נְעוּרִים 34 youth (2·46) 655

בַּעֲבוּר in order that (15·46) 721

Chapter 47

הַצִּיג 2 to set (4·15·16) 426

מִרְעֶה 4 pasture (1·13) 945

כָּבֵד grievous (9·39) 458

מֵיטָב 6 best (2·5) 406

כַּמָּה 8 how much? how many? (1·13) 552

מְגוּרִים 9 sojourning (6·11) 158

הִשִּׂיג to reach (4·49·49) 673

מֵיטָב 11 best (2·5) 406

כִּלְכֵּל 12 to sustain (3·23·36) 465

טַף children (8·41) 381

כָּבֵד 13 grievous (9·39) 458

להה to faint, languish (1·1·2) 529

לקט 14 to gather (1·21·36) 544

שֶׁבֶר grain (7·9) 991

שבר to buy grain (13·16·21) 991

יהב 15 to give (8·27·27) 396

אָפֵס to cease, fail (2·5) 67

יהב 16 to give (8·27·27) 396

אָפֵס to cease, fail (2·5) 67

נהל 17 to refresh with food (1·9·10) 624

כחד 18 to hide (1·15·30) 470

בִּלְתִּי except (4·24) 116

גְּוִיָּה body (1·12) 156

הֵא 23 behold (1·2) 210

תְּבוּאָה 24 product, yield (1·43) 100

אֹכֶל food (16·44) 38

לַאֲשֶׁר to those who (4·38) 81

טַף children (8·41) 381

פרה 27 to be fruitful (10·22·29) 826

יָרֵךְ 29 thigh, loins (9·34) 437

קְבוּרָה 30 grave (3·14) 869

מִטָּה 31 bed (3·29) 641

Chapter 48

מִטָּה 2 bed (3·29) 641

שַׁדַּי 3 Almighty (6·48) 994

הפרה 4 to make fruitful (5·7·29) 826

מוֹלֶדֶת 6 kindred (9·22) 409

בְּעוֹד 7 within yet (4·20) 728

כִּבְרָה a distance (2·3) 460

בָּזֶה 9 in this |place|, here (3·19) 260

זָקֵן 10 old age (1·1) 279

נשק to kiss (4·5·32) 676

חבק to embrace (3·10·13) 287

פלל 11 to judge (1·4·5) 813

בֶּרֶךְ	12 knee (3·25) 139	
צָעִיר	14 young (8·22) 859	
שָׂכֵל	to lay crosswise (1·1·1) 968	
מֵעוֹד	15 ever since (1·2) 728	
דָּגָה	16 to multiply (1·1·1) 185	
תָּמַךְ	17 to grasp (1·20·21) 1069	
מָאָן	19 to refuse (3·45·45) 549	
אוּלָם	but, indeed (2·19) 19	
מְלֹא	multitude (1·38) 571	
שְׁכֶם	22 shoulder (6·22) 1014	

Chapter 49

אוֹן	3 manly vigor (1·10) 20
שְׂאֵת	dignity (2·7) 673
עַז	strong (1·22) 738
פַּחַז	4 wantonness, recklessness (1·1) 808
מִשְׁכָּב	bed (1·46) 1012
יָצוּעַ	couch, bed (1·5) 426
מְכֵרָה	5 name of a weapon (1·1) 468
סוֹד	6 council (1·21) 691
יָחַד	to be united (1·2·3) 402
עָקַר	to hamstring (1·5·7) 785
עֶבְרָה	7 overflowing rage (1·34) 720
קָשָׁה	to be hard, severe (1·5·28) 904
עֹרֶף	8 back of neck (1·33) 791
גּוּר	9 whelp, young (1·7) 158
טֶרֶף	prey (1·17) 383
כָּרַע	to bow down (1·29·35) 502
רָבַץ	to lie down (5·24·30) 918
לָבִיא	lion (1·11) 522
מְחֹקֵק	10 commander's staff (1·7) 349
מִבֵּין	from between (1·21) 107
שִׁילֹה	he whose it is (1·1) 1010
יְקָהָה	obedience (1·2) 429
עַיִר	11 male ass (2·9) 747
שֹׂרֵקָה	choice vine (1·1) 977
אָתוֹן	she-ass (4·35) 87
לְבוּשׁ	garment (1·31) 528

עֵנָב	grape[s] (3·19) 772
סוּת	vesture (1·1) 691
חַכְלִילִי	12 dull (1·1) 314
לָבָן	white (3·28) 526
חָלָב	milk (2·44) 316
חוֹף	13 shore, coast (2·7) 342
אֳנִיָּה	ship (1·31) 58
יַרְכָה	further side (1·28) 438
גֶּרֶם	14 strength (1·5) 175
רָבַץ	to lie down (5·24·30) 918
מִשְׁפְּתַיִם	fireplaces, ash heaps (1·2) 1046
מְנוּחָה	15 resting-place (1·21) 629
נָעֵם	to be pleasant (1·8·8) 653
שְׁכֶם	shoulder (6·22) 1014
סָבַל	to bear a heavy load (1·7·9) 687
מַס	labor band (1·23) 586
דִּין	16 to judge (4·23·24[?]) 192
נָחָשׁ	17 serpent (6·31) 638
שְׁפִיפֹן	horned snake, viper (1·1) 1051
נָשַׁךְ	to bite (1·10·12) 675
עָקֵב	heel (3·14) 784
אָחוֹר	backwards (1·41) 30
קָוָה	18 to look eagerly for (1·40·45) 875
גְּדוּד	19 marauding band (1·33) 151
גּוּד	to attack (2·3[?]) 156
עָקֵב	rear, heel (3·14) 784
שָׁמֵן	20 fat, rich (1·10) 1032
מַעֲדָן	dainty food (1·3) 726
אַיָּלָה	21 doe (1·11) 19
אמר	rd.'אמר; אָמִיר=top, summit (1·1) 57
שֶׁפֶר	beauty (1·1) 1051
פרה	22 to be fruitful; pct. = fruit bearer, fruitful bough (10·22·29) 826
צעד	to climb [dub.] (1·7·8) 857
שׁוּר	wall (1·3) 1004
מרר	23 to show bitterness (1·3·14) 600
רבב	to shoot (1·1·1) 914

27

שֹׁטֵם	to bear a grudge against (3·3·6) 966
אֵיתָן	24 enduring, firm (1·14) 450
פֹזז	to be agile (1·1·2) 808
אָבִיר	strong (1·6) 7
שַׁדַּי	25 Almighty (6·48) 994
עַל	above (2·7) 752
תְּהוֹם	deep (4·36) 1062
רָבַץ	to lie down (5·24·30) 918
שַׁד	[female] breast (1·21) 994
רַחַם	womb (4·33) 933
גָּבַר	26 to be strong, prevail (5·17·25) 149
הֹרֶה	ptc. of הָרָה = parents, ancestors (1·3) 223
תַּאֲוָה	boundary (2·21[?]) 1063
קָדְקֹד	hairy crown, scalp (1·11) 869
נָזִיר	one devoted (1·15) 634
זְאֵב	27 wolf (1·8) 255
טָרַף	to tear (3·19·24) 382
עַד	booty, prey (1·3) 723
עַם	29 kinsman (6·34) 769
מְעָרָה	cave (11·40) 792
מְעָרָה	30 cave (11·40) 792
מְעָרָה	32 cave (11·40) 792
מִטָּה	33 bed (3·29) 641
גוע	to die (6·24·24) 157
עַם	kinsman (6·34) 769

Chapter 50

נָשַׁק	1 to kiss (7·26·32) 676
אֹפֵר	2 physician (2·5[?]) 950
חנט	to embalm (3·4·4) 334
חֲנֻטִים	3 embalming (1·1) 334
בְּכִית	4 weeping (1·1) 114
כָּרָה	5 to dig (2·13·14) 500
טַף	8 children (8·41) 381
כָּבֵד	9 numerous (9·39) 458
ספד	10 to lament (2·27·29) 704
מִסְפֵּד	wailing (1·16) 704
כָּבֵד	grievous (9·39) 458
אֵבֶל	mourning (4·24) 5
אֵבֶל	11 mourning (4·24) 5
כָּבֵד	vehement, sore (9·39) 458
מְעָרָה	13 cave (11·40) 792
לוּ	15 if (4·19) 530
שֹׁטֵם	to bear a grudge against (3·3·6) 966
גָּמַל	to deal out, to repay (2·34·37) 168
אָנָא	17 we beseech thee (1·7) 58
גָּמַל	to deal out, to repay (2·34·37) 168
כִּלְכֵּל	21 to sustain (3·23·36) 465
טַף	children (8·41) 381
שִׁלֵּשִׁים	23 those of the third generation (1·5) 1026
בֶּרֶךְ	knee (3·25) 139
חנט	26 to embalm (3·4·4) 334

EXODUS

Chapter 1

יָרֵךְ   5 thigh, loins (7·34) 437

פרה   7 to be fruitful (2·22·29) 826

שָׁרַץ   to swarm (2·14·14) 1056

עָצַם   to be numerous (2·16·18) 782

עָצוּם   9 mighty (1·31) 783

יהב   10 to come now (1·27·27) 396

התחכם   to deal wisely (1·2·26) 314

שֹׂנֵא   enemy (3·41) 971

מַס   11 slave gang (1·23) 586

סבלה   burden (6·6) 688

מִסְכְּנוֹת   storage (1·7) 698

פָּרַץ   12 to break over; increase (3·46·49) 829

קוּץ   to feel a sickening dread (1·8·8) 880

פֶּרֶךְ   13 harshness; severity (2·6) 827

מרר   14 to make bitter (1·3·14) 600

קָשֶׁה   severe (7·36) 904

חֹמֶר   mortar (1·17) 330

לְבֵנָה   brick (8·12) 527

פֶּרֶךְ   harshness; severity (2·6) 827

מְיַלֶּדֶת   15 midwife (7·9) 408

אֹבֶן   16 midwife's stool (1·2) 7

מְיַלֶּדֶת   17 midwife (7·9) 408

מְיַלֶּדֶת   18 midwife (7·9) 408

מְיַלֶּדֶת   19 midwife (7·9) 408

חָיֶה   lively; bearing quickly (1·1) 313

בְּטֶרֶם   19 before (1·39) 382

מְיַלֶּדֶת   20 midwife (7·9) 408

עָצַם   to be numerous (2·16·18) 782

מְיַלֶּדֶת   21 midwife (7·9) 408

יָלוֹד   22 born (1·5) 409

Chapter 2

הָרָה   2 to conceive (1·38·40) 247

צָפַן   to hide (1·23·28) 860

יֶרַח   month (1·12) 437

הצפן   3 to hide (1·2·28) 860

תֵּבָה   ark (2·28) 1061

גֹּמֶא   rush; reed; papyrus (1·4) 167

חמר   to cover; smear (1·5·5[?]) 330

חֵמָר   bitumen; asphalt (1·3) 330

זֶפֶת   pitch (1·3) 278

סוּף   reeds (2·4) 693

התיצב   4 to station oneself (6·48·48) 426

תֵּבָה   5 ark (2·28) 1061

סוּף   reeds (2·4) 693

חָמַל   6 to spare (1·40·40) 328

היניק   7 to nurse (4·10·18) 413

עַלְמָה   8 young woman (1·9) 761

היניק   9 to nurse (4·10·18) 413

שָׂכָר   hire; wages (2·29) 969

משה   10 to draw (1·1·3) 602

סבלה   11 burden (6·6) 688

טָמַן   12 to hide (1·28·31) 380

חוֹל   sand (1·22) 297

נצה   13 to struggle with each other (2·5·8) 663

אָכֵן   14 surely; truly (1·18) 38

בְּאֵר   15 well (1·36) 91

דָּלָה   16 to draw [water] (2·4·5) 194

רהט   trough (1·4) 923

גרש   17 to drive out (1·7·46) 176

דָּלָה   19 to draw [water] (2·4·5) 194

אֵי   20 where (1·39) 32

הוֹאִיל   21 to show willingness (1·18·18) 383

נָכְרִי   22 foreign (3·45) 648

נאנח   23 to sigh (1·12·12) 58

שַׁוְעָה   cry for help (1·11) 1003

נאקה   24 groaning (2·4) 611

Chapter 3

חֹתֵן	1	wife's father (15 · 21) 368
נָהַג		to drive (1 · 20 · 30) 624
לַבָּה	2	flame (1 · 1[?]) 529
סְנֶה		blackberry bush[?] (5 · 6) 702
סְנֶה	3	blackberry bush[?] (5 · 6) 702
סְנֶה	4	blackberry bush[?] (5 · 6) 702
הֲלֹם	5	hither; here (1 · 11) 240
נָשַׁל		to draw off (1 · 6 · 7) 675
נַעַל		sandle (2 · 22) 653
עֳנִי	7	affliction (3 · 36) 777
צְעָקָה	7	cry of distress (5 · 21) 858
נֹגֵשׂ		taskmaster (5 · 15) 620
מַכְאוֹב		pain (1 · 16) 456
רָחָב	8	wide; broad (1 · 21) 932
זוב		to flow (4 · 29 · 29) 264
חָלָב		milk (6 · 44) 316
צְעָקָה	9	cry of distress (5 · 21) 858
לַחַץ		oppression (1 · 11) 537
לָחַץ		to oppress (3 · 14 · 15) 537
זֵכֶר	15	memorial (2 · 33) 271
עֳנִי	17	affliction (3 · 36) 777
זוב		to flow (4 · 29 · 29) 264
חָלָב		milk (6 · 44) 316
נִקְרָה	18	to encounter; meet (1 · 6 · 27) 899
נִפְלָאוֹת	20	wonderful acts (2 · 43) 810
רֵיקָם	21	in empty condition; emptily (3 · 16) 938
שָׁכֵן	22	neighbor (2 · 20) 1015
שִׂמְלָה		clothes (6 · 29) 971

Chapter 4

נָחָשׁ	3	serpent (2 · 31) 638
זָנָב	4	tail (1 · 11) 275
חֵיק	6	fold of the garment at the breast (5 · 38) 300
מְצֹרָע		leprous (1 · 15) 863

שֶׁלֶג		snow (1 · 20) 1017
חֵיק	7	fold of the garment at the breast (5 · 38) 300
יַבָּשָׁה	9	dry ground (5 · 14) 387
בִּי	10	I pray!; excuse me (2 · 12) 106
תְּמוֹל		yesterday; afore-time (7 · 23) 1069
שִׁלְשֹׁם		three days ago; specif. = the day before yesterday (6 · 25) 1026
מֵאָז		since (3 · 18) 23
כָּבֵד		heavy (9 · 39) 458
אִלֵּם	11	dumb; unable to speak (1 · 6) 48
חֵרֵשׁ		deaf (1 · 9) 361
פִּקֵּחַ		seeing (2 · 2) 824
עִוֵּר		blind (1 · 25) 734
הוֹרָה	12	to teach (5 · 45 · 45[?]) 434
בִּי	13	I pray!; excuse me (2 · 12) 106
הוֹרָה	15	to teach (5 · 45 · 45[?]) 434
חֹתֵן	18	wife's father (15 · 21) 368
מוֹפֵת	21	wonder (5 · 36) 68
מֵאָן	23	to refuse (8 · 45 · 45) 549
מָלוֹן	24	lodging-place (1 · 8) 533
פָּגַשׁ		to meet; encounter (2 · 10 · 14) 803
צֹר	25	flint [used as a knife] (1 · 6) 866
עָרְלָה		foreskin (1 · 16) 790
חָתָן		daughter's husband; bridegroom (2 · 20) 368
רָפָה	26	to relax; withdraw (1 · 14 · 44) 951
חָתָן		bridegroom; daughter's husband (2 · 20) 368
מוּלָה		circumcision (1 · 1) 558
פָּגַשׁ	27	to meet; encounter (2 · 10 · 14) 803
נָשַׁק		to kiss (2 · 26 · 32) 676
עֳנִי	31	affliction (3 · 36) 777
קָדַד		to bow down (3 · 15 · 15) 869

Chapter 5

חָגַג	1	to keep a pilgrim feast (4 · 16 · 16) 290

30

פָּגַע	3 to fall upon (3·40·46) 803		שְׁלְשֹׁם	three days ago; specif. = the day before yesterday (6·25) 1026
דֶּבֶר	plague (3·46) 184			
הִפְרִיעַ	4 to cause to refrain (1·2·16) 828		שֹׁטֵר	15 official; officer (5·25) 1009
סִבְלָה	burden (6·6) 688		תֶּבֶן	16 straw (8·17) 1061
סִבְלָה	5 burden (6·6) 688		לְבֵנָה	brick (8·12) 527
נֹגֵשׂ	6 taskmaster (5·15) 620		נרפה	17 to be idle (2·2·44) 951
שֹׁטֵר	official; officer (5·25) 1009		תֶּבֶן	18 straw (8·17) 1061
תֶּבֶן	7 straw (8·17) 1061		תֹּכֶן	measurement (1·2) 1067
לבן	to make brick (2·3·3) 527		לְבֵנָה	brick (8·12) 527
לְבֵנָה	brick (8·12) 527		שֹׁטֵר	19 official; officer (5·25) 1009
תְּמוֹל	yesterday; formerly (7·23) 1069		גרע	to diminish (3·14·22) 175
שְׁלְשֹׁם	three days ago; specif. = the day before yesterday (6·25) 1026		לְבֵנָה	brick (8·12) 527
			פָּגַע	20 to meet; light upon (3·40·46) 803
קָשַׁשׁ	to gather stubble (2·6·8) 905		הִבְאִישׁ	21 to cause to stink (2·7·16) 92
מַתְכֹּנֶת	8 proportion (3·5) 1067		מֵאָז	23 since (3·18) 23
לְבֵנָה	brick (8·12) 527			
תְּמוֹל	yesterday; formerly (7·23) 1069			**Chapter 6**
שְׁלְשֹׁם	three days ago; specif. = the day before yesterday (6·25) 1026		גרש	1 to drive out (1·7·46) 176
			מָגוֹר	4 sojourning (1·11) 158
גרע	to diminish (3·14·22) 175		נְאָקָה	5 groaning (2·4) 611
נרפה	to be idle (2·2·44) 951		סִבְלָה	6 burden (6·6) 688
שָׁעָה	9 to gaze (1·12·15) 1043		שפט	judgement (3·16) 1048
נֹגֵשׂ	10 taskmaster (5·15) 620		סִבְלָה	7 burden (6·6) 688
שֹׁטֵר	official; officer (5·25) 1009		מוֹרָשָׁה	8 possession (1·9) 440
תֶּבֶן	straw (8·17) 1061		קֹצֶר	9 shortness (1·1) 894
תֶּבֶן	11 straw (8·17) 1061		קָשֶׁה	severe (7·36) 904
מֵאֲשֶׁר	from that which (3·17) 84		עָרֵל	12 uncircumcised (3·35) 790
נגרע	to be withdrawn (1·7·22) 175		תּוֹלְדוֹת	16 generations (3·39) 410
קָשַׁשׁ	12 to gather stubble (2·6·8) 905		תּוֹלְדוֹת	19 generations (3·39) 410
קַשׁ	stubble, chaff (2·16) 905		דֹּדָה	20 aunt (1·3) 187
תֶּבֶן	straw (8·17) 1061		עָרֵל	30 uncircumcised (3·35) 790
נֹגֵשׂ	13 taskmaster (5·15) 620			
אוץ	to press; hasten (1·8·10) 21			**Chapter 7**
תֶּבֶן	straw (8·17) 1061		הִקְשָׁה	3 to make stiff; stubborn (2·21·28) 904
שֹׁטֵר	14 official; officer (5·25) 1009		מוֹפֵת	wonder (5·36) 68
נֹגֵשׂ	taskmaster (5·15) 620		שפט	4 judgment (3·16) 1048
לבן	to make brick (2·3·3) 527		מוֹפֵת	9 wonder (5·36) 68
תְּמוֹל	yesterday; formerly (7·23) 1069		תַּנִּין	serpent (3·15) 1072
			תַּנִּין	10 serpent (3·15) 1072

31

כִּשֵּׁף 11 to practice sorcery (2·6·6) 506

חַרְטֹם magician (7·11) 355

לְהָטִים mysteries (1·1[?]) 532

תַּנִּין 12 serpent (3·15) 1072

בָּלַע to swallow down (2·20·41[?]) 118

כָּבֵד 14 heavy, hard (9·39) 458

מֵאֵן to refuse (8·45·45) 549

נָחָשׁ 15 serpent (2·31) 638

בְּזֹאת 17 by; through this (1·15) 260

דָּגָה 18 fish [collective] (2·15) 185

בָּאַשׁ to stink (4·5·16) 92

נִלְאָה to be weary (1·10·19) 521

אֲגַם 19 pool; pond (2·8) 8

דָּגָה 21 fish [collective] (2·15) 185

בָּאַשׁ to stink (4·5·16) 92

חַרְטֹם 22 magician (7·11) 355

לָט mystery (3·7) 532

לָזֹאת 23 for this (1·3) 260

חָפַר 24 to dig; search for (1·22·22) 343

מֵאֵן 27 to refuse (8·45·45) 549

נָגַף to strike (7·24·48) 619

צְפַרְדֵּעַ frog (11·13) 862

שָׁרַץ 28 to swarm (2·14·14) 1056

צְפַרְדֵּעַ frog (11·13) 862

חֶדֶר room; chamber (1·34) 293

מִשְׁכָּב lying down (2·46) 1012

מִטָּה bed (1·29) 641

תַּנּוּר stove; firepot (1·15) 1072

מִשְׁאֶרֶת kneading trough (2·4) 602

צְפַרְדֵּעַ 29 frog (11·13) 862

Chapter 8

אֲגַם 1 pool; pond (2·8) 8

צְפַרְדֵּעַ frog (11·13) 862

צְפַרְדֵּעַ 2 frog (11·13) 862

חַרְטֹם 3 magician (7·11) 355

לָט mystery (3·7) 532

צְפַרְדֵּעַ frog (11·13) 862

הֶעְתִּיר 4 to make supplication (6·7·20) 801

צְפַרְדֵּעַ frog (11·13) 862

הִתְפָּאֵר 5 to glorify oneself (1·7·13) 802

לְמָתַי against when (1·1) 607

הֶעְתִּיר to make supplication (6·7·20) 801

צְפַרְדֵּעַ frog (11·13) 862

צְפַרְדֵּעַ 7 frog (11·13) 862

צְפַרְדֵּעַ 8 frog (11·13) 862

צְפַרְדֵּעַ 9 frog (11·13) 862

צָבַר 10 to heap up (1·7·7) 840

חֹמֶר heap (2·12) 330

בָּאַשׁ to stink (4·5·16) 92

רְוָחָה 11 respite; relief (1·2) 926

כֵּן 12 gnat (3·5) 487

כִּנָּם 13 gnats (2·2) 487

כֵּן gnat (3·5) 487

חַרְטֹם 14 magician (7·11) 355

לָט mystery (3·7) 532

כֵּן gnat (3·5) 487

כִּנָּם 14 gnats (2·2) 487

חַרְטֹם 15 magician (7·11) 355

אֶצְבַּע finger (3·31) 840

הִתְיַצֵּב 16 to set oneself (6·48·48) 426

עָרֹב 17 a swarm (7·9) 786

הִפְלָה 18 to make separate; set apart (3·3·4) 811

עָרֹב a swarm (7·9) 786

פְּדוּת 19 ransom (1·4) 804

עָרֹב 20 a swarm (7·9) 786

כָּבֵד heavy (9·39) 458

סָקַל 22 to stone (4·12·22) 709

הֶעְתִּיר 24 to make supplication (6·7·20) 801

הֶעְתִּיר 25 to make supplication (6·7·20) 801

עָרֹב a swarm (7·9) 786

הֵתֵל to mock; trifle with (1·1·1[?]) 1068

עָתַר 26 to pray; supplicate (2·5·20) 801

עָרֹב a swarm (7·9) 786

Chapter 9

מֵאֵן 2 to refuse (8·45·45) 549

דֶּבֶר 3 plague (3·46) 184

כָּבֵד	grievous (9·39) 458		הַמְטִיר	to rain (3·16·17) 565
הִפְלָה	4 to make separate; to set apart (3·3·4) 811		בָּרָד	24 hail (17·29) 135
מָחֳרָת	6 the morrow (4·32) 564		כָּבֵד	grievous (9·39) 458
חֹפֶן	8 hollow of hand (1·6) 342		מֵאָז	since (3·18) 23
פִּיחַ	soot (2·2) 806		בָּרָד	25 hail (17·29) 135
כִּבְשָׁן	kiln (3·4) 461		עֵשֶׂב	herb (5·33) 793
זָרַק	to toss (6·32·34) 284		בָּרָד	26 hail (17·29) 135
אָבָק	9 dust (1·6) 7		הֶעְתִּיר	28 to make supplication (6·7·20) 801
שְׁחִין	boil (4·13) 1006		בָּרָד	hail (17·29) 135
פָּרַח	to break out (2·29·34) 827		בָּרָד	29 hail (17·29) 135
אֲבַעְבֻּעֹ	blisters; boils (2·2) 101		טֶרֶם	30 not yet (3·16) 382
פִּיחַ	10 soot (2·2) 806		פִּשְׁתָּה	31 flax (2·4) 834
כִּבְשָׁן	kiln (3·4) 461		שְׂעֹרָה	barley (2·34) 972
זָרַק	to toss (6·32·34) 284		אָבִיב	young ears (5·8) 1
שְׁחִין	boil (4·13) 1006		גִּבְעֹל	bud (1·1) 149
אֲבַעְבֻּעֹ	blisters; boils (2·2) 101		כֻּסֶּמֶת	32 spelt (1·3) 493
פָּרַח	to break out (2·29·34) 827		אָפִיל	late [of crops] (1·1) 66
חַרְטֹם	11 magician (7·11) 355		בָּרָד	33 hail (17·29) 135
שְׁחִין	boil (4·13) 1006		מָטָר	rain (2·37) 564
הִתְיַצֵּב	13 to set oneself (6·48·48) 426		נִתַּךְ	to be poured (1·8·21) 677
מַגֵּפָה	14 plague (1·26) 620		מָטָר	34 rain (2·37) 564
בַּעֲבוּר	for the sake of (6·46) 21		בָּרָד	hail (17·29) 135
דֶּבֶר	15 plague (3·46) 184			
נִכְחַד	to be destroyed (1·9·30) 470			

Chapter 10

אוּלָם	16 but; but indeed (1·19) 19		הִתְעַלֵּל	2 to make a toy of (1·7·17) 759
בַּעֲבוּר	for the sake of (6·46) 721		מָתַי	3 when? (2·42) 607
הִסְתּוֹלֵל	17 to exalt oneself (1·1·10) 699		מֵאֵן	to refuse (8·45·45) 549
הַמְטִיר	18 to rain (3·16·17) 565		מֵאֵן	4 to refuse (8·45·45) 549
בָּרָד	hail (17·24) 135		אַרְבֶּה	locust (7·24) 916
כָּבֵד	grievous (9·39) 458		פְּלֵיטָה	5 escaped remnant (1·28) 812
לְמִן	from (1·14) 583		בָּרָד	hail (17·29) 135
נוֹסַד	to be founded (1·2·42) 413		צָמַח	to sprout (1·15·33) 855
הָעֵז	19 to bring into safety (1·4·5) 731		מָתַי	7 when? (2·42) 607
בָּרָד	19 hail (17·29) 135		מוֹקֵשׁ	snare (3·27) 430
בָּרָד	22 hail (17·29) 135		טֶרֶם	not yet (3·16) 382
עֵשֶׂב	herb (5·33) 793		טַף	10 children (3·41) 381
בָּרָד	23 hail (17·29) 135		גֵּרֵשׁ	11 to drive away (9·33·33[?]) 176
			אַרְבֶּה	12 locust (7·24) 916

33

עֵשֶׂב	herb (5·33) 793
בָּרָד	hail (17·29) 135
נָהַג	13 to drive away (2·10·30) 624
אַרְבֶּה	locust (7·24) 916
אַרְבֶּה	14 locust (7·24) 916
כָּבֵד	numerous (9·39) 458
חָשַׁךְ	15 to have a dark color; to be dark (1·11·17) 364
עֵשֶׂב	herb (5·33) 793
בָּרָד	hail (17·29) 135
יֶרֶק	green (1·8) 438
העתיר	17 to make supplication (6·7·20) 801
עתר	18 to pray; supplicate (2·5·20) 801
אַרְבֶּה	19 locust (7·24) 916
המש	21 to feel (1·3·4[?]) 606
אֲפֵלָה	22 darkness (1·10) 66
מוֹשָׁב	23 dwelling place (4·43) 444
הצג	24 to be detained (1·1·16) 426
טַף	children (3·41) 381
פַּרְסָה	26 hoof (1·21) 828

Chapter 11

כָּלָה	1 complete destruction (1·22) 478
גרש	to drive out (9·33·46) 176
רְעוּת	2 fellow [woman] (1·6) 946
רחה	5 [hand] mill (1·5) 932
צְעָקָה	6 cry of distress (5·21) 858
חָרַץ	7 to sharpen; to sharpen tongue = to utter a sound (1·5·10) 358
כֶּלֶב	dog (2·32) 476
הִפְלָה	to make separate; to set apart (3·3·4) 811
חָרִי	8 burning (1·6) 354
מוֹפֵת	9 wonder (5·36) 68
מוֹפֵת	10 wonder (5·36) 68

Chapter 12

עָשׂוֹר	3 tenth day (1·15) 797

שֶׂה	one of a flock; sheep; goat (13·44) 961
מעט	4 to be small (1·8·22) 589
שֶׂה	one of a flock; sheep; goat (13·44) 961
שָׁכֵן	neighbor (2·20) 1015
מִכְסָה	number (1·2) 493
כסס	to compute (1·1·1) 493
שֶׂה	5 one of a flock; sheep; goat (13·44) 961
מְזוּזָה	7 doorpost (4·20) 265
מַשְׁקוֹף	lintel[?] (3·3) 1054
צָלִי	8 roasted (2·3) 852
מרר	bitter herb (1·5[?]) 601
נָא	9 raw (1·1) 644
בָּשֵׁל	boiled (1·2·27) 143
בָּשֵׁל	to be boiled (1·4·27) 143
צָלִי	roasted (2·3) 852
כרע	leg (2·9) 502
כָּכָה	11 thus (2·34) 462
מָתְנַיִם	loins (2·50) 608
חגר	to gird on (2·44·44) 291
נַעַל	sandal (2·22) 653
מַקֵּל	staff (1·18) 596
חִפָּזוֹן	hurried flight (1·3) 342
פֶּסַח	passover (6·49) 820
שפט	12 judgment (3·16) 1048
פָּסַח	13 to pass over (3·5·7) 820
נֶגֶף	blow; plague (2·7) 620
מַשְׁחִית	destruction (2·19) 1008
זָכָרוֹן	14 memorial day; memorial (8·24) 272
חגג	to keep a pilgrim feast (4·16·16) 290
שְׂאֹר	15 leaven (3·5) 959
חָמֵץ	that which is leavened (5·11) 329
מִקְרָא	16 convocation (2·22) 896
לְבַדּוֹ	alone (3·35) 94
בְּעֶצֶם	17 selfsame; itself (3·17) 783

שְׂאֹר 19 leaven (3·5) 959

מַחְמֶצֶת anything leavened (2·2) 330

אֶזְרָח native (3·17) 280

מַחְמֶצֶת 20 anything leavened (2·2) 330

מוֹשָׁב dwelling place (4·43) 444

מָשַׁךְ 21 to proceed (2·30·36) 604

פֶּסַח passover (6·49) 820

אֲגֻדָּה 22 bunch; band (1·4) 8

אֵזוֹב hyssop (1·10) 23

טָבַל to dip (1·15·16) 371

סַף basin (1·6) 706

מַשְׁקוֹף lintel[?] (3·3) 1054

מְזוּזָה doorpost (4·20) 265

נָגַף 23 to strike (7·24·48) 619

מַשְׁקוֹף lintel[?] (3·3) 1054

מְזוּזָה doorpost (4·20) 265

פָּסַח to pass over (3·5·7) 820

מַשְׁחִית destroyer (2·19) 1008

פֶּסַח 27 passover (6·49) 820

פָּסַח to pass over (3·5·7) 820

נָגַף to strike (7·24·48) 619

קדד 27 to bow down (3·15·15) 869

שְׁבִי 29 captive (1·46) 985

צְעָקָה 30 cry of distress (5·21) 858

בָּצֵק 34 dough (2·5) 130

טֶרֶם ere; before that (3·16) 382

חָמֵץ to be leavened (2·3·4) 329

משאר kneading trough (2·4) 602

שִׂמְלָה wrapper; mantle (6·29) 971

שְׁכֶם shoulder (1·22) 1014

שִׂמְלָה 35 clothes (5·29) 971

רַגְלִי 37 on foot (1·12) 920

טַף children (3·41) 381

עֵרֶב 38 mixture; mixed company (1·5) 786

כָּבֵד heavy (9·39) 458

אָפָה 39 to bake (2·9·12) 66

בָּצֵק dough (2·5) 130

עֻגָה cake of bread (1·7) 728

חָמֵץ to be leavened (2·3·4) 329

גרש to drive out (1·7·46) 176

התמהמה to tarry (1·9·9) 554

צֵידָה provision (1·9) 845

מוֹשָׁב 40 time of dwelling (4·43) 444

בְּעֶצֶם 41 selfsame; itself (3·17) 783

פֶּסַח 43 passover (6·49) 820

נֵכָר foreignness (1·36) 648

מוּל 44 to circumcise (1·12·29) 557

תּוֹשָׁב 45 sojourner (1·14) 444

שָׂכִיר 45 hired laborer (2·18) 969

פֶּסַח 48 passover (6·49) 820

נִמּוֹל to be circumcised (1·17·29) 557

אֶזְרָח native (3·17) 280

עָרֵל uncircumcised (3·35) 790

אֶזְרָח 49 native (3·17) 280

בְּעֶצֶם 51 selfsame; itself (3·17) 783

Chapter 13

פֶּטֶר 2 firstborn (8·11) 809

רֶחֶם womb (4·32) 933

חֹזֶק 3 strength (3·5) 305

חָמֵץ that which is leavened (5·11) 329

זוב 5 to flow (4·29·29) 264

חָלָב milk (6·44) 316

חָמֵץ 7 that which is leavened (5·11) 329

שְׂאֹר leaven (3·5) 959

בַּעֲבוּר 8 for the sake of (6·46) 721

זִכָּרוֹן 9 memorial (8·24) 272

פֶּטֶר 12 firstborn (8·11) 809

רֶחֶם womb (4·32) 933

שֶׁגֶר offspring; young [of beasts] (1·5) 993

פֶּטֶר 13 firstborn (8·11) 809

שֶׂה one of a flock; sheep, goat (13·44) 961

ערף to break the neck (2·6·6) 791

חֹזֶק 14 strength (3·5) 305

35

הִקְשָׁה 15 to make stiff; stubborn (2 · 21 · 28) 904

פֶּטֶר firstborn (8 · 11) 809

רֶחֶם womb (4 · 32) 933

טוֹטָפוֹת 16 bands (1 · 3) 377

חֹזֶק strength (3 · 5) 305

נחה 17 to lead (4 · 14 · 40) 634

חֲמֻשִׁים 18 in battle array (1 · 4 · 5[?]) 332

נחה 21 to lead (4 · 14 · 40) 634

הֵאִיר to light up; shine (3 · 34 · 40) 21

הֵמִישׁ 22 to remove (2 · 20[?] · 20) 559

Chapter 14

נֹכַח 2 in front of (3 · 22) 647

נבוך 3 to be confused; perplexed (1 · 3 · 3) 100

בָּחוּר 7 chosen (1 · 19[?]) 103

שָׁלִישׁ adjutant; officer (2 · 16) 1026

רָם 8 high; exalted (1 · 31)[?] 926

הִשִּׂיג 9 to overtake (2 · 48 · 48) 673

מִבְּלִי 11 from want of (1 · 25) 115

הִתְיַצֵּב 13 to take one's stand (6 · 48 · 48) 426

הֶחֱרִישׁ 14 to be silent (2 · 38 · 46) 361

יַבָּשָׁה 16 dry ground (5 · 14) 387

הֵאִיר 20 to light up; shine (3 · 34 · 40) 21

עַז 21 strong; mighty (1 · 22) 738

חָרָבָה dry ground (1 · 8) 351

יַבָּשָׁה 22 dry ground (5 · 14) 387

תָּוֶךְ 23 midst; middle (1 · 33) 1063

אַשְׁמֹרֶת 24 watch (1 · 7) 1038

הִשְׁקִיף to look down (1 · 12 · 22) 1054

הָמַם to confuse; discomfit (2 · 13 · 13) 243

אוֹפָן 25 wheel (1 · 34) 66

מֶרְכָּבָה chariot (2 · 44) 939

נָהַג to drive away (2 · 10 · 30) 624

כְּבֵדֻת heaviness (1 · 1) 459

אֵיתָן 27 steady flow (1 · 14) 450

נֵעֵר to shake off (1 · 3 · 10) 654

יַבָּשָׁה 29 dry ground (5 · 14) 387

Chapter 15

שִׁירָה 1 song (1 · 13) 1010

גָּאָה to be lifted up; exalted (2 · 5 · 5) 144

רָמָה to cast (2 · 4 · 4) 941

זִמְרָה 2 melody; song (1 · 4) 274

הִנְיָה to adorn (1 · 1 · 1[?]) 627

מֶרְכָּבָה 4 chariot (2 · 44) 939

יָרָה to throw (2 · 13 · 25[?]) 434

מבחר choicest (1 · 12) 104

שָׁלִישׁ adjutant; officer (2 · 16) 1026

טבע to be sunk (1 · 1 · 10) 371

תְּהוֹם 5 sea; abyss (2 · 36) 1062

מְצוּלָה depth (1 · 12) 846

נֶאְדָּר 6 majestic (2 · 2) 12

רעץ to shatter (1 · 2 · 2) 950

גָּאוֹן 7 exaltation (1 · 49) 144

הָרַס to throw down (3 · 40 · 43) 248

קָם adversary (2 · 12) 878

חָרוֹן [burning of] anger (2 · 41) 354

קַשׁ stubble; chaff (2 · 16) 905

נֶעֶרְמוּ 8 to be heaped up (1 · 1 · 1) 790

נֵד heap of waters (1 · 6) 622

נֹזֵל flood (1 · 5) 633

קפא to condense (1 · 2 · 3) 891

תְּהוֹם sea; abyss (2 · 36) 1062

הִשִּׂיג 9 to overtake (2 · 48 · 48) 673

הֵרִיק to make empty (1 · 17 · 19) 937

נָשַׁף 10 to blow (1 · 2 · 2) 676

צלל to sink (1 · 1 · 1) 853

עֹפֶרֶת lead (metal) (1 · 9) 780

אַדִּיר majestic (1 · 27) 12

נֶאְדָּר 11 majestic (2 · 2) 12

נוֹרָא fearful (2 · 44) 431

פֶּלֶא wonder (1 · 13) 810

בָּלַע 12 to swallow down (2 · 20 · 41[?]) 118

נחה 13 to lead (4 · 14 · 40) 634

זוּ	which (2 · 16) 262
נהל	to lead to a station (1 · 9 · 10) 624
נָוֶה	habitation (1 · 45) 627
רָגַז	14 to quake (1 · 30 · 41) 919
חִיל	writhing (1 · 6) 297
נִבְהַל	15 to be dismayed (1 · 1 · 39) 96
רַעַד	trembling (1 · 2) 944
נָמוֹג	to melt (1 · 8 · 17) 556
אֵימָה	16 terror; dread (2 · 17) 33
פַּחַד	dread (1 · 49) 808
דמם	to be struck dumb; astonished (1 · 23 · 30) 198
זוּ	which (2 · 16) 262
מָכוֹן	17 fixed place (1 · 17) 467
עַד	18 forever (1 · 48) 723
יַבָּשָׁה	19 dry ground (5 · 14) 387
נְבִיאָה	20 prophetess (1 · 6) 612
תֹּף	timbrel; tamborine (2 · 17) 1074
מחולה	dance (2 · 8) 298
ענה	21 to sing (3 · 13 · 16) 777
גָּאָה	to be lifted up; exalted (2 · 5 · 5) 144
רָמָה	to cast (2 · 4 · 4) 941
מַר	23 bitter (1 · 37) 600
נלון	24 to murmur (3 · 8 · 18) 534
הורה	25 to teach (5 · 45 · 45[?]) 434
מתק	to be sweet (1 · 4 · 6) 608
נִסָּה	to test (5 · 36 · 36) 650
הֶאֱזִין	26 to listen (1 · 41 · 41) 24
מַחֲלָה	sickness (2 · 4) 318
רֹפֵא	physician (1 · 5)[?] 950
תָּמָר	25 palm tree; date palm (1 · 12) 1041

Chapter 16

נלון	2 to murmur (3 · 8 · 18) 534
סִיר	3 pot (3 · 29) 696
שֹׂבַע	satiety; abundance (1 · 8) 959
הִמְטִיר	4 to rain (3 · 16 · 17) 565
לקט	to gather (9 · 14 · 36) 544

נִסָּה	to test (5 · 36 · 36) 650
מִשְׁנֶה	5 double (2 · 35) 1041
לקט	to gather (9 · 14 · 36) 544
תלנה	7 murmuring (5 · 8) 534
הלין	to murmur (4 · 10 · 18) 534
תלנה	8 murmuring (5 · 8) 534
הלין	to murmur (4 · 10 · 18) 534
תלנה	9 murmuring (5 · 8) 534
תלנה	12 murmuring (5 · 8) 534
שְׂלָו	13 quail (1 · 4) 969
שכבה	layer [of dew] (2 · 9) 1012
טַל	dew (2 · 31) 378
שכבה	14 layer [of dew] (2 · 9) 1012
טַל	dew (2 · 31) 378
דַּק	small; fine (2 · 14) 201
חספס	to be scalelike (1 · 1 · 1) 341
כְּפוֹר	hoar frost (1 · 3) 499
מָן	15 what (1 · 1) 577
לקט	16 to gather (9 · 14 · 36) 544
אֹכֶל	food; food supply (4 · 44) 38
עֹמֶר	omer (6 · 6) 771
גֻּלְגֹּלֶת	head [in counting]="for each man" (2 · 12) 166
לַאֲשֶׁר	to whom (1 · 38) 81
לקט	17 to gather (9 · 14 · 36) 544
הֶמְעִיט	to make small (3 · 13 · 22) 589
עֹמֶר	18 omer (6 · 6) 771
הֶעְדִּיף	to have a surplus (1 · 1 · 9) 727
הֶמְעִיט	to make small (3 · 13 · 22) 589
הֶחְסִיר	to cause to lack (1 · 2 · 24) 341
אֹכֶל	food; food supply (4 · 44) 38
לקט	to gather (9 · 14 · 36) 544
רמם	20 to be wormy (1 · 1 · 1) 942
תּוֹלֵעָה	worm, grub (27 · 41) 1069
בָּאַשׁ	to stink (4 · 5 · 16) 92
קָצַף	to be wroth (1 · 28 · 34) 893
לקט	21 to gather (9 · 14 · 36) 544
כְּפִי	in proportion to (3 · 16) 804

אֹכֶל food; food supply (4·44) 38

חָמַם to be or grow warm (1·23·26) 328

נָמַס to melt (1·19·21) 587

לקט 22 to gather (9·14·36) 544

מִשְׁנֶה double (2·35) 1041

עֹמֶר omer (6·6) 771

שַׁבָּתוֹן 23 Sabbath observance (3·11) 992

אָפָה to bake (2·9·12) 66

בָּשַׁל to boil; cook (4·20·27) 143

עָדַף to remain over; be in excess (4·8·9) 727

הִבְאִישׁ 24 to emit a stinking odor (2·7·16) 92

רִמָּה worm (1·7) 942

לקט 26 to gather (9·14·36) 544

לקט 27 to gather (9·14·36) 544

אָנָה 28 whither? where? (1·39) 33

מֵאֵן to refuse (8·45·45) 549

מָן 31 manna (5·14) 577

גַּד coriander (1·2) 151

לָבָן white (1·28) 526

טַעַם taste (1·13) 381

צַפִּיחִת flat cake; wafer (1·1) 860

עֹמֶר 32 omer (6·6) 771

צִנְצֶנֶת 33 jar (1·1) 857

עֹמֶר omer (6·6) 771

מָן manna (5·14) 577

מָן manna (5·14) 577

עֹמֶר 36 omer (6·6) 771

אֵיפָה ephah (1·38) 35

Chapter 17

מַסַּע 1 journey by stages (3·12) 652

נָסָה 2 to test (5·36·36) 650

צָמֵא 3 to be thirsty (1·10·10) 854

הלין to murmur (4·10·18) 534

צָמָא thirst (1·17) 854

סקל 4 to stone (4·12·22) 709

נָסָה 7 to test (5·36·36) 650

גָּבַר 11 to prevail (2·17·25) 149

כָּבֵד 12 heavy (9·39) 458

תָּמַךְ to hold up; support (1·20·21) 1069

חָלַשׁ 13 to disable (1·3·3) 325

זִכָּרוֹן 14 memorial; reminder (8·24) 272

מָחָה to exterminate (3·22·35) 562

זֵכֶר remembrance; memory (2·23) 271

נֵס 15 standard (1·21) 651

כֵּס 16 throne (1·1) 490

Chapter 18

חֹתֵן 1 wife's father (15·21) 368

חֹתֵן 2 wife's father (15·21) 368

שִׁלּוּחִים a sending away (1·3) 1019

נָכְרִי 3 foreign (3·45) 648

עֵזֶר 4 help; one who helps (1·21) 740

חֹתֵן 5 wife's father (15·21) 368

חֹתֵן 6 wife's father (15·21) 368

חֹתֵן 7 wife's father (15·21) 368

נָשַׁק to kiss (2·26·32) 676

חֹתֵן 8 wife's father (15·21) 368

אודה cause (1·11) 15

תְּלָאָה weariness; hardship (1·15) 521

חדה 9 to rejoice (1·2·3) 292

זוד 11 to act presumptuously; rebelliously (1·2·10) 267

חֹתֵן 12 wife's father (15·21) 368

מָחֳרָת 13 the morrow (4·32) 564

יָרָה to throw (2·13·25[?]) 434

חֹתֵן 14 wife's father (15·21) 368

חֹתֵן 15 wife's father (15·21) 368

חֹתֵן 17 wife's father (15·21) 368

נָבֵל 18 to sink down (2·20·24[?]) 615

כָּבֵד heavy (9·39) 458

מוּל 19 in front of (6·25) 557

הִזְהִיר 20 to teach; warn (1·13·21) 264

יָרֵא 21 fear (1·45) 431

בֶּצַע unjust gain (1·23) 130

חֹתֵן	24 wife's father (15·21) 368
קָשָׁה	26 hard; difficult (7·36) 904
חֹתֵן	27 wife's father (15·21) 368

Chapter 19

נֶשֶׁר	4 eagle (1·26) 676
סְגֻלָּה	5 possession (1·8) 688
עָב	9 thickness (1·30) 716
בַּעֲבוּר	in order that (6·46) 721
שִׂמְלָה	10 clothes (6·29) 971
הִגְבִּיל	12 to set bounds (2·2·5) 148
סָקַל	13 to stone (4·12·22) 709
נִסְקַל	to be stoned (4·4·22) 709
יָרָה	to shoot (2·13·25[?]) 434
נוֹרָה	to be shot through (1·1·25[?]) 434
מָשַׁךְ	to draw out (2·30·36) 604
יוֹבֵל	ram's horn (1·27) 385
שִׂמְלָה	14 clothes (6·29) 971
בָּרָק	16 lightning (1·20) 140
כָּבֵד	heavy (9·39) 458
חָרַד	16 to tremble (2·23·39) 353
הִתְיַצֵּב	17 to station oneself (6·48·48) 426
תַּחְתִּי	lower; lowest (1·19) 1066
עָשַׁן	18 to smoke (1·6·6) 798
עָשָׁן	smoke (2·25) 798
כִּבְשָׁן	kiln (3·4) 461
חָרַד	to tremble (2·23·39) 353
חָזֵק	19 strong (1·2) 304
הֵעִיד	21 to affirm solemnly; warn (2·40·45) 729
הָרַס	to break through (3·20·43) 248
פָּרַץ	22 to break out upon (3·46·49) 829
הֵעִיד	23 to exhort solemnly; admonish (2·40·45) 729
הִגְבִּיל	to set bounds (2·2·5) 148
הָרַס	24 to break through (3·30·43) 248
פָּרַץ	to break out upon (3·46·49) 829

Chapter 20

פֶּסֶל	4 idol; image (1·31) 820
תְּמוּנָה	likeness; representation (1·10) 568
מִמַּעַל	above; on top of (3·29) 751
קַנָּא	5 jealous (3·6) 888
שִׁלֵּשׁ	those of the third generation; i.e., grandsons (2·5) 1026
רִבֵּעַ	pertaining to the fourth (2·4) 918
שֹׂנֵא	enemy (3·41) 971
אֹהֵב	6 lover; friend (1·36[?]) 12
נִקָּה	7 to leave unpunished (2·12·36) 667
רָצַח	13 to murder; slay (1·38·43) 953
נָאַף	14 to commit adultery (1·16·30) 610
גָּנַב	15 to steal (4·30·39) 170
חָמַד	17 to desire (3·16·21) 326
לַפִּיד	18 torch (1·13) 542
עָשֵׁן	smoking (1·2) 798
נוּעַ	to tremble (1·22·38) 631
לְבַעֲבוּר	20 in order to (1·3) 721
נִסָּה	to test (5·36·36) 650
בַּעֲבוּר	in order that (6·46) 721
יִרְאָה	fear (1·45) 432
עֲרָפֶל	21 heavy cloud (1·15) 791
גָּזִית	25 a hewing; cutting (1·11) 159
הֵנִיף	to wield (4·32·34[?]) 631
מַעֲלָה	26 step (1·45[?]) 752

Chapter 21

חָפְשִׁי	2 free (4·17) 344
חִנָּם	freely (2·32) 336
גַּף	3 body; self (2·2) 172
גַּף	4 body; self (2·2) 172
חָפְשִׁי	5 free (4·17) 344
מְזוּזָה	6 doorpost (4·20) 265
רָצַע	to bore; pierce (1·1·1) 954
מַרְצֵעַ	awl (1·2) 954
יָעַד	8 to designate (2·5·28) 416

39

נָכְרִי	foreign (3·45) 648	
בגד	to act or deal treacherously (1·42·42) 93	
יָעַד	9 to designate (2·5·28) 416	
שְׁאֵר	10 flesh (1·17) 984	
כְּסוּת	covering (2·8) 492	
ענה	cohabitation (1·1) 773	
גרע	to diminish (3·14·22) 175	
חִנָּם	11 freely (2·32) 336	
צָדָה	13 to lie in wait (1·2·2) 841	
אָנָה	to cause |or allow| to meet (1·4·4) 58	
הֵזִיד	14 to act insolently (2·10·12) 267	
עָרְמָה	craftily (1·5) 791	
גנב	16 to steal (4·30·39) 120	
אֶגְרֹף	18 fist (1·2) 175	
מִשְׁכָּב	bed (2·46) 1012	
מִשְׁעֶנֶת	19 staff (1·12) 1044	
נִקָּה	to be exempt from punishment (1·23·36) 667	
שֶׁבֶת	cessation (1·7)[?] 992	
נקם	20 to avenge (1·13·34) 667	
נקם	to be avenged (1·12·34) 667	
הֻקַּם	21 to be avenged (1·3·34) 667	
נצה	22 to struggle with each other (2·5·8) 663	
נָגַף	to strike (7·24·48) 619	
הָרָה	pregnant (1·15[?]) 247	
אָסוֹן	mischief; evil; harm (2·5) 62	
ענש	to fine; punish (1·6·9) 778	
נענש	to be fined; punished (1·3·9) 778	
פָּלִיל	judge (1·3) 813	
אָסוֹן	23 mischief; evil; harm (2·5) 62	
כְּוִיָּה	25 burning (2·2) 465	
פֶּצַע	bruise; wound (2·8) 822	
חַבּוּרָה	stripe; blow (2·7) 289	
חָפְשִׁי	26 free (4·17) 344	
חָפְשִׁי	27 free (4·17) 344	

נָגַח	28 to gore (4·4·11) 618	
סָקַל	to stone (4·12·22) 709	
נִסְקַל	to be stoned (4·4·22) 709	
נָקִי	free from punishment (2·43) 667	
נַגָּח	29 addicted to goring (2·2) 618	
תְּמוֹל	yesterday; aforetime (7·23) 1069	
שִׁלְשֹׁם	three days ago; specif. = the day before yesterday (6·25) 1026	
הוּעַד	"and protest be entered" (1·1·45) 729	
נִסְקַל	to be stoned (4·4·22) 709	
כֹּפֶר	30 ransom (2·13) 497	
פִּדְיֹן	ransom (1·3) 804	
נָגַח	31 to gore (4·4·11) 618	
נָגַח	32 to gore (4·4·11) 618	
נִסְקַל	to be stoned (4·4·22) 709	
כָּרָה	33 to dig (1·13·14) 500	
נָגַף	35 to strike (7·24·48) 619	
חָצָה	to divide (2·11·15) 345	
נַגָּח	36 addicted to goring (2·2) 618	
תְּמוֹל	yesterday (7·23) 1069	
שִׁלְשֹׁם	three days ago; specif. = the day before yesterday (6·25) 1026	
גנב	37 to steal (4·30·37) 170	
שֶׂה	one of a flock; sheep; goat (13·44) 961	
טבח	37 to slaughter (1·11·11) 370	

Chapter 22

מַחְתֶּרֶת	1 burglary (1·2) 369	
גַּנָּב	thief (3·17) 170	
זָרַח	2 to rise (1·18·18) 280	
גְּנֵבָה	thing stolen (2·2) 170	
גְּנֵבָה	3 thing stolen (2·2) 170	
שֶׂה	one of a flock; sheep; goat (13·44) 961	
בְּעִיר	4 beast (1·6) 129	
בֵּעֵר	to consume (1·26·28[?]) 129	

מֵיטָב — the best (2·6) 406

קוֹץ — 5 thornbush (1·11) 881

גָּדִישׁ — heap; stack [of sheaves] (1·4) 155

קָמָה — standing grain (1·10) 879

בְּעֵרָה — burning (1·1) 129

גָּנַב — 6 to be stolen away (1·4·39) 170

גַּנָּב — thief (3·17) 170

גַּנָּב — 7 thief (3·17) 170

שֶׂה — 8 one of a flock; sheep; goat (13·44) 961

שַׂלְמָה — outer garment (2·16) 971

אֲבֵדָה — a lost thing (1·4) 2

הִרְשִׁיעַ — to condemn as guilty (1·25·34) 957

שֶׂה — 9 one of a flock; sheep; goat (13·44) 961

נִשְׁבָּה — to be taken captive (1·8·37) 985

שְׁבוּעָה — 10 oath; curse (1·30) 989

גָנב — 11 to steal (4·30·39) 170

נגנב — to be stolen (1·1·39) 170

טָרַף — 12 to tear (1·19·24) 382

נטרף — to be torn (1·2·24) 382

טְרֵפָה — animal torn (2·9) 383

שָׂכִיר — 14 hired (2·18) 969

שָׂכָר — hire; wages (2·29) 969

פִּתָּה — 15 to seduce (1·17·27) 834

בְּתוּלָה — virgin (2·50) 143

ארש — to be betrothed (1·5·11) 76

מהר — to acquire by paying a purchase price (2·3·3) 555

מֵאֵן — 16 to refuse (8·45·45) 549

שָׁקַל — to weigh out (1·19·22) 1053

מֹהַר — purchase price (1·3) 555

בְּתוּלָה — virgin (2·50) 143

כִּשֵּׁף — 17 to practice sorcery (2·6·6) 506

הֶחֱרַם — 19 to be put under the ban (1·3·49) 355

בִּלְתִּי — except (1·24) 116

לְבַדּוֹ — alone (3·35) 94

הוֹנָה — 20 to maltreat (1·14·18) 413

לָחַץ — to oppress (3·14·15) 537

יָתוֹם — 21 orphan (2·42) 450

צְעָקָה — 22 cry of distress (5·21) 858

יָתוֹם — 23 orphan (2·42) 450

הִלְוָה — 24 to lend (1·9·14) 531

נֹשֶׁה — creditor (1·4[?]) 674

נֶשֶׁךְ — interest (1·12) 675

חָבַל — 25 to bind by pledge (1·11·12) 286

שַׂלְמָה — outer garment (2·16) 971

כְּסוּת — 26 covering (2·8) 492

שִׂמְלָה — wrapper; mantle (6·29) 971

בַּמֶּה — wherein (2·29) 552

חַנּוּן — gracious (2·13) 337

מְלֵאָה — 28 full produce (1·3) 571

דֶּמַע — juice (1·1) 199

אָחַר — to keep back (1·15·17) 29

טְרֵפָה — 30 animal torn (2·9) 383

כֶּלֶב — dog (2·32) 476

Chapter 23

שֶׁמַע — 1 hearing; report (1·17) 1034

דַּל — 3 the poor (2·48) 195

הָדַר — to pay honor to (1·4·6) 213

פָּגַע — 4 to meet; light upon (3·40·46) 803

תָּעָה — to wander about (1·26·49) 1073

שֹׂנֵא — 5 enemy (3·41) 971

רָבַץ — to lie down (1·24·30) 918

מַשָּׂא — load (1·43) 672

נָקִי — 7 clean (2·43) 667

הִצְדִּיק — to declare righteous; to justify (1·12·41) 842

שֹׁחַד — 8 bribe (2·23) 1005

עִוֵּר — to blind (1·5·5) 734

פִּקֵּחַ — seeing (2·2) 824

סִלֵּף — to subvert (1·7·7) 701

לָחַץ — 9 to oppress (3·14·15) 537

תְּבוּאָה — 10 product; yield (1·43) 100

שׁמט 11 to let drop; let fall (1·7·9) 1030

נָטַשׁ to let alone (1·33·40) 643

זַיִת olives; olive tree (3·38) 268

נפשׁ 12 to refresh oneself (2·3·3) 661

חגג 14 to keep a pilgrim feast (4·16·16) 290

רֵיקָם 15 in empty condition; emptily (3·16) 938

קָצִיר 16 harvest (3·49) 894

בִּכּוּרִים first fruits (4·17) 114

אָסִיף ingathering; harvest (2·2) 63

זכור 17 male (2·4) 271

חָמֵץ 18 that which is leavened (5·11) 329

בִּכּוּרִים 19 firstfruits (4·17) 114

בשׁל to boil (4·20·27) 143

גְּדִי kid (2·16) 152

חָלָב milk (6·44) 316

הֵמַר 21 to show bitterness (1·3·14) 600

איב 22 to be hostile to (1·2·2) 33

צור to show hostility to; to treat as foe (1·5·5) 849

צֹרֵר vexer, harasser (1·17) 865

הכחיד 23 to annihilate (1·6·30) 470

הרס 24 to overthrow; to tear down (2·3·43) 248

מַצֵּבָה pillar (3·35) 663

מַחֲלָה 25 sickness (2·4) 318

שׁכל 26 to show abortion; to miscarry (1·18·24) 1013

עָקָר barren (1·11) 785

אֵימָה 27 terror; dread (2·17) 33

עֹרֶף back of neck (5·33) 791

צִרְעָה 28 hornets (1·3) 864

גרשׁ to drive out (9·33·46) 176

גרשׁ 29 to drive out (9·33·46) 176

רבב to be; become many (1·23·24) 912

גרשׁ 30 to drive out (9·33·46) 176

פרה to be fruitful (2·22·29) 826

גרשׁ 31 to drive out (9·33·46) 176

מוֹקֵשׁ lure (3·27) 430

Chapter 24

לְבַדּוֹ 2 alone (3·35) 94

מַצֵּבָה 4 pillar (3·35) 663

אַגָּן 6 basin (1·3) 8

זָרַק to throw; scatter abundantly (6·32·34) 284

זָרַק 8 to throw; scatter abundantly (6·32·34) 284

לְבֵנָה 10 tile, pavement (8·12) 527

סַפִּיר sapphire (3·11) 705

טֹהַר purity (1·3) 372

אציל 11 noble (1·1[?]) 69

לוּחַ 12 tablet (14·40) 531

הורה to teach (5·45·45[?]) 434

מְשָׁרֵת 13 servant (2·20) 1058

בָּזֶה 14 in this [place]; here (1·19) 261

Chapter 25

נָדַב 2 to incite (3·3·17) 621

תְּכֵלֶת 4 violet (34·49) 1067

אַרְגָּמָן purple thread (26·39) 71

תּוֹלֵעָה coccus ilicis [yielding scarlet color] (27·41) 1069

שָׁנִי scarlet (26·42) 1040

שׁשׁ linen (33·37) 1058

אדם 5 to be reddened; dyed red (6·7·10) 10

תַּחַשׁ dugong[?] (6·14) 1065

שִׁטָּה acacia (wood) (26·28) 1008

מָאוֹר 6 light (7·19) 22

בֶּשֶׂם balsam (6·30) 141

מִשְׁחָה ointment (13·21) 603

סם spice (11·16) 702

שֹׁהַם 7 onyx (7·11) 995

מלוא setting (8·15) 571

אֵפוֹד		ephod; a priestly garment (29·49) 65
חֹשֶׁן		breast piece (23·25) 365
תַּבְנִי	9	pattern (3·20) 125
שִׁטָּה	10	acacia [wood] (26·28) 1008
קוֹמָה		height (10·45) 879
צָפָה	11	to overlay (25·42·46) 860
זֵר		border (10·10) 267
טַבַּע	12	ring (35·44) 371
צֵלָע		side (19·39) 854
בַּד	13	pole; stave (27·41) 94
שִׁטָּה		acacia [wood] (26·28) 1008
צָפָה		to overlay (25·42·46) 860
בַּד	14	pole; stave (27·41) 94
טַבַּע		ring (35·44) 371
צֵלָע		side (19·39) 854
טַבַּע	15	ring (35·44) 371
בַּד		pole; stave (27·41) 94
כַּפֹּרֶ	17	propitiatory (18·27) 498
מִקְשָׁ	18	hammered work[?] (6·9) 904
קָצָה		end (21·28) 892
כַּפֹּרֶ		propitiatory (18·27) 498
קָצָה	19	end (21·28) 892
כַּפֹּרֶ		propitiatory (18·27) 498
לְמַע	20	upward (2·34) 751
סכך		to cover (3·12·18[?]) 696
כַּפֹּרֶ		propitiatory (18·27) 498
כַּפֹּרֶ	21	propitiatory (18·27) 498
מִלְמַ		above (6·24) 751
נועד	22	to meet at an appointed place (4·18·28) 416
כַּפֹּרֶ		propitiatory (18·27) 498
מִבֵּין		from between (1·21) 107
שִׁטָּה	23	acacia [wood] (26·28) 1008
קוֹמָה		height (10·45) 879
צָפָה	24	to overlay (25·42·46) 860
זֵר		border (10·10) 267
מִסְגֶּ	25	rim (6·17) 689
טֶפַח		handbreadth (2·9) 381
זֵר		border (10·10) 267
טַבַּעַת	26	ring (35·44) 371
לְעֻמַּת	27	close by; side by side with (5·31) 769
מִסְגֶּרֶת		rim (6·17) 689
טַבַּעַת		ring (35·44) 371
בַּד		pole; stave (27·41) 94
בַּד	28	pole; stave (27·41) 94
שִׁטָּה		acacia [wood] (26·28) 1008
צָפָה		to overlay (25·42·46) 860
קְעָרָה	29	dish; platter (2·17) 891
קַשְׂוָה		jug; jar (2·4) 903
מְנַקִּיה		sacrificial bowl (2·4) 667
הֻסַּךְ		to be poured out (2·2·24) 650
מְנוֹרָה	31	lampstand (18·39) 633
מִקְשָׁה		hammered work[?] (6·9) 904
יָרֵךְ		base (7·34) 437
גְּבִיעַ		cup (8·14) 149
כַּפְתּוֹר		knob (14·16) 499
פֶּרַח		bud; sprout (8·17) 827
צַד	32	side (9·31) 841
מְנוֹרָה		lampstand (18·39) 633
גְּבִיעַ	33	cup (8·14) 149
שָׁקֵד		pu. ptc. = shaped as almond [blossoms] (6·6·17) 1052
כַּפְתּוֹר		knob (14·16) 499
פֶּרַח		bud; sprout (8·17) 827
מְנוֹרָה		lampstand (18·39) 633
מְנוֹרָה	34	lampstand (18·39) 633
גְּבִיעַ		cup (8·14) 149
שָׁקֵד		pu. ptc. = shaped as almond [blossoms] (6·6·17) 1052
כַּפְתּוֹר	34	knob (14·16) 499
פֶּרַח		bud; sprout (8·17) 827
כַּפְתּוֹר	35	knob (14·16) 499
מְנוֹרָה		lampstand (18·39) 633
כַּפְתּוֹר	36	knob (14·16) 499

מְקֻשָׁה hammered work[?] (6·9) 904

נֵר 37 lamp (11·44) 632

הֵאִיר to shine (3·34·40) 21

מֶלְקָחַיִם 38 snuffers (2·6) 544

מַחְתָּה snuff holder (4·21) 367

תַּבְנִית 40 pattern (3·20) 125

Chapter 26

שֵׁשׁ 1 linen (33·37) 1058

הָשְׁזֹר to be twisted (21·21·21) 1004

תְּכֵלֶת violet (34·49) 1067

אַרְגָּמָן purple thread (26·39) 71

תּוֹלֵעָה coccus ilicis [yielding scarlet color] (27·41) 1069

שָׁנִי scarlet (26·42) 1040

חֹשֵׁב workman (11·12) 362

חבר 3 to unite; be joined (4·11·28) 287

לוּלִי 4 loop (13·13) 533

תְּכֵלֶת violet (34·49) 1067

קָצָה end (21·28) 892

חֹבֶרֶת a thing that joins or is joined; curtain pieces (4·4) 289

קִיצוֹן at the end; outermost (4·4) 894

מַחְבֶּרֶת thing joined (8·8) 289

לוּלִי 5 loop (13·13) 533

מַחְבֶּרֶת thing joined (8·8) 289

הִקְבִּיל to show oppositeness in corresponding to one another (2·2·13) 867

קֶרֶס 6 hook (10·10) 902

חִבַּר 9 to unite; join (8·9·29) 287

חִבַּר to unite; join (8·9·29) 287

כָּפַל to double over (3·3·4) 495

מוּל the forefront of (6·25) 557

לוּלִי 10 loop (13·13) 533

קִיצוֹן at the end of; outermost (4·4) 894

חֹבֶרֶת a thing that joins or is joined; curtain pieces (4·4) 289

קֶרֶס 11 hook (10·10) 902

לוּלִי loop (13·13) 533

חִבַּר to unite; join (8·9·29) 287

סֶרַח 12 excess (1·1) 710

עֹדֵף to remain over; be in excess (4·8·9) 727

סרח to overrun (1·3·4[?]) 710

עֹדֵף 13 to remain over; be in excess (4·8·9) 727

סָרוּחַ overhang (1·3[?]) 710

צַד side (9·31) 841

מִכְסֶה 14 covering (8·16) 492

אָדֹם to be reddened; dyed red (6·7·10) 10

תַּחַשׁ dugong[?] (6·14) 1065

מִלְמַעְלָה above (6·24) 751

קֶרֶשׁ 15 board (43·46) 903

שִׁטָּה acacia [wood] (26·28) 1008

קֶרֶשׁ 16 board (43·46) 903

קֶרֶשׁ 17 board (43·46) 903

שֻׁלָּב to be bound; joined (2·2·2) 1016

קֶרֶשׁ 18 board (43·46) 903

תֵּימָן [toward] the south (5·24) 412

קֶרֶשׁ 19 board (43·46) 903

צֶלַע 20 side (19·39) 854

קֶרֶשׁ board (43·46) 903

קֶרֶשׁ 21 board (43·46) 903

יַרְכָה 22 extreme parts (6·28) 438

קֶרֶשׁ board (43·46) 903

קֶרֶשׁ 23 board (43·46) 903

[?]קצע pu. ptc. = corner post (2·2·3) 893

יַרְכָה extreme parts (6·28) 438

תֹּאֲמִים 24 double (2·6)[?] 1060

מִלְמַטָּה beneath (6·6) 641

תָּם complete (2·15) 1070

טַבַּעַת ring (35·44) 371

מְקֻצָּע corner-buttress (2·11) 893

קֶרֶשׁ	25 board (43·46) 903	
בְּרִיחַ	26 bar (15·41) 138	
שִׁטָּה	acacia [wood] (26·28) 1008	
קֶרֶשׁ	board (43·46) 903	
צֵלָע	side (19·39) 854	
בְּרִיחַ	27 bar (15·41) 138	
קֶרֶשׁ	board (43·46) 903	
צֵלָע	side (19·39) 854	
ירכה	extreme parts (6·28) 438	
בְּרִיחַ	28 bar (15·41) 138	
תִּיכוֹן	middle (2·12) 1064	
קֶרֶשׁ	board (43·46) 903	
קֶרֶשׁ	29 board (43·46) 903	
צִפָּה	to overlay (25·42·46) 860	
טַבַּעַת	ring (35·44) 371	
בְּרִיחַ	bar (15·41) 138	
פָּרֹכֶת	31 curtain (15·25) 827	
תְּכֵלֶת	violet (34·49) 1067	
אַרְגָּמָן	purple thread (26·39) 71	
תּוֹלֵעָה	coccus ilicis [yielding scarlet color] (27·41) 1069	
שָׁנִי	scarlet (26·42) 1040	
שֵׁשׁ	linen (33·37) 1058	
השזר	to be twisted (21·21·21) 1004	
חֹשֵׁב	workman (11·12[?]) 362	
שִׁטָּה	32 acacia [wood] (26·28) 1008	
צפה	to be overlaid (1·2·46) 860	
וו	hook; pin; peg (13·13) 255	
פָּרֹכֶת	33 curtain (15·25) 827	
קרס	hook (10·10) 902	
הבדיל	to divide (1·32·42) 95	
כַּפֹּרֶת	34 propitiatory (18·27) 498	
פָּרֹכֶת	35 curtain (15·25) 827	
מְנוֹרָה	lampstand (18·39) 633	
נוֹכַח	in front of (3·22) 647	
צֵלָע	side (19·39) 854	
תֵּימָן	[toward] the south (5·24) 412	
מָסָךְ	36 screen (16·25) 697	

תְּכֵלֶת	violet (34·49) 1067	
אַרְגָּמָן	purple thread (26·39) 71	
תּוֹלֵעָה	coccus ilicis [yielding scarlet color] (27·41) 1069	
שָׁנִי	scarlet (26·42) 1040	
שֵׁשׁ	linen (33·37) 1058	
השזר	to be twisted (21·21·21) 1004	
רקם	to variegate; weave (8·8·9) 955	
מָסָךְ	37 screen (16·25) 697	
שִׁטָּה	acacia [wood] (26·28) 1008	
צִפָּה	to overlay (25·42·46) 860	
וו	hook; pin; peg (13·13) 255	

Chapter 27

שִׁטָּה	1 acacia [wood] (26·28) 1008	
רבע	to be squared (6·9·12) 917	
קוֹמָה	height (10·45) 879	
פִּנָּה	2 corner (2·30) 819	
צִפָּה	to overlay (25·42·46) 860	
סִיר	3 pot (3·29) 696	
דִּשֵּׁן	to take away the fat ashes (1·5·11) 206	
יע	shovel (2·9) 418	
מִזְרָק	basin (2·32) 284	
מזלגה	three-pronged fork (2·5) 272	
מַחְתָּה	fire pan (4·21) 367	
מִכְבָּר	4 grating (6·6) 460	
רֶשֶׁת	network (4·22) 440	
טַבַּעַת	ring (35·44) 371	
קָצָה	end (21·28) 892	
כַּרְכֹּב	5 rim (2·2) 501	
מִלְמַטָּה	beneath (6·6) 641	
רֶשֶׁת	network (4·22) 440	
בַּד	6 poles; staves (27·41[?]) 94	
שִׁטָּה	acacia [wood] (26·28) 1008	
צִפָּה	to overlay (25·42·46) 860	
בַּד	7 poles; staves (27·41[?]) 94	
טַבַּעַת	ring (35·44) 371	

צֶלָע	side (19·39) 854
נבב	8 to hollow out (2·4·4) 612
לוּחַ	board (14·40) 531
תֵּימָן	9 [toward] the south (5·24) 412
קלע	curtain; hanging (13·16) 887
שֵׁשׁ	linen (33·37) 1058
השזר	to be twisted (21·21·21) 1004
וו	10 hook; pin; peg (13·13) 255
חשוק	fillet; ring (8·8) 366
קלע	11 curtain; hanging (13·16) 887
וו	hook; pin; peg (13·13) 255
חשוק	fillet; ring (8·8) 366
קלע	12 curtain; hanging (13·16) 887
קדם	13 eastward (2·26) 870
קלע	14 curtain; hanging (13·16) 887
קלע	15 curtain; hanging (13·16) 887
מָסָךְ	16 screen (16·25) 697
תְּכֵלֶת	violet (34·49) 1067
אַרְגָּמָן	purple thread (26·39) 71
תּוֹלֵעָה	coccus ilicis [yielding scarlet color] (27·41) 1069
שָׁנִי	scarlet (26·42) 1040
שֵׁשׁ	linen (33·37) 1058
השזר	to be twisted (21·21·21) 1004
רקם	to variegate; weave (8·8·9) 955
חשק	17 to be furnished with fillets or rings (2·2·11) 366
וו	hook; pin; peg (13·13) 255
קוֹמָה	18 height (10·45) 879
שֵׁשׁ	linen (33·37) 1058
השזר	to be twisted (21·21·21) 1004
יָתֵד	19 peg; pin (8·24) 450
זַיִת	20 olives (3·38) 268
זַךְ	pure; unmixed (2·11) 269
כָּתִית	beaten (2·5) 510
מָאוֹר	light (7·19) 22
נֵר	lamp (11·44) 632
פָּרֹכֶת	21 curtain (15·25) 827

Chapter 28

כֹּהֵן	1 to act as priest (12·23·23) 464
כֹּהֵן	3 to act as priest (12·23·23) 464
חֹשֶׁן	4 breast piece (23·25) 365
אֵפוֹד	ephod; priestly garment (29·49) 65
מְעִיל	robe (9·28) 591
כְּתֹנֶת	tunic (8·30) 509
תַּשְׁבֵּץ	checkered; plaited (1·1) 990
מִצְנֶפֶת	turban (8·12) 857
אַבְנֵט	girdle (5·9) 126
כֹּהֵן	to act as priest (12·23·23) 464
תְּכֵלֶת	5 violet (34·49) 1067
אַרְגָּמָן	purple thread (26·39) 71
תּוֹלֵעָה	coccus ilicis [yielding scarlet color] (27·41) 1069
שָׁנִי	scarlet (26·42) 1040
שֵׁשׁ	linen (33·37) 1058
אֵפוֹד	6 ephod; priestly garment (29·49) 65
תְּכֵלֶת	violet (34·49) 1067
אַרְגָּמָן	purple thread (26·39) 71
תּוֹלֵעָה	coccus ilicis [yielding scarlet color] (27·41) 1069
שָׁנִי	scarlet (26·42) 1040
שֵׁשׁ	linen (33·37) 1058
השזר	to be twisted (21·21·21) 1004
חֹשֵׁב	workman (11·12[?]) 362
חבר	7 to unite; be joined (4·11·28) 287
קָצָה	end (21·28) 892
חבר	to be united; joined (2·4·28) 287
חֵשֶׁב	8 girdle; ingenious work (7·8) 363
אֲפֻדָּה	ephod; high priestly garment (2·3) 65
תְּכֵלֶת	violet (34·49) 1067
אַרְגָּמָן	purple thread (26·39) 71
תּוֹלֵעָה	coccus ilicis [yielding scarlet color] (27·41) 1069
שָׁנִי	scarlet (26·42) 1040

שֵׁשׁ	linen (33·37) 1058		סַפִּיר	sapphire (3·11) 705
הֹשׁז	to be twisted (21·21·21) 1004		יַהֲלֹם	jasper[?] (2·3) 240
שֹׁהַם	9 onyx (7·11) 995		טוּר	19 row (12·26) 377
פָּתַח	to engrave (3·8·9) 836		לֶשֶׁם	precious stone (2·2) 545
תּוֹלד	10 generations (3·39) 410		שְׁבוּ	precious stone (2·2) 986
חָרָשׁ	11 graver, artificer (3·38) 360		אַחְלָמָה	amethyst[?] (2·2) 21
פִּתּוּח	engraving (6·11) 836		טוּר	20 row (12·26) 377
חֹתָם	engraving of a seal (6·13) 368		תַּרְשִׁישׁ	yellow jasper[?] (2·7) 1076
פָּתַח	to engrave (3·8·9) 836		שֹׁהַם	onyx (7·11) 995
מְשׁ	checkered work (8·9) 990		יָשְׁפֵה	jasper (2·3) 448
אֵפוֹ	12 ephod; priestly garment (29·49) 65		שבץ	pu. ptc. = inwoven (1·1·2) 990
זִכָּרוֹ	memorial (8·24) 272		מלאה	setting of jewel (3·3) 571
מְשׁ	13 checkered work (8·9) 990		פִּתּוּחַ	21 engraving (6·11) 836
שַׁרשׁ	14 chain (4·8) 1057		חוֹתָם	engraving of a seal (6·13) 368
מִגְבָּ	the twisted (1·1) 148		חֹשֶׁן	22 breast piece (23·25) 365
עֲבֹת	cordage; cord (8·24) 721		שרשרה	chain (4·8) 1057
מְשׁ	checkered work (8·9) 990		גַּבְלֻת	twisting (2·2) 148
חֹשֶׁן	15 breast piece (23·25) 365		עֲבֹת	cordage; cord (8·24) 721
חֹשֵׁ	workman (11·12[?]) 362		חֹשֶׁן	23 breast piece (23·25) 365
אֵפוֹ	ephod; priestly garment (29·49) 65		טַבַּעַת	ring (35·44) 371
תְּכֵל	violet (34·49) 1067		קָצֶה	end (21·28) 892
אַרגָּ	purple thread (26·39) 71		עֲבֹת	24 cordage; cord (8·24) 721
תּוֹלַ	coccus ilicis [yielding scarlet color] (27·41) 1069		טַבַּעַת	ring (35·44) 371
שָׁנִי	scarlet (26·42) 1040		קָצֶה	end (21·28) 892
שֵׁשׁ	linen (33·37) 1058		חֹשֶׁן	breast piece (23·25) 365
הֹשׁז	to be twisted (21·21·21) 1004		קָצֶה	25 end (21·28) 892
רבע	16 ptc. pass. = to be squared (6·9·12) 917		עֲבֹת	cordage; cord (8·24) 721
כָּפַל	to double (3·3·4) 495		מִשְׁבְּצוֹת	checkered work (8·9) 990
זֶרֶת	span (4·7) 284		אֵפוֹד	ephod; priestly garment (29·49) 65
מִלֵּא	17 setting of jewel (3·3) 571		מוּל	the forefront of (6·25) 557
טוּר	row (12·26) 377		טַבַּעַת	26 ring (35·44) 371
אֹדֶם	carnelian [ruby] (2·3) 10		קָצֶה	end (21·28) 892
פִּטְדָ	topaz (2·4) 809		חֹשֶׁן	breast piece (23·25) 365
בָּרֶקֶ	emerald (2·3) 140		אֵפוֹד	ephod; priestly garment (29·49) 65
טוּר	18 row (12·26) 377		טַבַּעַת	27 ring (35·44) 371
נֹפֶךְ	ruby[?] (2·4) 656		אֵפוֹד	ephod; priestly garment (29·49) 65
			מִלְמַטָּה	beneath (6·6) 641
			מִמּוּל	on the forefront of (2·9) 557

47

לְעֻמַּת — close by; side by side with (5·31) 769

מַחְבֶּרֶת — place of joining (8·8) 289

מִמַּעַל — above; on top of (3·29) 751

חֵשֶׁב — girdle; ingenious work (7·8) 363

רכס — 28 to bind (2·2·2) 940

חֹשֶׁן — breast piece (23·25) 365

טַבַּעַת — ring (35·44) 371

אֵפוֹד — ephod; priestly garment (29·49) 65

פָּתִיל — cord (5·11) 836

תְּכֵלֶת — violet (34·49) 1067

חֵשֶׁב — girdle; ingenious work (7·8) 363

נזחח — to be displaced (2·2·2) 267

חֹשֶׁן — 29 breast piece (23·25) 365

זִכָּרֹן — memorial (8·24) 272

חֹשֶׁן — 30 breast piece (23·25) 365

אוּרִים — Urim (1·7) 22

תֻּמִּים — Thummim[?] (1·5) 1070

מְעִיל — 31 robe (9·28) 591

אֵפוֹד — ephod; priestly garment (29·49) 65

כָּלִיל — entirety (2·15) 483

תְּכֵלֶת — violet (34·49) 1067

אֹרֵג — 32 weaver (4·10[?]) 70

כְּפִי — in proportion to (3·16) 804

תַּחְרָא — corselet? (2·2) 1065

שׁוּל — 33 skirt [of robe] (6·11) 1002

רִמּוֹן — pomegranate (8·32) 941

תְּכֵלֶת — violet (34·49) 1067

אַרְגָּמָן — purple thread (26·39) 71

תּוֹלֵעָה — coccus ilicis [yielding scarlet color] (27·41) 1069

שָׁנִי — scarlet (26·42) 1040

פַּעֲמֹן — bell (7·7) 822

פַּעֲמֹן — 34 bell (7·7) 822

רִמּוֹן — pomegranate (8·32) 941

שׁוּל — skirt [of robe] (6·11) 1002

מְעִיל — robe (9·28) 591

צִיץ — 36 shining plate [of gold] (2·15) 847

פָּתַח — to engrave (3·8·9) 836

פִּתּוּחַ — engraving (6·11) 836

חוֹתָם — engraving of a seal (6·13) 368

פָּתִיל — 37 cord (5·11) 836

תְּכֵלֶת — violet (34·49) 1067

מִצְנֶפֶת — turban of high priest (8·12) 857

מוּל — the forefront (6·25) 557

מֵצַח — 38 forehead (2·13) 594

מַתָּנָה — gift (1·17) 682

שׁבץ — 39 to weave in checker[?] (1·1·2) 990

כְּתֹנֶת — tunic (8·30) 509

שֵׁשׁ — linen (33·37) 1058

מִצְנֶפֶת — turban of high priest (8·12) 857

אַבְנֵט — girdle (5·9) 126

רקם — to variegate; weave (8·8·9) 955

כְּתֹנֶת — 40 tunic (8·30) 509

אַבְנֵט — girdle (5·9) 126

מִגְבָּעוֹת — turban of common priest (3·4) 149

כֹּהֵן — 41 to act as priest (12·23·23) 464

מכנס — 42 drawers (2·5) 488

בַּד — white linen (2·23) 94

מָתְנַיִם — loins (2·50) 608

יָרֵךְ — thigh (7·34) 437

Chapter 29

כֹּהֵן — 1 to act as priest (12·23·23) 464

חַלָּה — 2 a kind of cake (2·14) 319

בָּלַל — to mix (2·42·42[?]) 117

רָקִיק — a thin cake; wafer (2·8) 956

סַל — 3 basket (4·15) 700

כְּתֹנֶת — 5 tunic (8·30) 509

מְעִיל — robe (9·28) 591

אֵפוֹד — ephod; priestly garment (29·49) 65

חֹשֶׁן — breast piece (23·25) 365

אפד — to gird on [an ephod] (1·2·2) 65

חֵשֶׁב — girdle; ingenious work (7·8) 363

מִצְנֶפֶת — 6 turban of high priest (8·12) 857

נֵזֶר — crown (2·24) 634

מִשְׁחָה 7 ointment (13·21) 603

כְּתֹנֶת 8 tunic (8·30) 509

חגר 9 to gird on (2·44·44) 291

אַבְנֵט girdle (5·9) 126

חבש to bind; bind on (1·27·31) 289

מִגְבָּעָה turban of a common priest (3·4) 149

כְּהֻנָּה priesthood (2·13) 464

סָמַךְ 10 to lay (3·41·48) 701

אֶצְבַּע 12 finger (3·31) 840

יְסוֹד base (1·19) 414

יֹתֶרֶת 13 appendage (2·11) 452

כָּבֵד liver (2·14) 458

כִּלְיָה kidney (2·30) 480

פֶּרֶשׁ 14 offal [contents of stomach] (1·7) 831

סָמַךְ 15 to lay (3·41·48) 701

זָרַק 16 to toss; scatter abundantly (6·32·34) 284

נָתַח 17 to cut in pieces (1·9·9) 677

נֵתַח piece of a divided carcass (2·12) 677

כְּרָעַיִם leg (2·9) 502

נִיחוֹחַ 18 soothing (3·43) 629

סָמַךְ 19 to lay (3·41·48) 701

תְּנוּךְ 20 tip, i.e., lobe of ear (2·8) 1072

יְמָנִי right (3·33) 412

בֹּהֶן thumb; great toe (2·14) 97

זָרַק to toss; scatter abundantly (6·32·34) 284

מִשְׁחָה 21 ointment (13·21) 603

הִזָּה to sprinkle (1·20·24) 633

אַלְיָה 22 fat tail (1·5) 46

יֹתֶרֶת appendage (2·11) 452

כָּבֵד liver (2·14) 458

כִּלְיָה kidney (2·30) 480

שׁוֹק leg (2·19) 1003

מִלֻּא installation (8·15) 571

חַלָּה 23 a kind of cake (2·3) 319

רָקִיק thin cake; wafer (2·8) 956

סַל basket (4·15) 700

הֵנִיף 24 to wave (4·32·34[?]) 631

תְּנוּפָה wave offering; wave breast (6·30) 632

נִיחוֹחַ 25 soothing (3·43) 629

חָזֶה 26 breast (2·13) 303

מִלֻּא installation (8·15) 571

הֵנִיף to wave (4·32·34[?]) 631

תְּנוּפָה wave offering; wave breast (6·30) 632

מָנָה portion (1·12) 584

חָזֶה 27 breast (2·13) 303

תְּנוּפָה wave offering; wave breast (6·30) 632

שׁוֹק leg (2·19) 1003

הוּנַף to be waved (1·1·34[?]) 631

מִלֻּא installation (8·15) 571

מֵאֲשֶׁר from that which (3·17) 84

מִלֻּא 31 installation (8·15) 571

בִּשֵּׁל to cook (4·20·27) 143

סַל 32 basket (4·15) 700

מִלֻּא 34 installation (8·15) 571

כָּכָה 35 thus (2·34) 462

כִּפֻּרִים 36 atonement (3·8) 498

עִשָּׂרוֹן 40 tenth part (1·28) 798

בָּלַל to mix (2·41·42) 117

כָּתִית beaten (2·5) 510

רֶבַע fourth part (1·7) 917

הִין hin; liquid measure (3·22) 228

נִיחוֹחַ 41 soothing (3·43) 629

נוֹעַד 42 to meet at an appointed place (4·18·28) 416

נוֹעַד 43 to meet at an appointed place (4·18·28) 416

כֹּהֵן 44 to act as priest (12·23·23) 464

Chapter 30

מקטר 1 place of sacrificial smoke (1·1) 883

שִׁטָּה		acacia [wood] (26·28) 1008		מוֹר		myrrh (1·12) 600	
רבע	2	ptc. pass. = to be squared (6·9·12) 917		דְּרוֹר		fine-flowing (1·1[?]) 204	
קוֹמָה		height (10·45) 879		קִנָּמוֹן .		cinnamon (1·3) 890	
צָפָה	3	to overlay (25·42·46) 860		מַחֲצִית		half (5·16) 345	
גָּג		top; roof (2·29) 150		קִדָּה	24	cassia [a spice] (1·2) 869	
זֵר		circlet; border (10·10) 267		זַיִת		olive[s] (3·38) 268	
טַבַּעַת	4	ring (35·44) 371		הִין		hin; liquid measure (3·22) 228	
זֵר		circlet; border (10·10) 267		מִשְׁחָה	25	ointment (13·21) 603	
צֵלָע		side (19·39) 854		רֹקַח		spice mixture; perfume (2·2) 955	
צַד		side (9·31) 841		מִרְקַחַת		ointment mixture (1·3) 955	
בַּד		pole; stave (27·41) 94		רקח		to mix; compound (4·6·8) 955	
בַּד	5	pole; stave (27·41) 94		מְנוֹרָה	27	lampstand (18·39) 633	
שִׁטָּה		acacia [wood] (26·28) 1008		כִּיּוֹר	28	basin (9·23) 468	
צָפָה		to overlay (25·42·46) 860		כֵּן		base (7·17) 487	
פָּרֹכֶת	6	curtain (15·25) 827		כִּהֵן	30	to act as priest (12·23·23) 464	
כַּפֹּרֶת		propitiatory (18·27) 498		מִשְׁחָה	31	ointment (13·21) 603	
נועד		to meet at an appointed place (4·18·28) 416		סוך	32	to be poured (1[?]·1[?]·9) 691	
סַם	7	spice (11·16) 702		מַתְכֹּנֶת		proportion (3·5) 1067	
נֵר		lamp (11·44) 632		רקח	33	to mix; compound (4·6·8) 955	
נֵר	8	lamp (11·44) 632		עַם		kinsman (3·34) 769	
נָסַךְ	9	to pour out (1·7·24) 650		סַם	34	spice (11·16) 702	
כִּפֻּרִים	10	atonement (3·8) 498		נָטָף		an odoriferous gum (1·1) 643	
כֹּפֶר	12	ransom (2·13) 497		שְׁחֵלֶת		an ingredient of the holy incense (1·1) 1006	
נֶגֶף		plague (2·7) 620		חֶלְבְּנָה		a kind of gum (1·1) 317	
מַחֲצִית	13	half (5·16) 345		לְבֹנָה		frankincense (1·21) 526	
גֵּרָה		a gerah; one-twentieth of a shekel (1·5) 176		זַךְ		pure; unmixed (2·11) 269	
עָשִׁיר	15	rich (1·23) 799		בַּד		part (1·3[?]) 94	
דַּל		low; weak; poor (2·48) 195		רֹקַח	35	spice mixture; perfume (2·2) 955	
המעיט		to make small (3·13·22) 589		רקח		to mix; compound (4·6·8) 955	
מַחֲצִית		half (5·16) 345		מלח		to be salted (1·1·3) 572	
כִּפֻּרִים	16	atonement (3·8) 498		שׁחק	36	to beat fine; pulverize (1·4·4) 1007	
זִכָּרוֹן		memorial (8·24) 272		הֵדַק		to pulverize (1·8·13) 200	
כִּיּוֹר	18	basin (9·23) 468		נועד		to meet at an appointed place (4·18·28) 416	
כֵּן		base (7·17) 487		מַתְכֹּנֶת	37	proportion (3·5) 1067	
בֶּשֶׂם	23	spice; balsam (6·30) 141		הֵרִיחַ	38	to smell (1·11·14) 926	
				עַם		kinsman (3·34) 769	

Chapter 31

תְּבוּנָה	3 understanding (3·42)	108
חָרֹשֶׁת	5 carving; skillful working (4·4)	360
כַּפֹּרֶת	7 propitiatory (18·27)	498
מְנוֹרָה	8 lampstand (18·39)	633
כִּיּוֹר	9 basin (9·23)	468
כֵּן	base (7·17)	487
שְׂרָד	10 plaited; braided work[?] (4·4)	975
כָּהֵן	to act as priest (12·23·23)	464
מִשְׁחָה	11 ointment (13·21)	603
סַם	spice (11·16)	702
עַם	kinsman (3·34)	769
שַׁבָּתוֹן	15 Sabbath observance (3·11)	992
נפשׁ	17 to refresh oneself (2·3·3)	661
לוּחַ	18 tablet (14·40)	531
אֶצְבַּע	finger (3·31)	840

Chapter 32

נקהל	1 to assemble (1·19·39)	874
פרק	2 to tear off (1·3·10)	830
נֶזֶם	ring (3·17)	633
התפרק	3 to tear off (2·3·10)	830
נֶזֶם	ring (3·17)	633
צור	4 to fashion; delineate (1·2·2)	849
חֶרֶט	graving tool; stylus (1·2)	354
עֵגֶל	calf (6·35)	722
מַסֵּכָה	molten metal (3·25)	651
מָחֳרָת	6 the morrow (4·32)	564
צחק	sport; to play (1·7·13)	850
עֵגֶל	8 calf (6·35)	722
מַסֵּכָה	molten metal (3·25)	651
קָשֶׁה	9 stiff; stubborn (7·36)	904
עֹרֶף	neck (5·33)	791
חָרוֹן	12 [burning of] anger (2·41)	354
כּוֹכָב	13 star (1·37)	456
לוּחַ	15 tablet (14·40)	531
לוּחַ	16 tablet (14·40)	531

מִכְתָּב	handwriting (3·9)	508
חרת	to engrave (1·1·1)	362
רֵעַ	17 shouting (1·3)	929
עָנָה	18 to sing (3·13·16)	777
חֲלוּשָׁה	weakness; prostration (1·1)	325
עֵגֶל	19 calf (6·35)	722
מְחוֹלָה	dancing (2·8)	298
לוּחַ	tablet (14·40)	531
עֵגֶל	20 calf (6·35)	722
טחן	to grind (1·7·7)	377
דַּק	to be fine (1·4·13)	200
זרה	to scatter (1·9·38)	279
התפרק	24 to tear off (2·3·10)	830
עֵגֶל	calf (6·35)	722
פָּרַע	25 to let loose, i.e., remove restraint (2·13·16)	828
שִׁמְצָה	whisper; derision (1·1)	1036
יָרֵךְ	27 thigh (7·34)	437
מָחֳרָת	30 the morrow (4·32)	564
חֲטָאָה	sin (3·8)	308
אוּלַי	perhaps (1·45)	19
אָנָּא	31 ah, now! (1·13)	58
חֲטָאָה	sin (3·8)	308
מָחָה	32 to wipe (3·22·35)	562
מָחָה	33 to wipe (3·22·35)	562
נחה	34 to lead (4·14·40)	634
נָגַף	35 to smite (7·24·48)	619
עֵגֶל	calf (6·35)	722

Chapter 33

גרשׁ	2 to drive out (9·33·46)	176
זוב	3 to flow (4·29·29)	264
חָלָב	milk (6·44)	316
קָשֶׁה	stiff; stubborn (7·36)	904
עֹרֶף	neck (5·33)	791
הִתְאַבֵּל	4 to mourn (1·19·38)	5
עֲדִי	ornaments (3·13)	725
קָשֶׁה	5 stiff; stubborn (7·36)	904

עֹרֶף neck (5·33) 791

רֶגַע moment (1·22) 921

עֲדִי ornaments (3·13) 725

עֲדִי 6 ornaments (3·13) 725

מְשָׁרֵת 11 servant (2·20) 1058

הֵמִישׁ to depart (2·20[?]·20) 559

בַּמֶּה 16 whereby (2·29) 552

אֵפוֹא then (1·15) 66

נפלה to be distinct (1·1·4) 811

טוּב 19 goodness (1·32) 375

רָחַם to have compassion (2·41·46) 933

נקרה 22 crevice (1·2) 669

שׂכך to cover (1·1·1) 967

אָחוֹר 23 hinder parts (2·41) 30

Chapter 34

פָּסַל 1 to hew out (2·6·6) 820

לוּחַ tablet (14·40) 531

מוּל 3 in front of (8·33) 557

פָּסַל 4 to hew out (2·6·6) 20

לוּחַ tablet (14·40) 531

רַחוּם 6 compassionate (1·13) 933

חַנּוּן gracious (2·13) 337

חַטָּאָה 7 sinful thing (1·2) 308

נקה to leave unpunished (2·12·36) 667

שִׁלֵּשִׁים those of the third generation, i.e., grandsons (2·5) 1026

רִבֵּעַ pertaining to the fourth (2·4) 918

קדד 8 to bow down (3·15·15) 869

קָשֶׁה 9 stiff; stubborn (7·36) 904

עֹרֶף neck (5·33) 791

סלח to pardon (1·33·46) 699

נִפְלָאוֹת 10 wonderful acts (2·43) 810

נברא to be created (1·10·48) 135

גרש 11 to drive out (1·7·46) 176

מוֹקֵשׁ 12 bait (3·27) 430

נָתַץ 13 to pull down (1·31·42) 683

מַצֵּבָה pillar (3·35) 663

אֲשֵׁרָה a sacred pole (1·40) 81

קַנָּא 14 jealous (3·6) 888

מַסֵּכָה 17 molten metal (3·25) 651

פֶּטֶר 19 firstborn (8·11) 809

רֶחֶם womb (4·32) 933

שֶׂה one of flock; sheep; goat (13·44) 961

פֶּטֶר 20 firstborn (8·11) 809

שֶׂה one of flock; sheep; goat (13·44) 961

ערף to break the neck (2·6·6) 791

רֵיקָם in empty condition; emptily (3·16) 938

חָרִישׁ 21 ploughing (1·3) 361

קָצִיר harvest (3·49) 894

שָׁבוּעַ 22 week; period (1·20) 988

בִּכּוּרִים firstfruits (4·17) 114

קָצִיר harvest (3·49) 894

אָסִיף ingathering; harvest (2·2) 63

תְּקוּפָה circuit (1·4) 880

הִרְחִיב 24 to enlarge (1·21·25) 931

חָמַד to desire (3·16·21) 326

חָמֵץ 25 that which is leavened (5·11) 329

בִּכּוּרִים 26 firstfruits (4·17) 114

בשל to boil (4·20·27) 143

גְּדִי kid (2·16) 152

חָלָב milk (6·44) 316

לוּחַ 28 tablet (14·40) 531

לוּחַ 29 tablet (14·40) 531

קָרַן to send out rays (3·3·4) 902

קָרַן 30 to send out rays (3·3·4) 902

מַסְוֶה 33 veil (3·3) 691

מַסְוֶה 34 veil (3·3) 691

קָרַן 35 to sent out rays (3·3·4) 902

מַסְוֶה veil (3·3) 691

Chapter 35

הִקְהִל 1 to summon an assembly (1·20·39) 874

שַׁבָּ 2 Sabbath observance (3·11) 992

מוֹ 3 dwelling place (4·43) 444

נָדִי 5 willing (2·27) 622

תְּכֵ 6 violet (34·49) 1067

אַרְ purple thread (26·39) 71

תּוֹלַ coccus ilicis [yielding scarlet color] (27·41) 1069

שָׁנִי scarlet (26·42) 1040

שֵׁשׁ linen (33·37) 1058

אדם 7 to be red (6·7·10) 10

תַּחַ dugong[?] (6·14) 1065

שָׁטַ acacia [wood] (26·28) 1008

מָא 8 light (7·19) 22

בֶּשֶׂ spice; balsam (6·30) 141

מִשׁ ointment (13·21) 603

סם spice (11·16) 702

שֹׁהַ 9 onyx (7·11) 995

מִלּוֹ setting (8·15) 571

אֵפֹ ephod; priestly garment (29·49) 65

חֹשֶׁ breast piece (23·25) 365

מִכְסֶ 11 covering (8·16) 492

קֶרֶס hook (10·10) 902

קֶרֶשׁ board (43·46) 903

בְּרִי bar (15·41) 138

בַּד 12 pole; stave (27·41) 94

כַּפֹּרֶ propitiatory (18·27) 498

פָּרֹכֶ curtain (15·25) 827

מָסָךְ screen (16·25) 697

בַּד 13 pole; stave (27·41) 94

מְנוֹ 14 lampstand (18·39) 633

מָאוֹ light (7·19) 22

נֵר lamp (11·44) 632

בַּד 15 pole; stave (27·41) 94

מִשׁ ointment (13·21) 603

סם spice (11·16) 702

מָסָךְ screen (16·25) 697

מִכְבָּ 16 grating (6·6) 460

בַּד pole; stave (27·41) 94

כִּיּוֹר basin (9·23) 468

כֵּן base (7·17) 487

קֶלַע 17 curtain; hanging (13·16) 887

מָסָךְ screen (16·25) 697

יָתֵד 18 peg (8·24) 450

מֵיתָר cord (2·9) 452

שָׂרָד 19 plaited; braided work (4·4) 975

כִּהֵן to act as priest (12·23·23) 464

נָדַב 21 to incite (3·3·17) 621

נָדִיב 22 willing (2·27) 622

חָח hook (1·7) 296

נֶזֶם ring (3·17) 633

טַבַּעַת ring (35·44) 371

כּוּמָז name of a golden ornament (1·2) 484

הֵנִיף to wave (4·32·34[?]) 631

תְּנוּפָה offering; wave offering (6·30) 632

תְּכֵלֶת 23 violet (34·49) 1067

אַרְגָּמָן purple thread (26·39) 71

תּוֹלֵעָה coccus ilicis [yielding scarlet color] (27·41) 1069

שָׁנִי scarlet (26·42) 1040

שֵׁשׁ linen (33·37) 1058

אדם to be red (6·7·10) 10

תַּחַשׁ dugong[?] (6·14) 1065

שָׁטָה 24 acacia [wood] (26·28) 1008

טוה 25 to spin (2·2·2) 376

מַטְוֶה yarn (1·1) 376

תְּכֵלֶת violet (34·49) 1067

אַרְגָּמָן purple thread (26·29) 71

תּוֹלֵעָה coccus ilicis [yielding scarlet color] (27·41) 1069

שָׁנִי scarlet (26·42) 1040

שֵׁשׁ linen (33·37) 1058

טוה 26 to spin (2·2·2) 376

שֹׁהַם 27 onyx (7·11) 995

מִלּוּא setting (8·15) 571

אֵפוֹד ephod; priestly garment (29·49) 65

53

חֹשֶׁן   breast piece (23·25) 365

בֶּשֶׂם   28 spice; balsam (6·30) 141

מָאוֹר   light (7·19) 22

מִשְׁחָה   ointment (13·21) 603

סם   spice (11·16) 702

נָדַב   29 to incite (3·3·17) 621

נְדָבָה   freewill offering (2·27) 621

תְּבוּנָה   31 understanding (3·42) 108

חֲרֹשֶׁת   33 carving; skillful working (4·4) 360

מִלֻּא   setting (8·15) 571

הורה   34 to instruct (5·45·45[?]) 434

חָרָשׁ   35 graver; artificer (3·38) 360

חֹשֵׁב   workman (11·12[?]) 362

רקם   to variegate; weave (8·8·9) 955

תְּכֵלֶת   violet (34·49) 1067

אַרְגָּמָן   purple thread (26·39) 71

תּוֹלֵעָה   coccus ilicis [yielding scarlet color] (27·41) 1069

שָׁנִי   scarlet (26·42) 1040

שֵׁשׁ   linen (33·37) 1058

אֹרֵג   weaver (4·10[?]) 70

Chapter 36

תְּבוּנָה   1 understanding (3·42) 108

נְדָבָה   3 freewill offering (2·27) 621

דַּי   5 enough (2·39[?]) 191

נכלא   6 to be restrained (1·3·17) 476

דַּי   7 enough (2·39[?]) 191

שֵׁשׁ   8 linen (33·37) 1058

השזר   to be twisted (21·21·21) 1004

תְּכֵלֶת   violet (34·49) 1067

אַרְגָּמָן   purple thread (26·39) 71

תּוֹלֵעָה   coccus ilicis [yielding scarlet color] (27·41) 1069

שָׁנִי   scarlet (26·42) 1040

חֹשֵׁב   workman (11·12[?]) 362

חִבַּר   10 to unite; join (8·9·28) 287

לוּלִי   11 loop (13·13) 533

תְּכֵלֶת   violet (34·49) 1067

קָצָה   end (21·28) 892

מַחְבֶּרֶת   thing joined (8·8) 289

קִיצוֹן   at the end; outermost (4·4) 894

לוּלִי   12 loop (13·13) 533

מַחְבֶּרֶת   thing joined (8·8) 289

הקביל   to show oppositeness in; corresponding to one another (2·2·13) 867

קֶרֶס   13 hook (10·10) 902

חִבַּר   to unite; join (8·9·28) 287

חִבַּר   16 to unite; join (8·9·28) 287

לוּלִי   17 loop (13·13) 533

קִיצוֹן   at the end; outermost (4·4) 894

מַחְבֶּרֶת   place of joining (8·8) 289

חֹבֶרֶת   a thing that joins; curtain piece (4·4) 289

קֶרֶס   18 hook (10·10) 902

חִבַּר   to unite; join (8·9·28) 287

מִכְסֶה   19 covering (8·16) 492

אדם   to be red (6·7·10) 10

תַּחַשׁ   dugong[?] (6·14) 1065

מִלְמַעְלָה   above (6·24) 751

קֶרֶשׁ   20 board (43·46) 903

שִׁטָּה   acacia [wood] (26·28) 1008

קֶרֶשׁ   21 board (43·46) 903

קֶרֶשׁ   22 board (43·46) 903

שׁלב   to be bound; joined (2·2·2) 1016

קֶרֶשׁ   23 board (43·46) 903

תֵּימָן   [toward] the south (5·24) 412

קֶרֶשׁ   24 board (43·46) 903

צֶלָע   25 side (19·39) 854

קֶרֶשׁ   board (43·46) 903

קֶרֶשׁ   26 board (43·46) 903

ירכה   27 extreme parts (6·28) 438

קֶרֶשׁ   board (43·46) 903

קֶרֶשׁ   28 board (43·46) 903

קצע[?]   pu. ptc. = corner post (2·2·3) 893

54

יַרְכָה	extreme parts (6·28) 438
תּוֹאֲמִ	29 double (2·6)[?] 1060
מִלְמַטָּ	beneath (6·6) 641
טַבַּעַת	ring (35·44) 371
מִקְצֹעַ	corner buttress (2·11) 893
קֶרֶשׁ	30 board (43·46) 903
בְּרִיחַ	31 bar (15·41) 138
שִׁטָּה	acacia [wood] (26·28) 1008
קֶרֶשׁ	board (43·46) 903
צֶלַע	side (19·39) 854
בְּרִיחַ	32 bar (15·41) 138
קֶרֶשׁ	board (43·46) 903
צֶלַע	side (19·39) 854
יַרְכָה	extreme parts (6·28) 438
בְּרִיחַ	33 bar (15·41) 138
תִּיכֹן	middle (2·12) 1064
קֶרֶשׁ	board (43·46) 903
קֶרֶשׁ	34 board (43·46) 903
צָפָה	to overlay (25·42·46) 860
טַבַּעַ	ring (35·44) 371
בְּרִיחַ	bar (15·41) 138
פָּרֹכֶ	35 curtain (15·25) 827
תְּכֵלֶ	violet (34·49) 1067
אַרְגָּמ	purple thread (26·39) 71
תּוֹלַ	coccus ilicis [yielding scarlet color] (27·41) 1069
שָׁנִי	scarlet (26·42) 1040
שֵׁשׁ	linen (33·37) 1058
הָשֻׁז	to be twisted (21·21·21) 1004
חֹשֵׁב	workman (i 1·12[?]) 362
שִׁטָּ	36 acacia [wood] (26·28) 1008
צָפָה	to overlay (25·42·46) 860
וו	hook; pin; peg (13·13) 255
מָסָךְ	37 screen (16·25) 697
תְּכֵל	violet (34·49) 1067
אַרְגָּ	purple thread (26·39) 71
תּוֹלַ	coccus ilicis [yielding scarlet color] (27·41) 1069

שָׁנִי	scarlet (26·42) 1040
שֵׁשׁ	linen (33·37) 1058
הָשֻׁזר	to be twisted (21·21·21) 1004
רקם	to variegate; weave (8·8·9) 955
וו	38 hook; pin; peg (13·13) 255
צָפָה	to overlay (25·42·46) 860
חָשׁוּק	fillet; ring (8·8) 366

Chapter 37

שִׁטָּה	1 acacia [wood] (26·28) 1008
קוֹמָה	height (10·45) 879
צָפָה	2 to overlay (25·42·46) 860
זֵר	border (10·10) 267
טַבַּעַת	3 ring (35·44) 371
צֶלַע	side (19·39) 854
בַּד	4 pole; stave (27·41) 94
שִׁטָּה	acacia [wood] (26·28) 1008
צָפָה	to overlay (25·42·46) 860
בַּד	5 pole; stave (27·41) 94
טַבַּעַת	ring (35·44) 371
צֶלַע	side (19·39) 854
כַּפֹּרֶת	6 propitiatory (18·27) 498
מִקְשָׁה	7 hammered work? (6·9) 904
קָצָה	end (21·28) 892
כַּפֹּרֶת	propitiatory (18·27) 498
קָצָה	8 end (21·28) 892
כַּפֹּרֶת	propitiatory (18·27) 498
קָצָה	end (3·9) 892
לְמַעְלָה	9 upward (2·34) 751
סכך	to cover (3·12·18[?]) 696
כַּפֹּרֶת	propitiatory (18·27) 498
שִׁטָּה	10 acacia [wood] (26·28) 1008
קוֹמָה	height (10·45) 879
צָפָה	11 to overlay (25·42·46) 860
זֵר	border (10·10) 267
מִסְגֶּרֶת	12 border (6·17) 689
טֶפַח	handbreadth (2·9) 381
זֵר	border (10·10) 267

טַבַּעַת 13 ring (35·44) 371

לְעֻמַּת 14 close by; side by side with (5·31) 769

מִסְגֶּרֶת border (6·17) 689

טַבַּעַת ring (35·44) 371

בַּד pole; stave (27·41) 94

בַּד 15 pole; stave (27·41) 94

שִׁטָּה acacia [wood] (26·28) 1008

צִפָּה to overlay (25·42·46) 860

קְעָרָה 16 dish; platter (2·17) 891

מְנַקִּיָּה sacrificial bowl (2·4) 667

קַשְׂוָה jug; jar (2·4) 903

הֻסַּךְ to be poured out (2·2·24) 650

מְנוֹרָה 17 lampstand (18·39) 633

מִקְשָׁה hammered work[?] (6·9) 904

יָרֵךְ base (7·34) 437

גָּבִיעַ cup (7·13) 149

כַּפְתּוֹר bulb (14·16) 499

פֶּרַח bud; sprout (8·17) 827

צַד 18 side (9·31) 841

מְנוֹרָה lampstand (18·39) 633

גָּבִיעַ 19 cup (7·13) 149

שָׁקַד to be shaped as almond [blossoms] (6·6·17) 1052

כַּפְתּוֹר bulb (14·16) 499

פֶּרַח bud; sprout (8·17) 827

מְנוֹרָה lampstand (18·39) 633

מְנוֹרָה 20 lampstand (18·39) 633

גָּבִיעַ cup (7·13) 149

שָׁקַד to be shaped as almond [blossoms] (6·6·17) 1052

כַּפְתּוֹר bulb (14·16) 499

פֶּרַח bud; sprout (8·17) 827

כַּפְתּוֹר 21 bulb (14·16) 499

כַּפְתּוֹר 22 bulb (14·16) 499

מִקְשָׁה hammered work[?] (6·9) 904

נֵר 23 lamp (11·44) 632

מֶלְקָחַיִם snuffers (2·6) 544

מַחְתָּה snuff holder (4·21) 367

שִׁטָּה 25 acacia [wood] (26·28) 1008

רבע ptc. pass. = to be squared (6·9·12) 917

קוֹמָה height (10·45) 879

צִפָּה 26 to overlay (25·42·46) 860

גָּג top; roof (2·29) 150

זֵר border (10·10) 267

טַבַּעַת 27 ring (35·44) 371

זֵר border (10·10) 267

צֵלָע side (19·39) 854

צַד side (9·31) 841

בַּד pole; stave (27·41) 94

בַּד 28 pole; stave (27·41) 94

שִׁטָּה acacia [wood] (26·28) 1008

צִפָּה to overlay (25·42·46) 860

מִשְׁחָה 29 ointment (13·21) 603

סַם spice (11·16) 702

רקח to mix; compound (4·6·8) 955

Chapter 38

שִׁטָּה 1 acacia [wood] (26·28) 1008

רבע ptc. pass. = to be squared (6·9·12) 917

קוֹמָה height (10·45) 879

פִּנָּה 2 corner (2·30) 819

צִפָּה to overlay (25·42·46) 860

סִיר 3 pot (3·27) 696

יָע shovel (2·9) 418

מִזְרָק basin (2·32) 284

מִזְלָגָה three-pronged fork (2·5) 272

מַחְתָּה fire pan (4·21) 367

מִכְבָּר 4 grating (6·6) 460

רֶשֶׁת network (4·22) 440

כַּרְכֹּב rim (2·2) 501

מִלְמַטָּה beneath (6·6) 641

טַבַּעַת 5 ring (35·44) 371

קָצָה end (3·9) 892

מִכְבָּר	grating (6·6) 460
בַּד	pole; stave (27·41) 94
בַּד	6 pole; stave (27·41) 94
שִׁטָּה	acacia [wood] (26·28) 1008
צִפָּה	to overlay (25·42·46) 860
בַּד	7 pole; stave (27·41) 94
טַבַּעַת	ring (35·44) 371
צֵלָע	side (19·39) 854
נבב	to hollow out (2·4·4) 612
לוּחַ	plank (14·40) 531
כִּיּוֹר	8 basin (9·23) 468
כֵּן	base (7·17) 487
מַרְאָה	mirror (1·12) 909
צבא	to serve (2·12·14) 838
תֵּימָן	9 [toward] the south (5·24) 412
קלע	curtain; hanging (13·16) 887
שֵׁשׁ	linen (33·37) 1058
השזר	to be twisted (21·21·21) 1004
וו	10 hook; pin; peg (13·13) 255
חשוק	fillet; ring (8·8) 366
וו	11 hook; pin; peg (13·13) 255
חשוק	fillet; ring (8·8) 366
קלע	12 curtain; hanging (13·16) 887
וו	hook; pin; peg (13·13) 255
חשוק	fillet; ring (8·8) 366
קלע	14 curtain; hanging (13·16) 887
קלע	15 curtain; hanging (13·16) 887
קלע	16 curtain; hanging (13·16) 887
שֵׁשׁ	linen (33·37) 1058
השזר	to be twisted (21·21·21) 1004
וו	17 hook; pin; peg (13·13) 255
חשוק	fillet; ring (8·8) 366
צִפּוּי	metal plating (2·5) 860
חשק	to be furnished with fillets or rings (2·2·11) 366
מָסָךְ	18 screen (16·25) 697
רקם	to variegate; weave (8·8·9) 955
תְּכֵלֶת	violet (34·49) 1067
אַרְגָּמָן	purple thread (26·39) 71
תּוֹלֵעָה	coccus ilicis [yielding scarlet color] (27·41) 1069
שָׁנִי	scarlet (26·42) 1040
שֵׁשׁ	linen (33·37) 1058
השזר	to be twisted (21·21·21) 1004
קוֹמָה	height (10·45) 879
לְעֻמַּת	close by; side by side with (5·31) 769
קלע	curtain; hanging (13·16) 887
וו	19 hook; pin; peg (13·13) 255
צִפּוּי	metal plating (2·5) 860
חשוק	fillet; ring (8·8) 366
יָתֵד	20 peg (8·24) 450
פקודים	21 musterings, i.e., expenses (1·3)[?] 824
חָרָשׁ	23 graver; artificer (3·38) 360
חֹשֵׁב	workman (11·12[?]) 362
רקם	to variegate; weave (8·8·9) 955
תְּכֵלֶת	violet (34·49) 1067
אַרְגָּמָן	purple thread (26·39) 71
תּוֹלֵעָה	coccus ilicis [yielding scarlet color] (27·41) 1069
שָׁנִי	scarlet (26·42) 1040
שֵׁשׁ	linen (33·37) 1058
תְּנוּפָה	24 offering; wave offering (6·30) 632
בֶּקַע	26 half; half shekel (1·2) 132
גֻּלְגֹּלֶת	for each man; head; skull (2·12) 166
מַחֲצִית	half (5·16) 345
פָּרֹכֶת	27 curtain (15·25) 827
וו	28 hook; pin; peg (13·13) 255
צִפָּה	to overlay (25·42·46) 860
חֹשֵׁק	to furnish with fillets or rings (1·1·11) 365
תְּנוּפָה	29 offering; wave offering (6·30) 632
מִכְבָּר	30 grating (6·6) 460
יָתֵד	31 peg (8·24) 450

Chapter 39

תְּכֵלֶת	1 violet (34·49) 1067	
אַרְגָּמָן	purple thread (26·39) 71	
תּוֹלֵעָה	coccus ilicis [yielding scarlet color] (27·41) 1069	
שָׁנִי	scarlet (26·42) 1040	
שְׂרָד	plaited; braided work (4·4) 975	
אֵפוֹד	2 ephod; priestly garment (29·49) 65	
תְּכֵלֶת	violet (34·49) 1067	
אַרְגָּמָן	purple thread (26·39) 71	
תּוֹלֵעָה	coccus ilicis [yielding scarlet color] (27·41) 1069	
שָׁנִי	scarlet (26·42) 1040	
שֵׁשׁ	linen (33·37) 1058	
הֻשְׁזָר	to be twisted (21·21·21) 1004	
רקע	3 to hammer out (1·3·11) 955	
פַּח	plate [of metal] (1·2) 809	
קָצַץ	to cut in two (1·9·14) 893	
פָּתִיל	thread (5·11) 836	
תְּכֵלֶת	violet (34·49) 1067	
אַרְגָּמָן	purple thread (26·39) 71	
תּוֹלֵעָה	coccus ilicis [yielding scarlet color] (27·41) 1069	
שָׁנִי	scarlet (26·42) 1040	
שֵׁשׁ	linen (33·37) 1058	
חֹשֵׁב	workman (11·12[?]) 362	
חבר	4 to unite (4·11·28) 287	
קָצָה	end (3·9) 892	
חֻבָּר	to be joined together (2·4·28) 287	
חֵשֶׁב	5 girdle; ingenious work (7·8) 363	
אֲפֻדָּה	high priest's ephod (2·3) 65	
תְּכֵלֶת	violet (34·49) 1067	
אַרְגָּמָן	purple thread (26·39) 71	
תּוֹלֵעָה	coccus ilicis [yielding scarlet color] (27·41) 1069	
שָׁנִי	scarlet (26·42) 1040	
שֵׁשׁ	linen (33·37) 1058	

הֻשְׁזָר	to be twisted (21·21·21) 1004	
שֹׁהַם	6 onyx (7·11) 995	
מִשְׁבְּצוֹת	checkered work (8·9) 990	
פתח	to engrave (1·1·9) 836	
פִּתּוּחַ	engraving (6·11) 836	
חוֹתָם	seal; signet ring (6·13) 368	
אֵפוֹד	7 ephod; priestly garment (29·49) 65	
זִכָּרוֹן	memorial; reminder (8·24) 272	
חֹשֶׁן	8 breast piece (23·25) 365	
חֹשֵׁב	workman (11·12[?]) 362	
אֵפוֹד	ephod; priestly garment (29·49) 65	
תְּכֵלֶת	violet (34·49) 1067	
אַרְגָּמָן	purple thread (26·39) 71	
תּוֹלֵעָה	coccus ilicis [yielding scarlet color] (27·41) 1069	
שָׁנִי	scarlet (26·42) 1040	
שֵׁשׁ	linen (33·37) 1058	
הֻשְׁזָר	to be twisted (21·21·21) 1004	
רבע	9 ptc. pass. = to be squared (6·9·12) 917	
כָּפַל	to double over (3·3·4) 495	
חֹשֶׁן	breast piece (23·25) 365	
זֶרֶת	span (4·7) 284	
טוּר	10 row (12·26) 377	
אֹדֶם	carnelian (2·3) 10	
פִּטְדָה	topaz (2·4) 809	
בָּרֶקֶת	a precious stone; emerald (2·3) 140	
טוּר	11 row (12·26) 377	
נֹפֶךְ	ruby[?] (2·4) 656	
סַפִּיר	sapphire (3·11) 705	
יַהֲלֹם	jasper[?] (2·3) 240	
טוּר	12 row (12·26) 377	
לֶשֶׁם	precious stone (2·2) 545	
שְׁבוּ	precious stone (2·2) 986	
אַחְלָמָה	amethyst[?] (2·2) 21	
טוּר	13 row (12·26) 377	
תַּרְשִׁישׁ	yellow jasper[?] (2·7) 1076	
שֹׁהַם	onyx (7·11) 995	

יָשְׁפֵה	jasper (2·3) 448
מְשֻׁבְּצֹת	checkered work (8·9) 990
מִלֻאָה	setting of jewel (3·3) 571
פִּתּוּחַ	14 engraving (6·11) 836
חֹתָם	seal; signet ring (6·13) 368
חֹשֶׁן	15 breast piece (23·25) 365
שַׁרְשְׁרֹת	chain (4·8) 1057
גַּבְלֻת	twisting (2·2) 148
עֲבֹת	cordage; cord (8·24) 721
מְשֻׁבְּצֹת	16 checkered work (8·9) 990
טַבַּעַת	ring (35·44) 371
קָצָה	end (21·28) 892
חֹשֶׁן	breast piece (23·25) 365
עֲבֹת	17 cordage; cord (8·24) 721
טַבַּעַת	ring (35·44) 371
קָצָה	end (21·28) 892
חֹשֶׁן	breast piece (23·25) 365
קָצָה	18 end (21·28) 892
עֲבֹת	cordage; cord (8·24) 721
מְשֻׁבְּצֹת	checkered work (8·9) 990
אֵפוֹד	ephod; priestly garment (29·49) 65
מוּל	the forefront of (6·25) 557
טַבַּעַת	19 ring (35·44) 371
קָצָה	end (21·28) 892
חֹשֶׁן	breast piece (23·25) 365
אֵפוֹד	ephod; priestly garment (29·49) 65
טַבַּעַת	20 ring (35·44) 371
אֵפוֹד	ephod; priestly garment (29·49) 65
מִלְמַטָּה	beneath (6·6) 641
מִמּוּל	on the front of (2·9) 557
לְעֻמָּה	close by; side by side with (5·31) 789
מַחְבֶּרֶת	thing joined (8·8) 289
חֵשֶׁב	girdle; ingenious work (7·8) 363
רכס	21 to bind (2·2·2) 940
חֹשֶׁן	breast piece (23·25) 365
טַבַּעַת	ring (35·44) 371
אֵפוֹד	ephod; priestly garment (29·49) 65
פָּתִיל	cord (5·11) 836
תְּכֵלֶת	violet (34·49) 1067
חֵשֶׁב	girdle; ingenious work (7·8) 363
נזחח	to remove; displace (2·2·2) 267
מְעִיל	22 robe (9·28) 591
אֵפוֹד	ephod; priestly garment (29·49) 65
אֹרֵג	weaver (4·16[?]) 70
כָּלִיל	entirety (2·15) 483
תְּכֵלֶת	violet (34·49) 1067
מְעִיל	23 robe (9·28) 591
כְּפִי	in proportion to (3·16) 804
תַּחְרָא	corselet (2·2) 1065
שׁוּל	24 skirt [of robe] (6·11) 1002
מְעִיל	robe (9·28) 591
רִמּוֹן	pomegranate (8·32) 941
תְּכֵלֶת	violet (34·49) 1067
אַרְגָּמָן	purple thread (26·39) 71
תּוֹלֵעָה	coccus ilicis [yielding scarlet color] (27·41) 1069
שָׁנִי	scarlet (26·42) 1040
הֻשְׁזָר	to be twisted (21·21·21) 1004
פַּעֲמֹן	25 bell (7·7) 822
רִמּוֹן	pomegranate (8·32) 941
שׁוּל	skirt [of robe] (6·11) 1002
מְעִיל	robe (9·28) 591
פַּעֲמֹן	26 bell (7·7) 822
רִמּוֹן	pomegranate (8·32) 941
שׁוּל	skirt [of robe] (6·11) 1002
מְעִיל	robe (9·28) 591
כֻּתֹּנֶת	27 tunic (9·30) 509
שֵׁשׁ	linen (33·37) 1058
אֹרֵג	weaver (4·10[?]) 70
מִצְנֶפֶת	28 turban of high priest (8·12) 857
שֵׁשׁ	linen (33·37) 1058
פְּאֵר	headdress; turban (1·7) 802
מִגְבָּעוֹת	turban of common priest (3·4) 149
מכנס	drawers (2·5) 488
בַּד	white linen (2·23) 94

הֻשְׁזָר	to be twisted (21·21·21) 1004	
אַבְנֵט	29 girdle (5·9) 126	
שֵׁשׁ	linen (33·37) 1058	
הֻשְׁזָר	to be twisted (21·21·21) 1004	
תְּכֵלֶת	violet (34·49) 1067	
אַרְגָּמָן	purple thread (26·39) 71	
תּוֹלֵעָה	coccus ilicis [yielding scarlet color] (27·41) 1069	
שָׁנִי	scarlet (26·42) 1040	
רקם	to variegate; weave (8·8·9) 955	
צִיץ	30 shining plate [of gold] (2·15) 847	
נֵזֶר	crown (2·24) 634	
מִכְתָּב	writing (3·9) 508	
פִּתּוּחַ	engraving (6·11) 836	
חוֹתָם	seal; signet ring (6·13) 368	
פְּתִיל	31 cord (5·11) 836	
תְּכֵלֶת	violet (34·49) 1067	
מִצְנֶפֶת	turban of high priest (8·12) 857	
מִלְמַעְלָה	above (6·24) 751	
קֶרֶס	33 hook (10·10) 902	
קֶרֶשׁ	board (43·46) 903	
בְּרִיחַ	bar (15·41) 138	
מִכְסֶה	34 covering (8·16) 492	
אדם	to be reddened (6·7·10) 10	
תַּחַשׁ	dugong[?] (6·14) 1065	
פָּרֹכֶת	curtain (15·25) 827	
מָסָךְ	screen (16·25) 697	
בַּד	35 pole; stave (27·41) 94	
כַּפֹּרֶת	propitiatory (18·27) 498	
מְנוֹרָה	37 lampstand (18·39) 633	
נֵר	lamp (11·44) 632	
מַעֲרָכָה	row (1·18) 790	
מָאוֹר	light (7·19) 22	
מִשְׁחָה	38 ointment (13·21) 603	
סם	spice (11·16) 702	
מָסָךְ	screen (16·25) 697	
מִכְבָּר	39 grating (6·6) 460	
בַּד	pole; stave (27·41) 94	

כִּיּוֹר	basin (9·23) 468	
כֵּן	base (7·17) 487	
קֶלַע	40 curtain; hanging (13·16) 887	
מָסָךְ	screen (16·25) 697	
מֵיתָר	cord (2·9) 452	
יָתֵד	peg (8·24) 450	
שְׂרָד	41 plaited; braided work (4·4) 975	
כִּהֵן	to act as priest (12·23·23) 464	

Chapter 40

סכך	3 to cover (3·12·18[?]) 696	
פָּרֹכֶת	curtain (15·25) 827	
עֵרֶךְ	4 order; row (2·33) 789	
מְנוֹרָה	lampstand (18·39) 633	
נֵר	lamp (11·44) 632	
מָסָךְ	5 screen (16·25) 697	
כִּיּוֹר	7 basin (9·23) 468	
מָסָךְ	8 screen (16·25) 697	
מִשְׁחָה	9 ointment (13·21) 603	
כִּיּוֹר	11 basin (9·23) 468	
כֵּן	base (7·17) 487	
כִּהֵן	13 to act as priest (12·23·23) 464	
כֻּתֹּנֶת	14 tunic (9·30) 509	
כִּהֵן	15 to act as priest (12·23·23) 464	
כְּהֻנָּה	priesthood (2·13) 464	
קֶרֶשׁ	18 board (43·46) 903	
בְּרִיחַ	bar (15·41) 138	
מִכְסֶה	19 covering (8·16) 492	
מִלְמַעְלָה	above (6·24) 751	
בַּד	20 pole; stave (27·41) 94	
כַּפֹּרֶת	propitiatory (18·27) 498	
מִלְמַעְלָה	above (6·24) 751	
פָּרֹכֶת	21 curtain (15·25) 827	
מָסָךְ	screen (16·25) 697	
סכך	to screen out (1·5·18[?]) 696	
יָרֵךְ	22 side (7·34) 437	
פָּרֹכֶת	curtain (15·25) 827	
עֵרֶךְ	23 order; row (2·33) 789	

מְנוֹרָה 24 lampstand (18·39) 633

נֹכַח opposite to (4·27) 647

יָרֵךְ side (7·34) 437

נֵר 25 lamp (11·44) 632

פָּרֹכֶת 26 curtain (15·25) 827

סַם 27 spice (11·16) 702

מָסָךְ 28 screen (16·25) 697

כִּיּוֹר 30 basin (9·23) 468

מָסָךְ 33 screen (16·25) 697

מַסַּע 36 journey (3·12) 652

מַסַּע 38 journey (3·12) 652

L E V I T I C U S

Chapter 1

סָמַךְ	4 to lay (14·41·48)	701
זָרַק	5 to throw, scatter abundantly (12·32·34)	284
הִפְשִׁיט	6 to flay, skin (1·15·43)	832
נִתַּח	to cut up (3·9·9)	677
נֵתַח	piece of a divided carcass (6·12)	677
נֵתַח	8 piece of a divided carcass (6·12)	677
פֶּדֶר	suet (3·3)	804
כֶּרַע	9 leg (6·9)	502
נִיחוֹחַ	soothing (17·43)	629
כֶּשֶׂב	10 lamb (7·13)	461
יָרֵךְ	11 side (1·34)	437
זָרַק	to throw, scatter abundantly (12·32·34)	284
נִתַּח	12 to cut up (3·9·9)	677
נֵתַח	piece of a divided carcass (6·12)	677
פֶּדֶר	suet (3·3)	804
כֶּרַע	13 leg (6·9)	502
נִיחוֹחַ	soothing (12·43)	629
תּוֹר	14 turtle dove (9·14)	1076
יוֹנָה	dove (10·35)	401
מָלַק	15 to nip off (2·2·2)	577
נִמְצָה	to be drained (2·3·7)	594
מֻרְאָה	16 crop (1·1)	597
נוֹצָה	plumage (1·1)	663
קֶדֶם	eastward (2·26)	870
דֶּשֶׁן	fat ashes (5·15)	206
שִׁסַּע	17 to tear in two (1·3·8)	1042
הִבְדִּיל	to separate, divide (8·32·42)	95
נִיחוֹחַ	soothing (17·43)	629

Chapter 2

לְבֹנָה	1 frankincense (7·21)	526
קָמַץ	2 to enclose with hand, grasp (2·3·3)	888

קֹמֶץ	closed hand, fist (3·4)	888
לְבֹנָה	frankincense (7·21)	526
אַזְכָּרָה	memorial offering (6·7)	272
נִיחוֹחַ	soothing (17·43)	629
מַאֲפֶה	4 a thing baked (1·1)	66
תַּנּוּר	stove, firepot (4·15)	1072
חַלָּה	a kind of cake (7·13)	319
בָּלַל	to mix (9·42·42[?])	117
רָקִיק	thin cake, wafer (3·8)	956
מַחֲבַת	5 griddle (3·5)	290
בָּלַל	to mix (9·42·42[?])	117
פָּתַת	6 to break up, crumble (1·1)	837
פַּת	fragment, bit, morsel (2·14)	839
מַרְחֶשֶׁת	7 stewpan (2·2)	935
אַזְכָּרָה	9 memorial offering (6·7)	272
נִיחוֹחַ	soothing (17·43)	629
חָמֵץ	11 that which is leavened (4·11)	329
שְׂאֹר	leaven (1·5)	959
נִיחוֹחַ	12 soothing (17·43)	629
מֶלַח	13 salt (3·28)	571
מָלַח	to salt (1·1·3)	572
בִּכּוּרִים	14 first fruits (4·17)	114
אָבִיב	fresh young ears (1·8)	1
קָלָה	to roast, parch (1·3·4)	885
גֶּרֶשׂ	grits (2·2)	176
כַּרְמֶל	fruit, garden growth (2·3[?])	502
לְבֹנָה	15 frankincense (7·21)	526
אַזְכָּרָה	16 memorial offering (6·7)	272
גֶּרֶשׂ	grits (2·2)	176
לְבֹנֶה	frankincense (7·21)	526

Chapter 3

נְקֵבָה	1 female (12·22)	666
סָמַךְ	2 to lay (14·41·48)	701
זָרַק	to throw, scatter abundantly (12·32·34)	284
כִּלְיָה	4 kidney (13·30)	480
כֶּסֶל	loin (4·5[?])	492

יֹתֶרֶת appendage (9·11) 452

כָּבֵד liver (9·14) 458

נִיחוֹחַ 5 soothing (17·43) 629

נְקֵבָה 6 female (12·22) 666

כֶּשֶׂב 7 lamb (7·13) 461

סָמַךְ 8 to lay (14·41·48) 701

זָרַק to throw, scatter abundantly (12·32·34) 284

אַלְיָה 9 fat tail (4·5) 46

לְעֻמָּה close by, side by side with (1·32) 769

עָצֶה spine, or as sacrum [bone close to fat tail] (1·1) 782

כִּלְיָה 10 kidney (13·30) 480

כֶּסֶל loin (4·5[?]) 492

יֹתֶרֶת appendage (9·11) 452

כָּבֵד liver (9·14) 458

סָמַךְ 13 to lay (14·41·48) 701

זָרַק to throw, scatter abundantly (12·32·34) 284

כִּלְיָה 15 kidney (13·30) 480

כֶּסֶל loin (4·5[?]) 492

יֹתֶרֶת appendage (9·11) 452

כָּבֵד liver (9·14) 458

נִיחוֹחַ 16 soothing (17·43) 629

מוֹשָׁב 17 dwelling place (8·43) 444

Chapter 4

שְׁגָגָה 2 sin of error, inadvertence (6·19) 993

מָשִׁיחַ 3 anointed (4·40) 603

אַשְׁמָה guiltiness (4·19) 80

סָמַךְ 4 to lay (14·41·48) 701

מָשִׁיחַ 5 anointed (4·40) 603

טָבַל 6 to dip (6·15·16) 371

אֶצְבַּע finger (13·31) 840

הִזָּה to sprinkle (13·20·24) 633

פָּרֹכֶת curtain (7·25) 827

סַם 7 spice (2·16) 702

יְסוֹד base (8·19) 414

כִּלְיָה 9 kidney (3·13) 480

כֶּסֶל loin (4·5[?]) 492

יֹתֶרֶת appendage (9·11) 452

כָּבֵד liver (9·14) 458

כְּרַע 11 leg (6·9) 502

פֶּרֶשׁ offal [as ripped out in preparing victim] (3·7) 831

שֶׁפֶךְ 12 [place of] pouring (2·2) 1050

דֶּשֶׁן fat ashes (5·15) 206

שָׁגָה 13 to commit a sin of ignorance (1·7·21) 993

נֶעְלַם to be concealed (4·11·29) 761

אָשֵׁם to be guilty (10·31·33) 79

סָמַךְ 15 to lay (14·41·48) 701

מָשִׁיחַ 16 anointed (4·40) 603

טָבַל 17 to dip (6·15·16) 371

אֶצְבַּע finger (13·31) 840

הִזָּה to sprinkle (13·20·24) 633

פָּרֹכֶת curtain (7·25) 827

יְסוֹד 18 base (8·19) 414

נִסְלַח 20 to be forgiven (10·13·46) 699

שְׁגָגָה 22 sin of error, inadvertence (6·19) 993

אָשֵׁם to be guilty (10·31·33) 79

סָמַךְ 24 to lay (14·41·48) 701

אֶצְבַּע 25 finger (13·31) 840

יְסוֹד base (8·19) 414

נִסְלַח 26 to be forgiven (10·13·46) 699

שְׁגָגָה 27 sin of error, inadvertence (6·19) 993

אָשֵׁם to be guilty (10·31·33) 79

שְׂעִירָה 28 she-goat (2·2) 972

נְקֵבָה female (12·22) 666

סָמַךְ 29 to lay (14·41·48) 701

אֶצְבַּע 30 finger (13·31) 840

יְסוֹד base (8·19) 414

נִיחוֹחַ 31 soothing (17·43) 629

נִסְלַח to be forgiven (10·13·46) 699

נְקֵבָה 32 female (12·22) 666

סָמַךְ 33 to lay (14·41·48) 701

אֶצְבַּע 34 finger (13·31) 840

יְסוֹד base (8·19) 414

כֶּשֶׂב 35 lamb (7·13) 461

נִסְלַח to be forgiven (10·13·46) 699

Chapter 5

אָלָה 1 oath (1·36) 46

נְבֵלָה 2 corpse (19·48) 615

שֶׁרֶץ swarmers, swarming things (2·15) 1056

נֶעְלַם to be concealed (4·11·29) 761

אָשֵׁם to be guilty (10·31·33) 79

טֻמְאָה 3 uncleanness (18·37) 380

נֶעְלַם to be concealed (4·11·29) 761

אָשֵׁם to be guilty (10·31·33) 79

בטא 4 to speak rashly (2·3·4) 104

שְׁבֻעָה oath (1·30) 989

נֶעְלַם to be concealed (4·11·29) 761

אָשֵׁם to be guilty (10·31·33) 79

אָשֵׁם 5 to be guilty (10·31·33) 79

אָשָׁם 6 trespass offering (27·46) 79

נְקֵבָה female (12·22) 666

כִּשְׂבָּה ewe lamb (1·1) 461

דֵּי 7 sufficiency, enough (3·12) 191

שֶׂה sheep, goat (5·44) 961

אָשָׁם trespass offering (27·46) 79

תּוֹר turtle dove (9·14) 1076

יוֹנָה dove (10·35) 401

מָלַק 8 to nip off (2·2·2) 577

מִמּוּל off the front of (1·9) 557

עֹרֶף neck (1·33) 791

הִבְדִּיל to divide (8·32·42) 95

הִזָּה 9 to sprinkle (13·20·24) 633

נִמְצָה to be drained (2·3·7) 594

יְסוֹד base (8·19) 414

נִסְלַח 10 to be forgiven (10·13·46) 699

הִשִּׂיג 11 to reach (12·48·48) 673

תּוֹר turtle dove (9·14) 1076

יוֹנָה dove (10·35) 401

אֵיפָה ephah, a measure (3·38) 35

לְבֹנָה frankincense (7·21) 526

קָמַץ 12 to enclose with hand, grasp (2·3·3) 888

קֹמֶץ fist (3·4) 888

אַזְכָּרָה memorial offering (6·7) 272

נִסְלַח 13 to be forgiven (10·13·46) 699

מָעַל 15 to act unfaithfully (3·35·35) 591

מַעַל unfaithful act (3·29) 591

שְׁגָגָה sin of error, inadvertence (6·19) 993

אָשָׁם trespass offering (27·46) 79

עֵרֶךְ valuation, estimate (24·33) 789

אָשָׁם 16 trespass offering (27·46) 79

נִסְלַח to be forgiven (10·13·46) 699

אָשֵׁם 17 to be guilty (10·31·33) 79

עֵרֶךְ 18 valuation, estimate (24·33) 789

אָשָׁם trespass offering (27·46) 79

שְׁגָגָה sin of error, inadvertence (6·19) 993

שָׁגַג to sin, go astray (1·5·5) 992

נִסְלַח to be forgiven (10·13·46) 699

אָשָׁם 19 trespass offering (27·46) 79

אָשֹׁם to commit an offence (10·31·33) 79

מָעַל 21 to act unfaithfully (10·13·42) 591

מַעַל unfaithful act (3·35·35) 591

כִּחֵשׁ to deceive (3·19·22) 471

עָמִית associate, fellow, relation (11·12) 765

פִּקָּדוֹן deposit, store (2·3) 824

תְּשׂוּמֶת pledge, security (1·1) 965

גָּזֵל robbery (1·4) 160

עָשַׁק to oppress, wrong (3·36·37) 798

אֲבֵדָה 22 a lost thing (2·4) 2

כִּחֵשׁ to deceive (3·19·22) 471

אָשֵׁם 23 to be guilty (10·31·33) 79

גְּזֵלָה plunder, spoil (1·6) 160

גזל to tear away, seize (2·29·30) 159

עֹשֶׁק	gain from extortion (1·15) 799
עָשַׁק	to oppress, wrong (3·36·37) 798
פִּקָּדוֹן	deposit, store (2·3) 824
אֲבֵדָה	a lost thing (2·4) 2
לַאֲשֶׁר 24	to (one whom) (3·38) 82
אַשְׁמָה	guiltiness (4·19) 80
אָשָׁם 25	tresspass offering (27·46) 79
עֵרֶךְ	estimate, valuation (24·33) 789
נִסְלַח 26	to be forgiven (10·13·46) 699
אַשְׁמָה	guiltiness (4·19) 80

Chapter 6

מוֹקֵד 2	hearth (1·3) 428
הוּקַד	to be burning (3·5·8) 428
מַד 3	garment (1·12) 551
בַּד	white linen (8·23) 94
מִכְנָס	drawers (2·5) 488
דֶּשֶׁן	fat ashes (5·15) 206
פָּשַׁט 4	to strip off, put off (2·24·43) 833
דֶּשֶׁן	fat ashes (5·15) 206
הוּקַד 5	to be burning (3·5·8) 428
כבה	to be extinguished (2·14·24) 459
הוּקַד 6	to be burning (3·5·8) 428
כבה	to be extinguished (2·14·24) 459
קֹמֶץ 8	fist (3·4) 888
לְבֹנָה	frankincense (7·21) 526
נִיחוֹחַ	soothing (17·43) 629
אַזְכָּרָה	memorial offering (6·7) 272
נאפה 10	to be baked (3·3·12) 66
חָמֵץ	that which is leavened (4·11) 329
אָשָׁם	trespass offering (27·46) 79
אֵפָה 13	ephah, a measure (3·38) 35
מַחֲצִית	half (2·16) 345
מַחֲבַת 14	griddle (3·5) 290
הרבך	to be well mixed (2·3·3) 916
תֻּפִינִים	[dub.] baken pieces (1·1) 1074
פַּת	fragment, bit, morsel (2·14) 837
נִיחוֹחַ	soothing (17·43) 629
מָשִׁיחַ 15	anointed (4·40) 603

כָּלִיל	whole offering (2·15) 483
כָּלִיל 16	whole offering (2·15) 483
נזה 20	to spatter (2·4·24) 633
חֶרֶשׂ 21	earthen vessel (5·16) 360
בֻּשַּׁל	to be boiled (2·4·27) 143
מֹרַק	to be well scoured (1·1·14) 599
שֻׁטַּף	to be rinsed (1·1·31) 1009

Chapter 7

אָשָׁם 1	trespass offering (27·46) 79
אָשָׁם 2	trespass offering (27·46) 79
זָרַק	to throw, scatter abundantly (12·32·34) 284
אַלְיָה 3	fat tail (4·5) 46
כִּלְיָה 4	kidney (13·30) 480
כֶּסֶל	loin (4·5[?]) 492
יֹתֶרֶת	appendage (9·11) 452
כָּבֵד	liver (9·14) 458
אָשָׁם 5	trespass offering (27·46) 79
אָשָׁם 7	trespass offering (27·46) 79
נאפה 9	to be baked (3·3·12) 66
תַּנּוּר	stove, firepot (4·15) 1092
מַרְחֶשֶׁת	stewpan (2·2) 935
מַחֲבַת	griddle (3·5) 290
בָּלַל 10	to mix (9·42·42[?]) 117
חָרֵב	dry, unmoistened (1·10?) 351
תּוֹדָה 12	thank offering (5·32) 392
חַלָּה	a kind of cake (8·14) 319
בָּלַל	to mix (9·42·42[?]) 117
רָקִיק	thin cake, wafer (3·8) 956
הרבך	to be well mixed (2·3·3) 916
חַלָּה 13	a kind of cake (8·14) 319
חָמֵץ	that which is leavened (4·11) 329
תּוֹדָה	thank offering (5·32) 392
זָרַק 14	to throw, scatter abundantly (12·32·34) 284
תּוֹדָה 15	thank offering (5·32) 392
נְדָבָה 16	freewill offering (5·27) 621

מָחֳרָת	on the morrow of, after (5·32) 564
פִּגּוּל	18 foul thing, refuse (2·4) 803
טֻמְאָה	20 uncleanness (18·37) 380
עַם	kinsman (12·34) 769
טֻמְאָה	21 uncleanness (18·37) 380
שֶׁקֶץ	detestable thing (9·11) 1054
עַם	kinsman (12·34) 769
כֶּשֶׂב	23 lamb (7·13) 461
נְבֵלָה	24 carcass (19·48) 615
טְרֵפָה	animal torn (3·9) 383
עַם	25 kinsman (12·34) 769
מוֹשָׁב	26 dwelling place (8·43) 444
עַם	27 kinsman (12·34) 769
חָזֶה	30 breast (9·13) 303
הֵנִיף	to wave (11·32·34[?]) 631
תְּנוּפָה	waving, wave offering (14·30) 632
חָזֶה	31 breast (9·13) 303
שׁוֹק	32 leg (8·19) 1003
שׁוֹק	33 leg (8·19) 1003
מָנָה	portion (2·12) 584
חָזֶה	34 breast (9·13) 303
תְּנוּפָה	waving, wave offering (14·30) 632
שׁוֹק	leg (8·19) 1003
מִשְׁחָה	35 consecrated portion (2·2[?]) 603
כִּהֵן	to minister as a priest (12·23·23) 464
אָשָׁם	37 trespass offering (27·46) 79
מִלּוּא	installation (6·15) 571

Chapter 8

מִשְׁחָה	2 ointment (7·21[?]) 603
סַל	basket (3·15) 700
הִקְהִיל	3 to summon an assembly (1·20·39) 874
נִקְהַל	4 to assemble (1·19·39) 874
כֻּתֹּנֶת	7 tunic (4·30) 509
חָגַר	to gird on (4·4·44) 291
אַבְנֵט	girdle (5·9) 126
מְעִיל	robe (1·28) 591
אֵפוֹד	priestly garment (2·49) 65
חֵשֶׁב	ingenious work, girdle (1·8) 363
אפד	to gird on an ephod (1·2·2) 65
חֹשֶׁן	8 breast piece (2·25) 365
אוּרִים	Urim (1·7) 22
תֻּמִּים	[dub.] Thummin (1·5) 1070
מִצְנֶפֶת	9 turban of high priest (3·12) 857
מוּל	the forefront of (1·23) 557
צִיץ	shining thing (1·15) 847
נֵזֶר	crown (2·24) 634
מִשְׁחָה	10 ointment (7·21) 603
נזה	11 to spatter (2·4·24) 633
כִּיּוֹר	basin (1·23) 468
כֵּן	base (1·17) 487
מִשְׁחָה	12 ointment (7·21) 603
כֻּתֹּנֶת	13 tunic (4·30) 509
חגר	to gird on (4·4·44) 291
אַבְנֵט	girdle (5·9) 126
חבש	to bind (on) (1·27·31) 289
מִגְבָּעוֹת	headgear (1·4) 149
סָמַךְ	14 to lay (14·41·48) 701
אֶצְבַּע	15 finger (13·31) 840
יְסוֹד	base (8·19) 414
יוֹתֶרֶת	16 appendage (9·11) 452
כָּבֵד	liver (9·14) 458
כִּלְיָה	kidney (13·30) 480
פֶּרֶשׁ	17 offal [as ripped out in preparing a victim] (3·7) 831
סָמַךְ	18 to lay (14·41·48) 701
זָרַק	19 to throw, scatter abundantly (12·32·34) 284
נִתַּח	20 to cut up (3·9·9) 677
נֵתַח	piece of a divided carcass (6·12) 677
פֶּדֶר	suet (3·3) 804
כֶּרַע	21 leg (6·9) 502
נִיחוֹחַ	soothing (17·43) 629
מִלּוּא	22 installation (6·15) 571
סָמַךְ	to lay (14·41·48) 701

תְּנוּךְ 23 tip, lobe of ear (6·8) 1072
יְמָנִי right (20·33) 412
בֹּהֶן thumb, great toe (12·14[?]) 97
תְּנוּךְ 24 tip, lobe of ear (6·8) 1072
יְמָנִי right (20·33) 412
בֹּהֶן thumb, great toe (12·14[?]) 97
זָרַק to throw, scatter abundantly (12·32·34) 284
אַלְיָה 25 fat tail (4·5) 46
יוֹתֶרֶת appendage (9·11) 452
כָּבֵד liver (9·14) 458
כִּלְיָה kidney (13·30) 480
שׁוֹק leg (8·19) 1003
סַל 26 basket (3·15) 700
חַלָּה kind of cake (8·14) 319
רָקִיק thin cake, wafer (3·8) 956
שׁוֹק leg (8·19) 1003
הֵנִיף 27 to wave (11·32·34[?]) 631
תְּנוּפָה waving, wave offering (14·30) 632
מִלּוּא 28 installation (6·15) 571
נִיחוֹחַ soothing (17·43) 629
חָזֶה 29 breast (9·13) 303
הֵנִיף to wave (11·32·34[?]) 631
תְּנוּפָה waving, wave offering (14·30) 632
מִלּוּא installation (6·15) 571
מָנָה portion (2·12) 584
מִשְׁחָה 30 ointment (7·21) 603
נזה to spatter (2·4·24) 633
בִּשֵּׁל 31 to cook, boil (1·20·27) 143
סַל basket (3·15) 700
מִלּוּא installation (6·15) 571
מִלּוּא 33 installation (6·15) 571

Chapter 9

עֵגֶל 2 calf (3·35) 722
עֵגֶל 3 calf (3·35) 722
בָּלַל 4 to mix (9·42·42[?]) 117
עֵגֶל 8 calf (3·35) 722

טָבַל 9 to dip (6·15·16) 371
אֶצְבַּע finger (13·31) 840
יְסוֹד base (8·19) 414
כִּלְיָה 10 kidney (13·30) 480
יוֹתֶרֶת appendage (9·11) 452
כָּבֵד liver (9·14) 458
זָרַק 12 to throw, scatter abundantly (12·32·34) 284
נֵתַח 13 piece of a divided carcass (6·12) 677
כֶּרַע 14 leg (6·9) 502
מִלְּבַד 17 besides (5·33) 94
זָרַק 18 to throw, scatter abundantly (12·32·34) 284
אַלְיָה 19 fat tail (4·5) 46
מְכַסֶּה covering (1·4) 492
כִּלְיָה kidney (13·30) 480
יוֹתֶרֶת 19 appendage (9·11) 452
כָּבֵד liver (9·14) 458
חָזֶה 20 breast (9·13) 303
חָזֶה 21 breast (9·13) 303
שׁוֹק leg (8·19) 1003
הֵנִיף to wave (11·32·34[?]) 631
תְּנוּפָה waving, wave offering (14·30) 632

Chapter 10

מַחְתָּה 1 censer (2·21) 367
דמם 3 to be silent (1·23·30) 198
כֻּתֹּנֶת 5 tunic (4·30) 509
פָּרַע 6 to let loose, remove restraint (3·13·16) 828
פרם to tear a garment (3·3·3) 827
קָצַף to be wroth (2·28·34) 893
שְׂרֵפָה burning (1·13) 977
מִשְׁחָה 7 ointment (7·21) 603
שֵׁכָר 9 intoxicating drink (1·23) 1016
הִבְדִּיל 10 to make a distinction (8·32·42) 95
חֹל profaneness (1·7) 320
הורה 11 to teach (2·45[?]·45[?]) 434

חָזֶה	14 breast (9·13)	303
תְּנוּפָה	waving, wave offering (14·30)	632
שׁוֹק	leg (8·19)	1003
שׁוֹק	15 leg (8·19)	1003
חָזֶה	breast (9·13)	303
תְּנוּפָה	waving, wave offering (14·30)	632
הֵנִיף	to wave (11·32·34[?])	631
קָצַף	16 to be wroth (2·28·34)	893
פְּנִימָה	18 towards the [in]side (1·5)	819

Chapter 11

הִפְרִיס	3 to divide [the hoof] (7·12·14)	828
פַּרְסָה	hoof (9·21)	828
שָׁסַע	to divide, cleave (3·5·8)	1042
שֶׁסַע	cleft (3·4)	1043
גֵּרָה	cud (7·11)	176
מִמַּעַל	4 above, on the top of (7·29)	751
גֵּרָה	cud (7·11)	176
הִפְרִיס	to divide [the hoof] (7·12·14)	828
פַּרְסָה	hoof (9·21)	828
שָׁפָן	5 rock badger (1·4)	1050
גֵּרָה	cud (7·11)	176
פַּרְסָה	hoof (9·21)	828
הִפְרִיס	to divide [the hoof] (7·12·14)	828
אַרְנֶבֶת	6 hare (1·2)	58
גֵּרָה	cud (7·11)	176
פַּרְסָה	hoof (9·21)	828
הִפְרִיס	to divide [the hoof] (7·12·14)	828
חֲזִיר	7 swine (1·7)	306
הִפְרִיס	to divide [the hoof] (7·12·14)	828
פַּרְסָה	hoof (9·21)	828
שָׁסַע	to divide, cleave (3·5·8)	1042
שֶׁסַע	cleft (3·4)	1043
גֵּרָה	cud (7·11)	176
נגרר	to chew (1·3·4)	176
נְבֵלָה	8 carcass (19·48)	615
סְנַפִּיר	9 fin (3·5)	703
קַשְׂקֶשֶׂת	scale [of fish] (3·8)	903

סְנַפִּיר	10 fin (3·5)	703
קַשְׂקֶשֶׂת	scale [of fish] (3·8)	903
שֶׁרֶץ	swarmers, swarming things (12·15)	1056
שֶׁקֶץ	detestable thing (9·11)	1054
שֶׁקֶץ	11 detestable thing (9·11)	1054
נְבֵלָה	carcass (19·48)	615
שָׁקַץ	to detest (4·6·6)	1055
סְנַפִּיר	12 fin (3·5)	703
קַשְׂקֶשֶׂת	scale [of fish] (3·8)	903
שֶׁקֶץ	detestable thing (9·11)	1054
שָׁקַץ	13 to detest (4·6·6)	1055
שֶׁקֶץ	detestable thing (9·11)	1054
נֶשֶׁר	eagle (1·26)	676
פֶּרֶס	bearded vulture (1·2)	828
עָזְנִיָּה	unclean bird of prey, apparently akin to vulture (1·2)	740
דָּאָה	14 bird of prey, kite (1·1)	178
אַיָּה	hawk, falcon (1·3)	17
מִין	species (9·31)	568
עֹרֵב	15 raven (1·12)	788
מִין	species (9·31)	568
יַעֲנָה	16 ostrich (1·8)	419
תַּחְמָס	male ostrich (1·2)	329
שַׁחַף	sea mew, gull (1·2)	1006
נֵץ	bird of prey (1·3)	665
מִין	species (9·31)	568
כּוֹס	17 a kind of owl (1·3)	468
שָׁלָךְ	cormorant (1·2)	1021
יַנְשׁוּף	a bird (1·3)	676
תִּנְשֶׁמֶת	18 unclean bird (1·2)	675
קָאָת	bird, usually a pelican (1·5)	866
רָחָם	carrion vulture (1·2)	934
חֲסִידָה	19 stork (1·6)	339
אֲנָפָה	an unclean bird (1·2)	60
מִין	species (9·31)	568
דּוּכִיפַת	unclean bird, hoopoe[?] (1·2)	189
עֲטַלֵּף	bat (1·3)	742

שֶׁרֶץ	20 swarmers, swarming things (12·15) 1056		(12·15) 1056	
שֶׁקֶץ	detestable thing (9·11) 1054		שַׂק	32 sack (1·48) 974
שֶׁרֶץ	21 swarmers, swarming things (12·15) 1056		חֶרֶשׂ	33 earthenware (5·16) 360
כֶּרַע	leg (6·9) 502		אֹכֶל	34 food (2·44) 38
מִמַּעַל	above, on the top of (7·29) 751		מַשְׁקֶה	drink (1·19) 1052
נתר	to leap (1·1·5) 684		נְבֵלָה	35 carcass (19·48) 615
אַרְבֶּה	22 a locust (1·24) 916		תַּנּוּר	stove, firepot (4·15) 1072
מִין	species (9·31) 568		כִּיר	cooking furnace (1·1) 468
סָלְעָם	locust (1·1) 701		התץ	to be broken down (1·1·42) 683
חַרְגֹּל	a kind of locust (1·1) 353		מַעְיָן	36 spring (1·23) 475
חָגָב	locust (1·5) 290		מִקְוֶה	collection, collected mass (1·7) 876
שֶׁרֶץ	23 swarmers, swarming things (12·15) 1056		נְבֵלָה	carcass (19·48) 615
שֶׁקֶץ	detestable thing (9·11) 1054		נְבֵלָה	37 carcass (19·48) 615
נְבֵלָה	24 carcass (19·48) 615		זֵרוּעַ	thing sown (1·2) 283
נְבֵלָה	25 carcass (19·48) 615		נְבֵלָה	38 carcass (19·48) 615
הפריס	26 to divide [the hoof] (7·12·14) 828		אָכְלָה	39 food, eating (2·18) 38
פַּרְסָה	the hoof (9·21) 828		נְבֵלָה	carcass (19·48) 615
שֶׁסַע	cleft (3·4) 1043		נְבֵלָה	40 carcass (19·48) 615
שסע	to divide, cleave (3·5·8) 1042		שֶׁרֶץ	41 swarmers, swarming things (12·15) 1056
גֵּרָה	cud (7·11) 176		שָׁרַץ	to swarm, teem (5·14·14) 1056
נְבֵלָה	27 carcass (19·48) 615		שֶׁקֶץ	detestable thing (9·11) 1054
נְבֵלָה	28 carcass (19·48) 615		גָּחוֹן	42 belly (1·2) 161
שֶׁרֶץ	29 swarmers, swarming things (12·15) 1056		שֶׁרֶץ	swarmers, swarming things (12·15) 1056
שָׁרַץ	to swarm (5·14·14) 1056		שָׁרַץ	to swarm, teem (5·14·14) 1056
חֹלֶד	weasel (1·1) 317		שֶׁקֶץ	detestable thing (9·11) 1054
עַכְבָּר	mouse (1·6) 747		שָׁקַץ	43 to make detestable (4·6·6) 1055
צָב	lizard (1·1) 839		שֶׁרֶץ	swarmers, swarming things (12·15) 1056
מִין	species (9·31) 568		שָׁרַץ	to swarm, teem (5·14·14) 1056
אֲנָקָה	30 ferret, shrew mouse (1·1) 60		שֶׁרֶץ	44 swarmers, swarming things (12·15) 1056
כֹּחַ	a kind of lizard (1·1) 470		רמשׂ	to creep, move about (3·16·16) 942
לְטָאָה	lizard (1·1) 538		רמשׂ	46 to creep, move about (3·16·16) 942
חֹמֶט	a kind of lizard (1·1) 328		שָׁרַץ	to swarm, teem (5·14·14) 1056
תִּנְשֶׁמֶת	lizard, chameleon (1·1) 675		הִבְדִּיל	47 to make a distinction (8·32·42) 95
שֶׁרֶץ	31 swarmers, swarming things			

Chapter 12

נִדָּה	2 impurity (13·30)	622
דְּוֹת	to be ill (1·1·1)	188
נִמּוֹל	3 to be circumcised (1·12·29)	557
עׇרְלָה	foreskin (2·16)	790
נְקֵבָה	5 female (12·22)	666
שָׁבוּעַ	week (1·20)	988
נִדָּה	impurity (13·30)	622
יוֹנָה	6 dove (10·35)	401
תּוֹר	turtle dove (9·14)	1076
מָקוֹר	7 flow (3·18)	881
נְקֵבָה	female (12·22)	666
דֵּי	8 sufficiency, enough (3·12)	191
שֶׂה	sheep, goat (5·44)	961
תּוֹר	turtle dove (9·14)	1076
יוֹנָה	dove (10·35)	401

Chapter 13

שְׂאֵת	2 swelling (7·7)	673
סַפַּחַת	eruption (2·2)	705
בַּהֶרֶת	bright spot (12·12)	97
צׇרַעַת	leprosy (29·35)	863
שֵׂעָר	3 hair (15·28)	972
לָבָן	white (20·28)	526
עָמֹק	deep (7·17)	771
צׇרַעַת	leprosy (29·35)	863
בַּהֶרֶת	4 bright spot (12·12)	97
לָבָן	white (20·28)	526
עָמֹק	deep (7·17)	771
שֵׂעָר	hair (15·28)	972
פָּשָׂה	5 to spread (18·18·18)	832
כֵּהָה	6 to grow faint (2·3·9[?])	462
פָּשָׂה	to spread (18·18·18)	832
מִסְפַּחַת	eruption (3·3)	705
פָּשָׂה	7 to spread (18·18·18)	832
מִסְפַּחַת	eruption (3·3)	705
פָּשָׂה	8 to spread (18·18·18)	832

מִסְפַּחַת	eruption (3·3)	705
צׇרַעַת	leprosy (29·35)	863
צׇרַעַת	9 leprosy (29·35)	863
שְׂאֵת	10 swelling (7·7)	673
לָבָן	white (20·28)	526
שֵׂעָר	hair (15·28)	972
מִחְיָה	10 the quick (2·8)	313
צׇרַעַת	11 leprosy (29·35)	863
נוֹשֶׁן	to be old (2·3·3[?])	445
פָּרַח	12 to break out (8·29·34)	827
צׇרַעַת	leprosy (29·35)	863
צׇרַעַת	13 leprosy (29·35)	863
לָבָן	white (20·28)	526
צׇרַעַת	15 leprosy (29·35)	863
לָבָן	16 white (20·28)	526
לָבָן	17 white (20·28)	526
שְׁחִין	18 a boil (4·13)	1006
שְׁחִין	19 a boil (4·13)	1006
שְׂאֵת	swelling (7·7)	673
לָבָן	white (20·28)	526
בַּהֶרֶת	bright spot (12·12)	97
אֲדַמְדָּם	reddish (6·6)	10
שָׁפָל	20 low (4·18)	1050
שֵׂעָר	hair (15·28)	972
לָבָן	white (20·28)	526
צׇרַעַת	leprosy (29·35)	863
שְׁחִין	a boil (4·13)	1006
פָּרַח	to break out (8·29·34)	827
שֵׂעָר	21 hair (15·28)	972
לָבָן	white (20·28)	526
שָׁפָל	low (9·18)	1050
כֵּהָה	faint (4·7)	462
פָּשָׂה	22 to spread (18·18·18)	832
בַּהֶרֶת	23 bright spot (12·12)	97
פָּשָׂה	to spread (18·18·18)	832
צׇרֶבֶת	scab/scar of a sore (2·2)	863
שְׁחִין	a boil (4·13)	1006
מִכְוָה	24 burn spot (5·5)	465

מִחְיָה	the quick (2·8) 313	
בַּהֶרֶת	bright spot (12·12) 97	
לָבָן	white (20·28) 526	
אֲדַמְדַּם	reddish (6·6) 10	
שֵׂעָר	25 hair (15·28) 972	
לָבָן	white (20·28) 526	
בַּהֶרֶת	bright spot (12·12) 97	
עָמֹק	deep (7·17) 771	
צָרַעַת	leprosy (29·35) 863	
מִכְוָה	burn spot (5·5) 465	
פָּרַח	to break out (8·29·34) 827	
בַּהֶרֶת	26 bright spot (12·12) 97	
שֵׂעָר	hair (15·28) 972	
לָבָן	white (20·28) 526	
שָׁפָל	low (4·18) 1050	
כֵּהָה	faint (4·7) 462	
פָּשָׂה	27 to spread (18·18·18) 832	
צָרַעַת	leprosy (29·35) 863	
בַּהֶרֶת	28 bright spot (12·12) 97	
פָּשָׂה	to spread (18·18·18) 832	
כֵּהָה	faint (4·7) 462	
שְׂאֵת	swelling (7·7) 673	
מִכְוָה	burn spot (5·5) 465	
צָרֶבֶת	scab/scar of a sore (2·2) 863	
זָקָן	29 chin, beard (5·18) 278	
עָמֹק	30 deep (7·17) 771	
שֵׂעָר	hair (15·28) 972	
צָהֹב	gleeming, yellow (3·3) 843	
דַּק	thin, small, fine (3·14) 201	
נֶתֶק	scab (14·14) 683	
צָרַעַת	leprosy (29·35) 863	
זָקָן	chin, beard (5·18) 278	
נֶתֶק	31 scab (14·14) 683	
עָמֹק	deep (7·17) 771	
שֵׂעָר	hair (15·28) 972	
שָׁחֹר	black (2·6) 1007	
פָּשָׂה	32 to spread (18·18·18) 832	
נֶתֶק	scab (14·14) 683	

שֵׂעָר	hair (15·28) 972	
צָהֹב	gleaming, yellow (3·3) 843	
עָמֹק	deep (7·17) 771	
הִתְגַּלָּח	33 to shave oneself (1·2·23) 164	
נֶתֶק	scab (14·14) 683	
גִּלַּח	to shave off (5·18·23) 164	
נֶתֶק	34 scab (14·14) 683	
פָּשָׂה	to spread (18·18·18) 832	
עָמֹק	deep (7·17) 771	
פָּשָׂה	35 to spread (18·18·18) 832	
נֶתֶק	scab (14·14) 683	
פָּשָׂה	36 to spread (18·18·18) 832	
נֶתֶק	scab (14·14) 683	
בִּקֵּר	to seek, look for (2·7·7) 133	
שֵׂעָר	hair (15·28) 972	
צָהֹב	gleaming, yellow (3·3) 843	
נֶתֶק	37 scab (14·14) 683	
שֵׂעָר	hair (15·28) 972	
שָׁחֹר	black (2·6) 1007	
צָמַח	to sprout, spring up (1·15·33) 855	
בַּהֶרֶת	38 bright spot (12·12) 97	
לָבָן	white (20·28) 526	
בַּהֶרֶת	39 bright spot (12·12) 97	
כֵּהָה	faint (4·7) 462	
לָבָן	white (20·28) 526	
בֹּהַק	harmless eruption on the skin (1·1) 97	
פָּרַח	to break out (8·29·34) 827	
נִמְרַט	40 to be made bald (2·2·14) 598	
קֵרֵחַ	bald (1·3) 901	
נִמְרַט	41 to be made bald (2·2·14) 598	
גִּבֵּחַ	having a bald forehead (1·1) 147	
קָרַחַת	42 baldness of head (4·4) 901	
גַּבַּחַת	bald forehead (4·4) 147	
לָבָן	white (20·28) 526	
אֲדַמְדָּם	reddish (6·6) 10	
צָרַעַת	leprosy (29·35) 863	
פָּרַח	to break out (8·29·34) 827	

קָרַחַת	baldness of head (4·4) 901
שְׂאֵת	43 swelling (7·7) 673
לָבָן	white (20·28) 526
אֲדַמְדָּם	reddish (6·6) 10
קָרַחַת	baldness of head (4·4) 901
גַּבַּחַת	bald forehead (4·4) 147
צָרַעַת	leprosy (29·35) 863
צָרוּעַ	44 leper (4·5) 863
צָרוּעַ	45 leper (4·5) 863
פרם	to tear/rend garment (3·3·3) 827
פָּרַע	to let loose, to remove restraint (3·13·16) 828
שָׂפָם	moustache (1·5) 974
עָטָה	to wrap, envelop [oneself] (1·11·14) 741
בָּדָד	46 isolation, separation (1·11) 94
מוֹשָׁב	dwelling place (8·43) 444
צָרַעַת	47 leprosy (29·35) 863
צֶמֶר	wool (4·16) 856
פֵּשֶׁת	flax, linen (4·16) 833
שְׁתִי	48 warp (9·9) 1059
עֵרֶב	woof (9·9) 786
פֵּשֶׁת	flax, linen (4·16) 833
צֶמֶר	wool (4·16) 856
יְרַקְרַק	49 greenish (2·3) 439
אֲדַמְדָּם	reddish (6·6) 10
שְׁתִי	warp (9·9) 1059
עֵרֶב	woof (9·9) 786
צָרַעַת	leprosy (29·35) 863
פָּשָׂה	51 to spread (18·18·18) 832
שְׁתִי	warp (9·9) 1059
עֵרֶב	woof (9·9) 786
צָרַעַת	leprosy (29·35) 863
הַמָאִיר	to pain (3·4·4) 549
שְׁתִי	52 warp (9·9) 1059
עֵרֶב	woof (9·9) 786
צֶמֶר	wool (4·16) 856
פֵּשֶׁת	flax, linen (4·16) 833

צָרַעַת	leprosy (29·35) 863
הַמָאִיר	to pain (3·4·4) 549
פָּשָׂה	53 to spread (18·18·18) 832
שְׁתִי	warp (9·9) 1059
עֵרֶב	woof (9·9) 786
פָּשָׂה	55 to spread (18·18·18) 832
פְּחֶתֶת	a boring, eating out (1·1) 809
קָרַחַת	baldness of head (4·4) 901
גַּבַּחַת	bald forehead (4·4) 147
כֵּהָה	56 to grow faint (2·3·9[?]) 462
שְׁתִי	warp (9·9) 1059
עֵרֶב	woof (9·9) 786
שְׁתִי	57 warp (9·9) 1059
עֵרֶב	woof (9·9) 786
פָּרַח	to break out (8·29·34) 827
שְׁתִי	58 warp (9·9) 1059
עֵרֶב	woof (9·9) 786
צָרַעַת	59 leprosy (29·35) 863
צֶמֶר	wool (4·16) 856
פֵּשֶׁת	flax, linen (4·16) 833
שְׁתִי	warp (9·9) 1059
עֵרֶב	woof (9·9) 786

Chapter 14

מְצֹרָע	2 leprous (1·15) 863
צָרַעַת	3 leprosy (29·35) 863
צָרוּעַ	leper (4·5) 863
צִפּוֹר	4 bird[s] (13·40) 861
שָׁנִי	scarlet (5·42) 1040
תּוֹלֵעָה	coccus ilicis [yielding scarlet color] (5·41) 1069
אֵזוֹב	hyssop (5·10) 23
צִפּוֹר	5 bird[s] (13·40) 861
חֶרֶשׂ	earthenware (5·16) 360
צִפּוֹר	6 bird[s] (13·40) 861
שָׁנִי	scarlet (5·42) 1040
תּוֹלֵעָה	coccus ilicis [yielding scarlet color] (5·41) 1069

אֵזוֹב	hyssop (5·10) 23
טָבַל	to dip (6·15·16) 371
הִזָּה	7 to sprinkle (13·20·24) 633
צָרַעַת	leprosy (29·35) 863
צִפּוֹר	bird[s] (3·40) 861
גִּלַּח	8 to shave off (5·18·23) 164
שֵׂעָר	hair (15·28) 972
גִּלַּח	9 to shave off (5·18·23) 164
שֵׂעָר	hair (15·28) 972
זָקָן	chin, beard (5·18) 278
גַּב	brow, anything curved (1·13) 146
כִּבְשָׂה	10 ewe lamb (1·7) 461
בָּלַל	to mix (9·42·42[?]) 117
לֹג	a liquid measure (5·5) 528
אָשָׁם	12 trespass offering (27·46) 79
לֹג	a liquid measure (5·5) 528
הֵנִיף	to wave (11·32·34[?]) 631
תְּנוּפָה	waving, wave offering (14·30) 632
אָשָׁם	13 trespass offering (27·46) 79
אָשָׁם	14 trespass offering (27·46) 79
תְּנוּךְ	tip, lobe of ear (6·8) 1072
יְמָנִי	right (20·33) 412
בֹּהֶן	thumb, great toe (12·14[?]) 97
לֹג	15 a liquid measure (5·5) 528
שְׂמֹאל	left, on the left (4·9) 970
טָבַל	16 to dip (6·15·16) 371
אֶצְבַּע	finger (13·31) 840
יְמָנִי	right (20·33) 412
שְׂמֹאל	left, on the left (4·9) 970
הִזָּה	to sprinkle (13·20·24) 633
תְּנוּךְ	17 tip, lobe of ear (6·8) 1072
יְמָנִי	right (20·33) 412
בֹּהֶן	thumb, great toe (12·14[?]) 97
אָשָׁם	trespass offering (27·46) 79
טֻמְאָה	19 uncleanness (18·37) 380
דַּל	21 poor (2·48) 195
הִשִּׂיג	to reach (12·48·48) 673
אָשָׁם	trespass offering (27·46) 79
תְּנוּפָה	waving, wave offering (14·30) 632
עִשָּׂרוֹן	tenth part (5·28) 798
בָּלַל	to mix (9·42·42[?]) 117
לֹג	a liquid measure (5·5) 528
תּוֹר	22 turtle dove (9·14) 1076
יוֹנָה	dove (10·35) 401
הִשִּׂיג	to reach (12·48·48) 673
אָשָׁם	24 trespass offering (27·46) 79
לֹג	a liquid measure (5·5) 528
הֵנִיף	to wave (11·32·34[?]) 631
תְּנוּפָה	waving, wave offering (14·30) 632
אָשָׁם	25 trespass offering (27·46) 79
תְּנוּךְ	tip, lobe of ear (6·8) 1072
יְמָנִי	right (20·33) 412
בֹּהֶן	thumb, great toe (12·14[?]) 97
שְׂמָאלִי	26 left, on the left (4·9) 970
הִזָּה	27 to sprinkle (13·20·24) 633
אֶצְבַּע	finger (13·31) 840
יְמָנִי	right (20·33) 412
שְׂמָאלִי	left, on the left (4·9) 970
תְּנוּךְ	28 tip, lobe of ear (6·8) 1072
יְמָנִי	right (20·33) 412
בֹּהֶן	thumb, great toe (12·14[?]) 97
אָשָׁם	trespass offering (27·46) 79
תּוֹר	30 turtle dove (9·14) 1076
יוֹנָה	dove (10·35) 401
הִשִּׂיג	to reach (12·48·48) 673
הִשִּׂיג	31 to reach (12·48·48) 673
צָרַעַת	32 leprosy (29·35) 863
צָרַעַת	34 leprosy (29·35) 863
בְּטֶרֶם	36 before (1·39) 382
שְׁקַעֲרוּרֹת	37 depression, hollow (1·1) 891
יְרַקְרַק	greenish (2·3) 439
אֲדַמְדָּם	reddish (6·6) 10
שָׁפָל	low (4·18) 1050
פָּשָׂה	39 to spread (18·18·18) 832
חָלַץ	to pull out, tear out (2·14·27) 322
הִקְצִיעַ	41 to scrape, scrape off (1·1·1) 892

73

הִקְצָה to scrape, scrape off (2·2·5) 891

טוּחַ 42 to coat (1·9·11) 376

פָּרַח 43 to break out (8·29·34) 827

חִלֵּץ to pull out, tear out (2·14·27) 322

הִקְצָה to scrape, scrape off (2·2·5) 891

נָטוֹחַ to be coated (2·2·11) 376

פָּשָׂה 44 to spread (18·18·18) 832

צָרַעַת leprosy (29·35) 863

הַמְאִיר to pain, prick (3·4·4) 549

נָתַץ 45 to pull down (1·31·42) 683

פָּשָׂה 48 to spread (18·18·18) 832

נָטוֹחַ to be coated (2·2·11) 376

צִפּוֹר 49 bird[s] (13·40) 861

שָׁנִי scarlet (5·42) 1040

תּוֹלֵעָה coccus ilicis [yielding scarlet color] (5·41) 1069

אֵזוֹב hyssop (5·10) 23

צִפּוֹר 50 bird[s] (13·40) 861

חֶרֶשׂ earthenware (5·16) 360

אֵזוֹב 51 hyssop (5·10) 23

שָׁנִי scarlet (5·42) 1040

תּוֹלֵעָה coccus ilicis [yielding scarlet color] (5·41) 1069

צִפּוֹר bird[s] (13·40) 861

טָבַל to dip (5·15·16) 371

הִזָּה to sprinkle (13·20·24) 633

צִפּוֹר 52 bird[s] (13·40) 861

אֵזוֹב hyssop (5·10) 23

שָׁנִי scarlet (5·42) 1040

תּוֹלֵעָה coccus ilicis [yielding scarlet color] (5·41) 1069

צִפּוֹר 53 bird[s] (13·40) 861

צָרַעַת 54 leprosy (29·35) 863

נֶתֶק scab (14·14) 683

צָרַעַת 55 leprosy (29·35) 863

שְׂאֵת 56 swelling (7·7) 673

סַפַּחַת eruption (2·2) 705

בַּהֶרֶת bright spot (12·12) 97

הוֹרָה 57 to teach (2·45[?]·45[?]) 434

צָרַעַת leprosy (29·35) 863

Chapter 15

זָב 2 to flow (5·29·29) 264

זוֹב issue, flux (13·13) 264

טֻמְאָה 3 uncleanness (18·37) 380

זוֹב issue, flux (13·13) 264

רָר to flow [like slime] (1·1·1) 938

הֶחְתִּים to show stoppage (1·1·27) 367

מִשְׁכָּב 4 bed (9·46) 1012

זָב to flow (5·29·29[?]) 264

מִשְׁכָּב 5 bed (9·46) 1012

זָב 6 one who has an issue (11·13[?]) 264

זָב 7 one who has an issue (11·13[?]) 264

רקק 8 to spit (1·1·1) 956

זָב one who has an issue (11·13[?]) 264

מֶרְכָּב 9 saddle (1·3) 939

זָב one who has an issue (11·13[?]) 264

זָב 11 one who has an issue (11·13[?]) 264

שָׁטַף to rinse off (1·28·31) 1009

חֶרֶשׂ 12 earthenware (5·16) 360

זָב one who has an issue (11·13[?]) 264

נשׁטף to be rinsed out, off (1·21·31) 1009

זָב 13 one who has an issue (11·13[?]) 264

זוֹב issue, flux (13·13) 264

תּוֹר 14 turtle dove (9·14) 1076

יוֹנָה dove (10·35) 401

זוֹב 15 issue, flux (13·13) 264

שְׁכָבָה 16 act of lying, sexual intercourse (6·9) 1012

שְׁכָבָה 17 act of lying, secual intercourse (6·9) 1012

שְׁכָבָה 18 act of lying, sexual intercourse (6·9) 1012

זָב 19 one who has an issue (11·13[?]) 264

זוֹב issue, flux (13·13) 264

נִדָּה impurity (13·30) 622

נִדָּה 20 impurity (13·30) 622

מִשְׁכָּב 21 bed (9·46) 1012

מִשְׁכָּב 23 bed (9·46) 1012
נִדָּה 24 impurity (13·30) 622
מִשְׁכָּב bed (9·46) 1012
זָב 25 to flow (5·29·29[?]) 264
זוֹב issue, flux (13·13) 264
בִּלְא outside of (1·29) 520
נִדָּה impurity (13·30) 622
טָמֵא uncleanness (18·37) 380
מִשְׁכָּב 26 bed (9·46) 1012
זוֹב issue, flux (13·13) 264
נִדָּה impurity (13·30) 622
טָמֵא uncleanness (18·37) 380
זוֹב 28 issue, flux (13·13) 264
תּוֹר 29 turtle dove (9·14) 1076
יוֹנָה dove (10·35) 401
זוֹב 30 issue, flux (13·13) 264
טָמֵא uncleanness (18·37) 380
הִזִּיר 31 to sacredly separate (1·6·10) 634
טָמֵא uncleanness (18·37) 380
זָב 32 one who has an issue (11·13[?]) 264
שְׁכָבָה act of lying, sexual intercourse (6·9) 1012
דָּוֶה 33 menstruous faint, unwell (2·5) 188
נִדָּה impurity (13·30) 622
זָב to flow (5·29·29[?]) 264
זוֹב issue, flux (13·13) 264
נְקֵבָה female (12·22) 666

Chapter 16

פָּרֹכֶת 2 curtain (7·25) 827
כַּפֹּרֶת propitiatory (7·27) 498
כֻּתֹּנֶת 4 tunic (4·30) 509
בַּד white linen (8·23) 94
מִכְנָס drawers (2·5) 488
אַבְנֵט girdle (3·9) 126
חָגַר to gird on (4·4·44) 291
מִצְנֶפֶת turban of high priest (3·12) 857
צָנַף to wrap, windup together (1·2·2) 857

מַחְתָּה 12 censer (2·21) 367
גַּחֶלֶת coal (1·18) 160
חֹפֶן hollow of hand (1·6) 342
סַם 12 spice (2·15) 702
דַּק small, fine (3·14) 201
פָּרֹכֶת curtain (7·25) 827
כַּפֹּרֶת 13 propitiatory (7·27) 498
הִזָּה 14 to sprinkle (13·20·24) 633
אֶצְבַּע finger (13·31) 840
כַּפֹּרֶת propitiatory (7·27) 498
קֶדֶם eastward (2·26) 870
פָּרֹכֶת 15 curtain (7·25) 827
הִזָּה to sprinkle (13·20·24) 633
כַּפֹּרֶת propitiatory (7·27) 498
טֻמְאָה 16 uncleanness (18·37) 380
הִזָּה 19 to sprinkle (13·20·24) 633
אֶצְבַּע finger (13·31) 840
טֻמְאָה uncleanness (18·37) 380
סָמַךְ 21 to lay (14·41·48) 701
עִתִּי timely, ready (1·1) 774
גְּזֵרָה 22 separation (1·1) 160
פָּשַׁט 23 to strip off, put off (2·24·43) 833
בַּד white linen (8·23) 94
פֶּרֶשׁ 27 offal [as ripped out in preparing victim] (3·7) 831
אֶזְרָח 29 native (7·17) 280
שַׁבָּתוֹן 31 sabbath observance (8·11) 992
כִּהֵן 32 to minister as priests (2·23·23) 464
בַּד white linen (8·23) 94

Chapter 17

כֶּשֶׂב 3 lamb (7·13) 461
זָרַק 6 to throw, scatter abundantly (12·32·34[?]) 284
נִיחוֹחַ soothing (17·43) 629
צוּד 13 to hunt (1·12·16) 844
צַיִד game (1·14) 844
נְבֵלָה 15 carcass (19·48) 615

טְרֵפָה	animal torn (3·9) 383	
אֶזְרָח	native (7·17) 280	

Chapter 18

שְׁאֵר 6 flesh relation, kinsman (7·17) 984

מוֹלֶדֶת 9 offspring (3·22) 409

מוֹלֶדֶת 11 begotten, offspring (3·22) 409

שְׁאֵר 12 flesh relation, kinsman (7·17) 984

שְׁאֵר 13 flesh relation, kinsman (7·17) 984

דּוֹדָה 14 aunt (2·3) 187

כַּלָּה 15 daughter-in-law (2·34) 483

שְׁאֵר 17 flesh relation, kinsman (7·17) 984

זִמָּה wickedness, device (5·28[?]) 273

צרר 18 to show hostility toward (1·10·10) 865

נִדָּה 19 impurity (13·30) 622

טֻמְאָה uncleanness (18·37) 380

עָמִית 20 associate, fellow (11·12) 765

שְׁכֹבֶת copulation (3·4) 1012

מִשְׁכָּב 22 bed (9·46) 1012

שְׁכֹבֶת 23 copulation (3·4) 1012

רבע to lie down (2·3·4) 918

תֶּבֶל confusion (2·2) 117

הֵקִיא 25 to vomit up, spue out, disgorge (3·7·8) 883

אֶזְרָח 26 native (7·17) 280

אֵל 27 these (1·10) 41

הֵקִיא 28 to vomit up, spue out, disgorge (3·7·8) 883

קִיא to vomit up, spue out, disgorge (1·1·8) 883

Chapter 19

אֱלִיל 4 worthless idols (2·20) 47

מַסֵּכָה molten metal (1·25) 651

מָחֳרָת 6 on the morrow, after (5·32) 564

פִּגּוּל 7 foul thing, refuse (2·4) 803

עַם 8 kinsman (12·34) 769

קצר 9 to reap, harvest (7·24·24) 894

קָצִיר harvest (7·49) 894

לֶקֶט gleaning (2·2) 545

לקט to gather (3·21·36) 544

עוֹלֵל 10 to glean (1·8·17) 760

פֶּרֶט broken off [ones], fallen grapes (1·1) 827

לקט to gather (3·21·36) 544

גנב 11 to steal (1·30·39) 170

כָּחַשׁ to deceive (3·19·22) 471

שׁקר to deal falsely (1·5·6) 1055

עָמִית associate, fellow relation (11·12) 765

עָשַׁק 13 to oppress, wrong (3·36·37) 798

גָּזַל to tear away, rob (2·29·30) 159

פְּעֻלָּה wages (1·14) 821

שָׂכִיר hired laborer (6·18) 969

חֵרֵשׁ 14 deaf (1·9) 361

עִוֵּר blind (2·25) 734

מִכְשׁוֹל stumbling block (1·14) 506

עָוֶל 15 injustice, unrighteousness (2·21) 732

דַּל low, poor (2·48) 195

הדר to honor (2·4·6) 213

עָמִית associate, fellow, relation (11·12) 765

רָכִיל 16 slanderer (1·6) 940

עַם kinsman (12·34) 769

עָמִית 17 associate, fellow, relation (11·12) 765

חֵטְא punishment for sin (4·33) 307

נקם 18 to take vengeance (2·13·34) 667

נטר to maintain (1·5·5[?]) 643

הִרְבִּיעַ 19 to cause to lie down (1·1·4) 918

כִּלְאַיִם two kinds (3·4) 476

שַׁעַטְנֵז mixed stuff (1·2) 1043

שִׁכְבָה 20 act of lying, sexual intercourse (6·9) 1012

נחרף to remain in harvest time (1·1·2[?]) 358

חֻפְשָׁה freedom (1·1) 344

בְּקֹרֶת punishment [after examination] (1·1) 134

אָשָׁם 21 trespass offering (27·46) 79

אָשָׁם 22 trespass offering (27·46) 79

נִסְלַח to be forgiven (10·13·46) 699

מַאֲכָל 23 food (1·30) 38

ערל to regard as uncircumcised (1·1·2) 790

עָרְלָה foreskin (2·16) 790

עָרֵל uncircumcised (2·35) 790

הִלּוּל 24 rejoicing praise (1·2) 239

תְּבוּאָה 25 product yield (11·43) 100

נִחֵשׁ 26 to practice divination (1·9·9) 638

עוֹנֵן to practice sooth-saying, divine (1·10·11) 778

הִקִּיף 27 to round off (1·16·17) 668

זָקָן beard (5·18) 278

שֶׂרֶט 28 incision (2·2) 976

קַעֲקַע incision, imprintment, tatoo (1·1) 891

זִמָּה 29 wickedness (5·28[?]) 273

אוֹב 31 necromancer (3·16) 15

יִדְּעֹנִי familiar spirit (3·11) 396

שֵׂיבָה 32 gray hair (1·20) 966

הדר to honor (2·4·6) 213

הוֹנָה 33 to oppress (3·14·18) 413

אֶזְרָח 34 native (7·17) 280

עָוֶל 35 injustice, unrighteousness (2·21) 732

מִשְׁקָל weight (2·48) 1054

מְשׂוּרָה measure (1·4) 601

מֹאזֵן 36 scales (1·15) 24

אֵיפָה ephah, quantity of wheat or barley (3·38) 35

הִין hin, a liquid measure (2·22) 228

Chapter 20

רגם 2 to kill by stoning, to stone (5·15·15) 920

הֶעְלִים 4 to conceal, hide (1·11·29) 761

אוֹב 6 necromancer (3·16) 15

יִדְּעֹנִי familiar spirit (3·11) 396

נאף 10 to commit adultery (3·16·30) 610

כַּלָּה 12 daughter-in-law (2·34) 483

תֶּבֶל confusion (2·2) 117

מִשְׁכָּב 13 bed (9·46) 1012

זִמָּה 14 wickedness (5·28[?]) 273

שִׁכְבַת 15 copulation (3·4) 1012

רבע 16 to lie down [for copulation] (2·3·4) 918

חֶסֶד 17 shame, reproach (1·2) 340

דָּוֶה 18 menstruous, unwell (2·5) 188

מָקוֹר source (3·18) 881

הֶעֱרָה to make naked (2·3·14) 788

שְׁאֵר 19 flesh relation, kinsman (7·17) 984

הֶעֱרָה to make naked (2·3·14) 788

דּוֹדָה 20 aunt (2·3) 187

עֲרִירִי stripped, i.e., childless (2·4) 792

נִדָּה 21 impurity (13·30) 622

עֲרִירִי stripped, i.e., childless (2·4) 792

הֵקִיא 22 to vomit up, spue out, disgorge (3·7·8) 883

קוּץ 23 to abhor (1·8·8) 880

זָב 24 to flow, issue (5·29·29[?]) 264

חָלָב milk (1·44) 316

הִבְדִּיל to make a distinction (between) (8·32·42) 95

הִבְדִּיל 25 to make a distinction (between) (8·32·42) 95

שִׁקֵּץ to make detestable (4·6·6) 1055

רמש to creep, move about (3·16·16) 942

הִבְדִּיל 26 to make a distinction (between) (8·32·42) 95

אוֹב 27 necromancer (3·16) 15

יִדְּעֹנִי familiar spirit (3·11) 396

רגם to kill by stoning, to stone (5·15· 920

Chapter 21

שְׁאֵר 2 flesh relation, kinsman (7·17) 984

בְּתוּלָה 3 virgin (2·50) 143

עַם 4 kinsman (12·34) 769

קרח 5 to make bald (1·2·5) 901

קָרְחָה baldness, bald spot |made in mourning| (1·11) 901

זָקָן beard (5·18) 278

גִּלַּח to shave off (5·18·23) 164

שׂרט to make incision (1·2·3) 976

שֶׂרֶט incision (2·2) 976

זוֹנָה 7 harlot (2·33|?|) 275

גרש to drive out, cast out (3·8·47) 176

מִשְׁחָה 10 ointment (13·21) 603

פָּרַע to let loose, remove restraint (3·13·16) 828

פרם to tear/rend garment (3·3·3) 827

נֵזֶר 12 consecration (2·24) 634

מִשְׁחָה ointment (13·21) 603

בְּתוּלִים 13 virginity, tokens of virginity (1·10) 144

גרש 14 to drive out, cast out (3·8·47) 176

זוֹנָה harlot (2·33|?|) 275

בְּתוּלָה virgin (2·50) 143

עַם kinsman (12·34) 769

עַם 15 kinsman (12·34) 769

מוּם 17 blemish (10·21) 548

מוּם 18 blemish (10·21) 548

עִוֵּר blind (2·25) 734

פִּסֵּחַ lame (1·14) 820

חָרֻם mutilated (1·1) 356

שׂרע to extend (2·2·3) 976

שֶׁבֶר 19 breaking, shattering (4·45) 991

גִּבֵּן 20 crook-backed (1·1) 148

דַּק withered, thin (3·14) 201

תְּבַלֻּל confusion, obscurity (1·1) 117

גָּרָב itch, scab (2·3) 173

יַלֶּפֶת an eruptive disease (2·2) 410

מָרוֹחַ dubious (1·1) 598

אֶשֶׁךְ testicle (1·1) 79

מוּם 21 blemish (10·21) 548

פָּרֹכֶת 23 curtain (7·25) 827

מוּם blemish (10·21) 548

Chapter 22

נזר 2 to hold sacredly aloof (1·4·10) 634

טֻמְאָה 3 uncleanness (18·37) 380

צָרוּעַ 4 leper (4·5) 863

זָב one that has as issue, flow (11·13|?| 264

שְׁכָבָה act of lying, sexual intercourse (6·9) 1072

שֶׁרֶץ 5 swarmers, swarming things (12·15) 1056

טֻמְאָה uncleanness (18·37) 380

נְבֵלָה 8 carcass (19·48) 615

טְרֵפָה animal torn (3·9) 383

חֵטְא 9 punishment for sin (4·33) 307

תּוֹשָׁב 10 sojourner (8·14) 444

שָׂכִיר hired laborer (6·18) 969

קִנְיָן 11 acquisition (1·9) 889

יָלִיד born (1·12) 409

גרש 13 to drive out, cast out (3·8·47) 176

נְעוּרִים youth (1·46) 655

שְׁגָגָה 14 sin of error, inadvertence (6·19) 993

אַשְׁמָה 16 trespass offering (4·19) 80

נֵזֶר 18 crown (2·24) 634

נְדָבָה freewill offering (5·27) 621

כֶּשֶׂב 19 lamb (7·13) 461

מוּם 20 blemish (10·21) 548

פלא 21 to make a special votive offering (1·3·5) 810

נְדָבָה freewill offering (5·27) 621

מוּם blemish (10·21) 548

עַוֶּרֶת 22 blindness (1·1) 734

שָׁבוּ broken (1·1) 991
חָרוּ cut, mutilated (1·4[?]) 358
יַבָּל running (1·1) 385
גָּרָב itch, scab (2·3) 173
יַלֶּפֶ an eruptive disease (2·2) 410
שֶׂה 23 sheep, goat (5·44) 961
שָׂרַע to extend (2·2·3) 976
קלט to be stunted (1·1·1) 886
נְדָבָ freewill offering (5·27) 621
מעך 24 to press (1·2·3) 590
כתר to crush (1·15·17) 510
נתק to pull away (1·3·27) 683
נֵכָר 25 foreignness (1·36) 648
מָשְׁ corruption (1·1) 1008
מוּם blemish (10·21) 548
כֶּשֶׂ lamb (7·13) 461
הָלְאָ 27 onwards (1·13) 229
שֶׂה 28 sheep, goat (5·44) 961
תּוֹדָ 29 thank offering (5·32) 392

Chapter 23

מִקְרָ 2 convocation (11·23) 896
שַׁבָּ 3 sabbath observance (8·11) 992
מוֹשׁ convocation (11·23) 896
מוֹשׁ dwelling place (8·43) 444
מִקְרָ 4 convocation (11·23) 896
פֶּסַ 5 passover [festival of] (1·49) 820
מִקְרָ 7 convocation (11·23) 896
מִקְרָ 8 convocation (11·23) 896
קצר 10 to reap, harvest (7·24·24) 894
קָצִי harvest (7·49) 894
עֹמֶר sheaf (4·8) 771
הֵנִי 11 to wave (11·32·34[?]) 631
עֹמֶר sheaf (4·8) 771
מָחֳרָ on the morrow, after (5·32) 564
עֹמֶר 12 sheaf (4·8) 771
עִשָּׂ 13 tenth part (5·28) 798
בָּלַל to mix (9·42·42[?]) 117

נִיחוֹחַ soothing (17·43) 629
הִין hin, a liquid measure (2·22) 228
קָלִי 14 parched grain (1·6) 885
כַּרְמֶל fruit, garden growth (2·3[?]) 502
מוֹשָׁב dwelling place (8·43) 444
מָחֳרָת 15 on the morrow, after (5·32) 564
עֹמֶר sheaf (4·8) 771
תְּנוּפָה waving, wave offering (14·30) 632
מָחֳרָת 16 on the morrow, after (5·32) 564
מוֹשָׁב 17 dwelling place (8·43) 444
תְּנוּפָה waving, wave offering (14·30) 632
חָמֵץ that which is leavened (4·11) 329
נאפה 17 to be baked (3·3·12) 66
בִּכּוּרִים firstfruits (4·17) 114
נִיחוֹחַ 18 soothing (17·43) 629
הֵנִיף 20 to wave (11·32·34[?]) 631
בִּכּוּרִים firstfruits (4·17) 114
תְּנוּפָה waving, wave offering (14·30) 632
בְּעֶצֶם 21 selfsame (4·17) 782
מִקְרָא convocation (11·22) 896
מוֹשָׁב dwelling place (8·43) 444
קצר 22 to reap, harvest (7·24·24) 894
קָצִיר harvest (7·49) 894
לֶקֶט gleaning (2·2) 545
לקט to gather (3·21·36) 544
שַׁבָּתוֹן 24 sabbath observance (8·11) 992
זִכָּרוֹן memorial, reminder (1·24) 272
תְּרוּעָה blast [for march] (2·36) 929
מִקְרָא convocation (11·22) 896
מִקְרָא 27 convocation (11·22) 896
עָשׂוֹר tenth day [of month] (3·15) 797
כִּפֻּרִים atonement (3·8) 498
בְּעֶצֶם 28 selfsame (4·17) 782
כִּפֻּרִים atonement (3·8) 498
בְּעֶצֶם 29 selfsame (4·17) 782
עַם kinsman (12·34) 769
בְּעֶצֶם 30 selfsame (4·17) 782
מוֹשָׁב 31 dwelling place (8·43) 444

שַׁבָּתוֹן 32 sabbath observance (8·11) 992

סֻכָּה 34 booth (4·31) 697

מִקְרָא 35 convocation (11·23) 896

מִקְרָא 36 convocation (11·23) 896

עֲצָרָה assembly (1·11) 783

מִקְרָא 37 convocation (11·23) 896

מִלְּבַד 38 besides (5·33) 94

נְדָבָה freewill offering (5·27) 621

תְּבוּאָה 39 product, yield (11·43) 100

חָגַג to keep a pilgrim feast (3·16·16) 290

שַׁבָּתוֹן sabbath observance (8·11) 992

הָדָר 40 ornament, honor (1·30) 214

כַּפָּה branch (1·4) 497

תָּמָר palm branches (1·12) 1071

עָנָף branches, boughs (1·7) 778

עָבוֹת leafy (1·4) 721

עֲרָבָה poplar (1·5) 788

חָגַג 41 to keep a pilgrim feast (3·16·16) 290

סֻכָּה 42 booth (4·31) 697

אֶזְרָח native (7·17) 280

סֻכָּה 43 booth (4·31) 697

Chapter 24

זַיִת 2 olives, olive tree (1·38) 268

זַךְ pure, unmixed (2·11) 269

כָּתִית beaten (1·5) 510

מָאוֹר light (1·19) 22

נֵר lamp (2·45) 632

פָּרֹכֶת 3 curtain (7·25) 827

מְנֹרָה 4 lampstand (1·39) 633

נֵר lamp (2·45) 632

אָפָה 5 to bake (2·9·12) 66

חַלָּה a kind of cake (8·14) 319

מַעֲרֶכֶת 6 row (2·9) 790

מַעֲרֶכֶת 7 row (2·9) 790

לְבֹנָה frankincense (7·21) 526

זַךְ pure, unmixed (2·11) 269

אַזְכָּרָה memorial offering (6·7) 272

נצה 10 to struggle with each other (1·5·8) 663

נקב 11 to pierce (3·3·19) 666

מִשְׁמָר 12 prison (1·20) 1038

פרש to declare distinctly (1·1·5) 831

סָמַךְ 14 to lay (14·41·48) 701

רגם to kill by stoning, to stone (5·15·1) 920

חֵטְא 15 punishment for sin (4·33) 307

נקב 16 to pierce (3·13·19) 666

רגם to kill by stoning, to stone (5·15·1) 920

אֶזְרָח native (7·17) 280

מוּם 19 blemish (10·21) 548

עָמִית associate, fellow, relation (11·12) 7

שֶׁבֶר 20 breaking, shattering (5·45) 991

מוּם blemish (10·21) 548

אֶזְרָח 22 native (7·17) 280

רגם 23 to kill by stoning, to stone (5·15·1) 920

Chapter 25

זמר 3 to trim, prune (2·3·3) 274

תְּבוּאָה product, yield (11·43) 100

שַׁבָּתוֹן 4 sabbath observance (8·11) 992

זמר to trim, prune (2·3·3) 274

סָפִיחַ 5 growth from spilled kernels (2·4) 7(

קצר to reap, harvest (7·24·24) 894

קָצִיר harvest (7·49) 894

עֵנָב grapes (1·19) 772

נָזִיר untrimmed vine (2·15) 634

בצר to cut off (2·7·7) 130

שַׁבָּתוֹן sabbath observance (8·11) 992

אָכְלָה 6 food, eating (2·18) 38

שָׂכִיר hired laborer (6·18) 969

תּוֹשָׁב sojourner (8·14) 444

תְּבוּאָה 7 product, yield (11·43) 100

תְּרוּעָה 9 blast [for march] (2·36) 929

כִּפֶּר	atonement (3·8) 498
דְּרוֹר	10 liberty, free run (1·7) 204
יוֹבֵל	ram's horn (20·27) 385
יוֹבֵל	11 ram's horn (20·27) 385
קָצַר	to reap, harvest (7·24·24) 894
סָפִיַח	growth from spilled kernels (2·4) 705
בָּצַר	to cut off (2·7·7) 130
נָזִיר	untrimmed vine (2·15) 634
יוֹבֵל	12 ram's horn (20·27) 385
תְּבוּאָ	product, yield (11·43) 100
יוֹבֵל	13 ram's horn (20·27) 385
מִמְכָּ	14 sale (7·10) 569
עָמִית	associate, fellow, relation (11·12) 765
הוֹנָה	to oppress (3·14·18) 413
יוֹבֵל	15 ram's horn (20·27) 385
עָמִית	associate, fellow, relation (11·12) 765
תְּבוּאָ	product, yield (11·43) 100
מִקְנָה	16 purchase (4·15) 889
מָעַט	to become small (1·8·22) 589
הִמְעִי	to make small (2·13·22) 589
תְּבוּאָ	product, yield (11·43) 100
הוֹנָה	17 to oppress (3·14·18) 413
עָמִית	associate, fellow, relation (11·12) 765
בֶּטַח	18 securely (3·43) 105
שֹׂבַע	19 satiety, fill (2·8) 959
בֶּטַח	securely (3·43) 105
תְּבוּאָ	20 product, yield (11·43) 100
תְּבוּאָ	21 product, yield (11·43) 100
תְּבוּאָ	22 product, yield (11·43) 100
יָשָׁן	old (4·8) 445
צְמִתָ	23 completion, finality (2·2) 856
תּוֹשָׁב	sojourner (8·14) 444
גְּאֻלָּה	24 redemption (9·14) 145
מָךְ	25 to grow poor (5·5·5) 557
גָּאַל	kinsman, redeemer (2·44[?]) 145
מִמְכָּ	sale (7·10) 569
גָּאַל	26 kinsman, redeemer (2·44[?]) 145
הִשִּׂיג	to reach (12·48·48) 673

כְּדִי	according to the sufficiency of, i.e. as much as it demands (1·5) 191
גְּאֻלָּה	right of redemption, redemption (9·14) 145
מִמְכָּר	27 sale (7·10) 569
עָדַף	to remain over, be in excess (1·8·9) 727
דַּי	28 sufficiency, enough (3·12) 191
מִמְכָּר	sale (7·10) 569
קָנֶה	owner [as purchaser] (2·7) 888
יוֹבֵל	ram's horn (20·27) 385
מוֹשָׁב	29 dwelling place (8·43) 444
גְּאֻלָּה	right of redemption, redemption (9·14) 145
מִמְכָּר	sale (7·10) 569
צְמִתֻת	30 completion, finality (2·2) 856
יוֹבֵל	ram's horn (20·27) 385
גְּאֻלָּה	31 right of redemption, redemption (9·14) 145
יוֹבֵל	ram's horn (20·27) 385
גְּאֻלָּה	32 right of redemption, redemption (9·14) 145
מִמְכָּר	33 sale (7·10) 569
יוֹבֵל	ram's horn (20·27) 385
מָךְ	35 to grow poor (5·5·5) 557
מוֹט	to totter (1·15·39) 556
תּוֹשָׁב	sojourner (8·14) 444
נֶשֶׁךְ	36 interest (2·12) 675
תַּרְבִּית	increment, interest (1·6) 916
נֶשֶׁךְ	37 interest (2·12) 675
מַרְבִּית	increment (1·5) 916
אֹכֶל	food (2·44) 38
מָךְ	39 to grow poor (5·5·5) 557
שָׂכִיר	40 hired laborer (6·18) 969
תּוֹשָׁב	sojourner (8·14) 444
יוֹבֵל	ram's horn (20·27) 385
מִמְכֶּרֶת	42 sale (1·1) 569
רדה	43 to have dominion, rule,

dominate (4·22·23) 921

פֶּרֶךְ harshness, severity (3·6) 827

תּוֹשָׁב 45 sojourner (8·14) 444

רדה 46 to have dominion, rule, dominate (4·22·23) 921

פֶּרֶךְ harshness, severity (3·6) 827

הִשִּׂיג 47 to reach (12·48·48) 673

תּוֹשָׁב sojourner (8·14) 444

מָךְ to grow poor (5·5·5) 557

עֵקֶר offshoot, member (1·1) 785

גְּאֻלָּה 48 right of redemption, redemption (9·14) 145

שְׁאֵר 49 flesh relation, kinsman (7·17) 984

הִשִּׂיג to reach (12·48·48) 673

קָנָה 50 owner [as purchaser] (2·7) 888

יוֹבֵל ram's horn (20·27) 385

מִמְכָּר sale (7·10) 569

שָׂכִיר hired laborer (6·18) 969

גְּאֻלָּה 51 price of redemption, redemption (9·14) 145

מִקְנָה purchase (4·15) 889

יוֹבֵל 52 ram's horn (20·27) 385

כְּפִי according to (1·16) 804

גְּאֻלָּה price of redemption, redemption (9·14) 145

שָׂכִיר 53 hired laborer (6·18) 969

רדה to have dominion, rule, dominate (4·22·23) 921

פֶּרֶךְ harshness, severity (3·6) 827

יוֹבֵל 54 ram's horn (20·27) 385

Chapter 26

אֱלִיל 1 worthless idol (2·20) 47

פֶּסֶל idol, image (1·31) 820

מַצֵּבָה pillar (1·35) 663

מַשְׂכִּית carved figure (1·6) 967

גֶּשֶׁם 4 rain, shower (1·36) 177

יְבוּל produce (2·13) 385

הִשִּׂיג 5 to reach (12·48·48) 673

דַּיִשׁ threshing (1·1) 190

בָּצִיר vintage (2·7) 131

שֹׂבַע satiety, fill (2·8) 959

בֶּטַח securely (3·43) 105

הֶחֱרִיד 6 drive in terror, terrify (1·16·39) 353

רְבָבָה 8 hundred (1·16) 914

הִפְרָה 9 to make fruitful (1·27·29) 826

יָשָׁן 10 old (4·8) 445

נושן to be old (2·3·3[?]) 445

גָּעַל 11 to abhor, loathe (5·8·10) 171

מוֹטָה 13 bar (1·10) 557

עֹל yoke (1·40) 760

קוֹמְמִיּוּת uprightness, upright (1·1) 879

גָּעַל 15 to abhor, loathe (5·8·10) 171

הֵפֵר to break, frustrate (2·41·44) 830

בֶּהָלָה 16 dismay, sudden terror (1·4) 96

שַׁחֶפֶת consumption (1·2) 1006

קַדַּחַת fever (1·2) 869

הֵדִיב to cause to pine away (1·1·1) 187

רִיק emptiness, vanity (2·12) 938

נִגַּף 17 to be smitten (1·23·48) 619

רדה to have dominion, rule, dominate (4·22·23) 921

שֹׂנֵא enemy (1·41) 971

יִסֵּר 18 to chastise (2·26·37) 415

גָּאוֹן 19 exaltation (1·49) 144

רִיק 20 emptiness, vanity (2·12) 938

יְבוּל produce (2·13) 385

קְרִי 21 opposition, contrariness, (7·7) 899

מַכָּה plague (1·48) 646

שכל 22 to make childless (1·18·24) 1013

המעיט to make small (2·13·22) 589

נוסר 23 to let oneself be chastened (1·5·41) 415

קְרִי opposition, contrariness (7·7) 899

קְרִי 24 opposition, contrariness (7·7) 899

נקם 25 to take vengeance (2·13·34) 667

דֶּבֶר	pestilence, plague (1·46) 184
אָפָה	26 to bake (2·9·12) 66
תַּנּוּר	stove, firepot (4·15) 1072
מִשְׁקָל	weight (2·48) 1054
קֶרִי	27 opposition, contrariness (7·7) 899
קֶרִי	28 opposition, contrariness (7·7) 899
יָסַר	to chastise (2·26·37) 415
חַמָּן	30 sun pillar (1·8) 329
פֶּגֶר	corpse, carcass (2·22) 803
גִּלּוּל	idol (1·48) 165
גָּעַל	to abhor, loathe (5·8·10) 171
חָרְבָּה	31 waste, desolation (2·42) 352
הֵרִיחַ	to smell (1·11·14) 926
נִיחֹחַ	soothing (17·43) 629
זָרָה	32 to scatter, disperse (1·25·38) 279
הֵרִיק	to make empty, empty out (1·17·19) 937
חָרְבָּה	33 waste, desolation (2·42) 352
רָצָה	34 to make acceptable (4·4·5) 953
הִרְצָה	to pay off (1·1·5) 953
מֹרֶךְ	36 weakness (1·1) 940
עָלֶה	leaf, leafage (1·17) 750
נִדַּף	to be driven about (1·6·9) 623
מָנוּס	flight, fleeing (1·2) 631
כְּמִפְּנֵי	37 as from, as from before (1·1) 816
תְּקוּמָה	standing, power to stand (1·1) 879
נָמַק	39 to pine away (2·9·10) 596
מַעַל	40 unfaithful act (3·29) 591
מָעַל	to act unfaithfully (3·35·35) 591
קֶרִי	opposition, contrariness (7·7) 899
קֶרִי	41 opposition, contrariness (7·7) 899
נִכְנַע	to humble oneself (1·25·36) 488
עָרֵל	uncircumcised (2·35) 790
רָצָה	to make acceptable (4·4·5) 953
רָצָה	43 to make acceptable (4·4·5) 953
בְּיַעַן	by the cause (1·3) 774
גָּעַל	to abhor, loathe (5·8·10) 171
גָּעַל	44 to abhor, to loathe (5·8·10) 171

הֵפֵר	to break, to frustrate (2·41·44) 830

Chapter 27

הִפְלִיא	2 to be a hard or difficult thing (1·2·5[?]) 810
עֵרֶךְ	estimate, valuation (24·33) 789
עֵרֶךְ	3 estimate, valuation (24·33) 789
נְקֵבָה	4 female (12·22) 666
עֵרֶךְ	estimate, valuation (24·33) 789
עֵרֶךְ	5 estimate, valuation (24·33) 789
נְקֵבָה	female (12·22) 666
עֵרֶךְ	6 estimate, valuation (24·33) 789
נְקֵבָה	female (12·22) 666
עֵרֶךְ	7 estimate, valuation (24·33) 789
נְקֵבָה	female (12·22) 666
מָךְ	8 to grow poor (5·5·5) 557
עֵרֶךְ	estimate, valuation (24·33) 789
הִשִּׂיג	to reach (12·48·48) 673
נָדַר	to make a vow (1·30·30) 623
הֶחֱלִיף	10 to change (1·10·26) 322
הֵמִיר	to exchange (4·12·13) 558
תְּמוּרָה	exchange, recompense (2·6) 558
עֵרֶךְ	12 estimate, valuation (24·33) 789
עֵרֶךְ	13 estimate, valuation (24·33) 789
עֵרֶךְ	15 estimate, valuation (24·33) 789
עֵרֶךְ	16 estimate, valuation (24·33) 789
חֹמֶר	a dry measure (1·12) 330
שְׂעֹרָה	barley (1·34) 972
יוֹבֵל	17 ram's horn (20·27) 385
עֵרֶךְ	estimate, valuation (24·33) 789
יוֹבֵל	18 ram's horn (20·27) 385
נִגְרַע	to be withdrawn (1·7·22) 175
עֵרֶךְ	estimate, valuation (24·33) 789
עֵרֶךְ	19 estimation, valuation (24·33) 789
יוֹבֵל	21 ram's horn (20·27) 385
חֵרֶם	devoted [to sanctuary] (4·29) 356
מִכְסָה	23 valuation (1·2) 493
עֵרֶךְ	estimation, valuation (24·33) 789

יוֹבֵל	ram's horn (20·27) 385	הֶחֱרִים	to devote for sacred use (1·46·49) 355
יוֹבֵל	24 ram's horn (20·27) 385		
לַאֲשֶׁר	to him, one who (3·38) 82 para.	חֵרֶם	29 devoted [to sanctuary] (4·29) 356
עֵרֶךְ	25 estimate, valuation (24·33) 789	הַחֲרַם	to be devoted (1·3·49) 355
גֵּרָה	a weight, one-twentieth of a shekel (1·5) 176	מַעֲשֵׂר	30 tithe (3·31) 798
		מַעֲשֵׂר	31 tithe (3·31) 798
בְּכֹר	26 to be made a firstborn (1·1·4) 114	מַעֲשֵׂר	32 tithe (3·31) 798
שֶׂה	sheep, goat (5·44) 961	בִּקֵּר	33 to seek to distinguish (2·7·7) 133
עֵרֶךְ	estimate, valuation (24·33) 789	הֵמִיר	to exchange (4·12·13) 558
חֵרֶם	28 devoted [to sanctuary] (4·29) 356	תְּמוּרָה	exchange, recompense (2·6) 558

NUMBERS

Chapter 1

גֻּלְגֹּ֫לֶת 2 each man, head (5·12) 166

אֶ֫לֶף 16 thousand (4·12[?]) 48

נקב 17 to be designated (1·6·19) 666

הקהּ 18 to summon an assembly (6·20·39) 874

גֻּלְגֹּ֫לֶת each man, head (5·12) 166

תּוֹלֵד 20 generations (13·39) 410

גֻּלְגֹּ֫לֶת each man, head (5·12) 166

תּוֹלֵד 22 generations (13·39) 410

גֻּלְגֹּ֫לֶת each man, head (5·12) 166

תּוֹלֵד 24 generations (13·39) 410

תּוֹלֵד 26 generations (13·39) 410

תּוֹלֵד 28 generations (13·39) 410

תּוֹלֵד 30 generations (13·39) 410

תּוֹלֵד 32 generations (13·39) 410

תּוֹלֵד 34 generations (13·39) 410

תּוֹלֵד 36 generations (13·39) 410

תּוֹלֵד 38 generations (13·39) 410

תּוֹלֵד 40 generations (13·39) 410

תּוֹלֵד 42 generations (13·39) 410

קָרֵב 51 approaching (5·11) 898

דֶּגֶל 52 standard, banner (13·14) 186

קֶ֫צֶף 53 wrath (3·29) 893

Chapter 2

דֶּגֶל 2 standard, banner (13·14) 186

מִנֶּגֶד some way off from, at a distance (1·26) 617

קֶ֫דֶם 3 eastward (8·26) 870

דֶּגֶל standard, banner (13·14) 186

דֶּגֶל 10 standard, banner (13·14) 186

תֵּימָן toward the south (3·24) 412

דֶּגֶל 17 standard, banner (13·14) 186

דֶּגֶל 18 standard, banner (13·14) 186

דֶּגֶל 25 standard, banner (13·14) 186

דֶּגֶל 31 standard, banner (13·14) 186

דֶּגֶל 34 standard, banner (13·14) 186

Chapter 3

תּוֹלֵדוֹת 1 generations (13·39) 410

כהן 3 to minister as a priest (2·23·23) 464

כהן 4 to minister as a priest (2·23·23) 464

כְּהֻנָּה 10 priesthood (6·13) 464

קָרֵב approaching (5·11) 898

פֶּטֶר 12 "first opens" i.e., firstborn (2·11) 809

רֶ֫חֶם womb (4·33) 933

מִכְסֶה 25 covering (7·16) 492

מָסָךְ screen (6·25) 697

קֶ֫לַע 26 curtain, hanging (2·16) 887

מָסָךְ screen (6·25) 697

מֵיתָר cord (4·9) 452

יָרֵךְ 29 side (6·34) 437

תֵּימָן toward the south (3·24) 412

מְנֹרָה 31 lampstand (6·39) 633

מָסָךְ screen (6·25) 697

פְּקֻדָּה 32 overseer (5·32) 824

יָרֵךְ 35 side (6·34) 437

פְּקֻדָּה 36 oversight, charge (5·32) 824

בְּרִיחַ bar (2·41) 138

יָתֵד 37 peg (2·24) 450

מֵיתָר cord (4·9) 452

קֶ֫דֶם 38 eastward (8·26) 870

קָרֵב approaching (5·11) 898

פְּדוּיִם 46 ransom (5·5) 804

עדף to remain over, be in excess (3·8·9) 727

גֻּלְגֹּ֫לֶת 47 each man, head (5·12) 166

גֵּרָה a weight, one-twentieth of a shekel (2·5) 176

פְּדוּיִם 48 ransom (5·5) 804

עֹדֵף   to remain over, be in excess (3·8·9) 727

פְּדוּיִם   49 ransom (1·3) 804

עֹדֵף   to remain over, be in excess (3·8·9) 727

פְּדוּיִם   ransom (5·5) 804

פְּדוּיִם   51 ransom (5·5) 804

Chapter 4

פָּרֹכֶת   5 curtain (2·25) 827

מָסָךְ   screen (6·25) 697

כָּלִיל   6 entirely (1·15) 483

תְּכֵלֶת   violet stuff, fabric (6·49) 1067

מִלְמָעְלָה   above (2·24) 751

בַּד   pole, stave (4·41) 94

תְּכֵלֶת   7 violet stuff, fabric (6·49) 1067

קְעָרָה   dish, platter (15·17) 891

מְנַקִּיָּה   sacrificial bowl (1·4) 667

קַשְׂוָה   jug, jar (1·4) 903

תּוֹלַעַה   8 coccus ilocus [yielding scarlet color] (2·41) 1069

שָׁנִי   scarlet (2·42) 1040

מִכְסֶה   covering (7·16) 492

תַּחַשׁ   a kind of leather or skin, and perhaps the animal yielding it (7·14) 1065

בַּד   pole, stave (4·41) 94

תְּכֵלֶת   9 violet stuff, fabric (6·49) 1067

מְנֹרָה   lampstand (6·39) 633

מָאוֹר   light (2·19) 22

נֵר   lamp (4·44) 632

מֶלְקָחַיִם   snuffers (1·6) 544

מַחְתָּה   fire pan (11·21) 367

מִכְסֶה   10 covering (7·16) 492

תַּחַשׁ   leather or skin, and perhaps the animal yielding it (7·14) 1065

מוֹט   pole (3·4) 557

תְּכֵלֶת   11 violet stuff, fabric (6·49) 1067

מִכְסֶה   covering (7·16) 492

תַּחַשׁ   leather or skin, and perhaps the animal yielding it (7·14) 1065

בַּד   pole, stave (4·41) 94

שָׁרֵת   12 vessels (1·2) 1058

תְּכֵלֶת   violet stuff, fabric (6·49) 1067

מִכְסֶה   covering (7·16) 492

תַּחַשׁ   leather or skin, and perhaps the animal yielding it (7·14) 1065

מוֹט   pole (3·4) 557

דִּשֵּׁן   13 to clear away the fat ashes (1·5·1) 206

אַרְגָּמָן   purple cloth (1·39) 71

מַחְתָּה   14 censer (11·21) 367

מִזְלָגָה   three-pronged fork (1·5) 272

יָע   shovel (1·9) 418

מִזְרָק   basin (15·32) 284

תַּחַשׁ   leather or skin, and perhaps the animal yielding it (7·14) 1065

בַּד   pole, stave (4·41) 94

פְּקֻדָּה   16 oversight, charge (5·32) 824

מָאוֹר   light (2·19) 22

סַם   spice (1·16) 702

מִשְׁחָה   ointment (1·21) 603

בֶּלַע   20 inf. = a swallowing, i.e., an instant (1·20·41) 118

צבא   23 to serve (4·12·14) 838

מִכְסֶה   25 covering (7·16) 492

תַּחַשׁ   leather or skin, and perhaps the animal yielding it (7·14) 1065

מִלְמָעְלָה   above (2·24) 751

מָסָךְ   screen (6·25) 697

קֶלַע   26 curtain, hanging (2·16) 887

מָסָךְ   screen (6·25) 697

מֵיתָר   cord (4·9) 452

בְּרִיחַ   31 bar (2·41) 138

יָתֵד   32 peg (2·24) 450

מֵיתָר   cord (4·9) 452

Chapter 5

צָרוּעַ	2 leper (1·5) 863	
זָב	one that has had an issue, flux (1·13[?]) 264	
נְקֵבָה	3 female (2·22) 666	
מָעַל	6 to act unfaithfully (3·35·35) 591	
אָשַׁם	to be, become guilty (2·31·33) 79	
אָשָׁם	7 compensation for trespass (4·46) 79	
לַאֲשֶׁר	to him who (1·38) 81	
אָשַׁם	to commit an offence (2·31·33) 79	
גָּאַל	8 kinsman, redeemer (8·44[?]) 145	
אָשָׁם	compensation for trespass (4·46) 79	
מִלְּבַד	besides (15·33) 94	
כִּפֻּרִים	atonement (2·8) 498	
שָׂטָה	12 to turn aside (4·6·6) 966	
מָעַל	to act unfaithfully (3·35·35) 591	
שְׁכָבָה	13 a lying (1·9) 1012	
נעלם	to be concealed (1·1·29) 761	
קִנְאָה	14 jealousy (9·43) 888	
קִנֵּא	to be jealous of (6·30·34) 888	
אֵיפָה	15 ephah, a certain quantity of wheat, barley (2·38) 35	
קֶמַח	flour, meal (1·14) 887	
שְׂעֹרָה	barley (1·34) 972	
לְבֹנָה	frankincense (1·21) 526	
קִנְאָה	jealousy (9·43) 888	
זִכָּרוֹן	memorial (5·24) 272	
חֶרֶשׂ	17 earthenware (1·16) 360	
קַרְקַע	floor (1·8) 903	
פָּרַע	18 to let go, let loose, i.e., remove restraint (1·13·16) 828	
זִכָּרוֹן	memorial (5·24) 272	
קִנְאָה	jealousy (9·43) 888	
מַר	bitterness (6·37) 600	
שָׂטָה	19 to turn aside (4·6·6) 966	
טָמְאָה	uncleanness (2·37) 380	
נָקָה	to be exempt from (3·23·36) 667	

מַר	bitterness (6·37) 600	
שָׂטָה	20 to turn aside (4·6·6) 966	
שְׁכֹבֶת	copulation (1·4) 1012	
מִבַּלְעֲדֵי	apart from, without (1·12) 116	
שְׁבֻעָה	21 curse (5·30) 989	
אָלָה	oath, curse (4·36) 46	
יָרֵךְ	thigh (6·34) 437	
צָבֶה	swelling, swollen (1·1) 839	
מֵעֶה	22 belly (1·31) 588	
הצבה	to swell, swell up (1·1·2) 839	
יָרֵךְ	thigh (6·34) 437	
אָמֵן	verily, truly (2·26) 53	
אָלָה	23 curse (4·36) 46	
מָחָה	to wipe (1·21·33) 562	
מַר	bitterness (6·37) 600	
מַר	24 bitterness (6·37) 600	
קִנְאָה	25 jealousy (9·43) 888	
הֵנִיף	to wave (6·32·34[?]) 631	
קָמַץ	26 to enclose with hand, grasp (1·3·3) 888	
אַזְכָּרָה	memorial offering (1·7) 272	
מָעַל	27 to act unfaithfully (3·35·35) 591	
מַר	bitterness (6·37) 600	
צבה	to swell, swell up (1·1·2) 839	
יָרֵךְ	thigh (6·34) 437	
אָלָה	execration, curse, oath (4·36) 46	
נָקָה	28 to be exempt from (3·23·36) 667	
קִנְאָה	29 jealousy (9·43) 888	
שָׂטָה	to turn aside (4·6·6) 966	
קִנְאָה	30 jealousy (9·43) 888	
קִנֵּא	to be jealous of (6·30·34) 888	
נָקָה	31 to be free from guilt (3·23·36) 667	

Chapter 6

הִפְלִיא	2 to do a hard or difficult thing (1·2·5) 810	
נָדַר	to vow (7·30·30) 623	
נָזִיר	one consecrated, devoted (6·16) 634	

הִזִּיר	to live as a Nazarite (5·6·10[?]) 634	
שֵׁכָר	3 intoxicating drink, strong drink (3·23) 1016	
הִזִּיר	to live as a Nazarite (5·6·10[?]) 634	
חֹמֶץ	vinegar (2·6) 330	
מִשְׁרָה	juice (1·1) 1056	
עֵנָב	grape[s] (4·19) 772	
לַח	moist (1·6) 535	
יָבֵשׁ	dried (2·9) 386	
נֵזֶר	4 consecration (12·24) 634	
חַרְצָן	grape-stones (1·1) 359	
זָג	name of some comparitively insignificant product of the vine, perh. skin of grape (1·1) 260	
נֵזֶר	5 consecration (12·24) 634	
תַּעַר	razor (2·13) 789	
הִזִּיר	to live as a Nazarite (5·6·10[?]) 634	
פֶּרַע	long hair [of head], locks (1·2) 828	
שֵׂעָר	hair (2·28) 972	
הִזִּיר	6 to live as a Nazarite (5·6·10[?]) 634	
נֵזֶר	7 consecration (12·24) 634	
נֵזֶר	8 consecration (12·24) 634	
פֶּתַע	9 suddenness (2·7) 837	
פִּתְאֹם	suddenly (2·25) 837	
נֵזֶר	consecration (12·24) 634	
גִּלַּח	to shave (3·18·23) 164	
תּוֹר	10 turtle dove (1·14) 1076	
יוֹנָה	dove (1·35) 401	
מֵאֲשֶׁר	11 from [or than] that which (1·17) 84	
הִזִּיר	12 to live as a Nazarite (5·6·10[?]) 634	
נֵזֶר	consecration (12·24) 634	
אָשָׁם	trespass offering (4·46) 79	
נָזִיר	13 one consecrated, devoted (6·16) 634	
נֵזֶר	consecration (12·24) 634	
סַל	15 basket (3·15) 700	
חַלָּה	a kind of cake (3·14) 319	
בָּלַל	to mix (26·42·42[?]) 117	
רָקִיק	thin cake, wafer (2·8) 956	

סַל	17 basket (3·15) 700	
גִּלַּח	18 to shave (3·18·23) 164	
נָזִיר	one consecrated, devoted (6·16) 634	
נֵזֶר	consecration (12·24) 634	
שֵׂעָר	hair (2·28) 972	
בָּשַׁל	19 cooked, boiled (1·2) 143	
חַלָּה	a kind of cake (3·14) 319	
סַל	basket (3·15) 700	
רָקִיק	thin cake, wafer (2·8) 956	
נָזִיר	one consecrated, devoted (6·16) 634	
הִתְגַּלָּח	to shave oneself (1·2·23) 164	
נֵזֶר	hair (12·24) 634	
הֵנִיף	20 to wave (6·32·34[?]) 631	
תְּנוּפָה	wave offering, wave breast (8·30) 632	
חָזֶה	breast (2·13) 303	
שׁוֹק	leg (2·19) 1003	
נָזִיר	one consecrated, devoted (6·16) 634	
נָזִיר	21 one consecrated, devoted (6·16) 634	
נָדַר	to vow (7·30·30) 623	
נֵזֶר	consecration (12·24) 634	
מִלְּבַד	besides (15·33) 94	
הִשִּׂיג	to reach, overtake (1·49) 673	
כְּפִי	according to (5·16) 804	
הֵאִיר	25 to make shine (2·34·40) 21	

Chapter 7

פְּקוּדִים	2 musterings (2·3) 823	
עֲגָלָה	3 cart (5·25) 722	
צָב	litter (1·2) 839	
כְּפִי	5 according to (5·16) 804	
עֲגָלָה	6 cart (5·25) 722	
עֲגָלָה	7 cart (5·25) 722	
כְּפִי	according to (5·16) 804	
עֲגָלָה	8 cart (5·25) 722	
כְּפִי	according to (5·16) 804	
חֲנֻכָּה	10 dedication, consecration (4·8) 335	
חֲנֻכָּה	11 dedication, consecration (4·8) 335	

קְעָרָה	13 dish, platter (15·17) 891	
מִשְׁקָל	weight (12·49) 1054	
מִזְרָק	basin (15·32) 284	
בָּלַל	to mix (26·42·42[?]) 117	
עַתּוּד	17 he-goat (13·29) 800	
קְעָרָה	19 dish, platter (15·17) 891	
מִשְׁקָל	weight (12·49) 1054	
מִזְרָק	basin (15·32) 284	
בָּלַל	to mix (26·42·42[?]) 117	
עַתּוּד	23 he-goat (13·29) 800	
קְעָרָה	25 dish, platter (15·17) 891	
מִשְׁקָל	weight (12·49) 1054	
מִזְרָק	basin (15·32) 284	
בָּלַל	to mix (26·42·42[?]) 117	
עַתּוּד	29 he-goat (13·29) 800	
קְעָרָה	31 dish, platter (15·17) 891	
מִשְׁקָל	weight (12·49) 1054	
מִזְרָק	basin (15·32) 284	
בָּלַל	to mix (26·42·42[?]) 117	
עַתּוּד	35 he-goat (13·29) 800	
קְעָרָה	37 dish, platter (15·17) 891	
מִשְׁקָל	weight (12·49) 1054	
מִזְרָק	basin (15·32) 284	
בָּלַל	to mix (26·42·42[?]) 117	
עַתּוּד	41 he-goat (13·29) 800	
קְעָרָה	43 dish, platter (15·17) 891	
מִשְׁקָל	weight (12·49) 1054	
מִזְרָק	basin (15·32) 284	
בָּלַל	to mix (26·42·42[?]) 117	
עַתּוּד	47 he-goat (13·29) 800	
קְעָרָה	49 dish, platter (15·17) 891	
מִשְׁקָל	weight (12·49) 1054	
מִזְרָק	basin (15·32) 284	
בָּלַל	to mix (26·42·42[?]) 117	
עַתּוּד	53 he-goat (13·29) 800	
קְעָרָה	55 dish, platter (15·17) 891	
מִשְׁקָל	weight (12·49) 1054	
מִזְרָק	basin (15·32) 284	
בָּלַל	to mix (26·42·42[?]) 117	
עַתּוּד	59 he-goat (13·29) 800	
קְעָרָה	61 dish, platter (15·17) 891	
מִשְׁקָל	weight (12·49) 1054	
מִזְרָק	basin (15·32) 284	
בָּלַל	to mix (26·42·42[?]) 117	
עַתּוּד	65 he-goat (13·29) 800	
קְעָרָה	67 dish, platter (15·17) 891	
מִשְׁקָל	weight (12·49) 1054	
מִזְרָק	basin (15·32) 284	
בָּלַל	to mix (26·42·42[?]) 117	
עַתּוּד	71 he-goat (13·29) 800	
קְעָרָה	73 dish, platter (15·17) 891	
מִשְׁקָל	weight (12·49) 1054	
מִזְרָק	basin (15·32) 284	
בָּלַל	to mix (26·42·42[?]) 117	
עַתּוּד	77 he-goat (13·29) 800	
קְעָרָה	79 dish, platter (15·17) 891	
מִשְׁקָל	weight (12·49) 1054	
מִזְרָק	basin (15·32) 284	
בָּלַל	to mix (26·42·42[?]) 117	
עַתּוּד	83 he-goat (13·29) 800	
חֲנֻכָּה	84 dedication, consecration (4·8) 335	
קְעָרָה	dish, platter (15·17) 891	
מִזְרָק	basin (15·32) 284	
קְעָרָה	85 dish, platter (15·17) 891	
מִזְרָק	basin (15·32) 284	
עַתּוּד	88 he-goat (13·29) 800	
חֲנֻכָּה	dedication, consecration (4·8) 335	
כַּפֹּרֶת	89 propitiatory (1·27) 498	
מִבֵּין	from between (2·21) 107	

Chapter 8

נֵר	2 lamp (4·44) 632	
מוּל	the forefront of (2·25) 557	
מְנוֹרָה	lampstand (6·39) 633	

הֵאִיר to light (2·34·40) 21

מוּל 3 the forefront of (2·25) 557

מְנוֹרָה lampstand (6·39) 633

נֵר lamp (4·44) 632

מְנוֹרָה 4 lampstand (6·39) 633

מִקְשָׁה perh. hammered work (3·9) 904

יָרֵךְ base (6·34) 437

פֶּרַח bud, sprout (2·17) 827

הִזָּה 7 to sprinkle (5·20·24) 633

תַּעַר razor (2·13) 789

בָּלַל 8 to mix (26·42·42[?]) 117

הִקְהִיל 9 to summon an assembly (6·20·39) 874

סָמַךְ 10 to lay (4·41·48) 701

הֵנִיף 11 to wave (6·32·34[?]) 631

תְּנוּפָה waving, wave offering (8·30) 632

סָמַךְ 12 to lay (4·41·48) 701

הֵנִיף 13 to wave (6·32·34[?]) 631

תְּנוּפָה waving, wave offering (8·30) 632

הִבְדִּיל 14 to separate (2·32·42) 95

הֵנִיף 15 to wave (6·32·34[?]) 631

תְּנוּפָה waving, wave offering (8·30) 632

פִּטְרָה 16 that which separates, first opens, i.e., firstborn (1·1) 809

רֶחֶם womb (4·33) 933

נֶגֶף 19 plague (3·7) 620

הֵנִיף 21 to wave (6·32·34[?]) 631

תְּנוּפָה waving, wave offering (8·30) 632

צבא 24 to serve (4·12·14) 838

כָּכָה 26 thus (5·34) 462

Chapter 9

פֶּסַח 2 festival of the passover (11·49) 820

פֶּסַח 4 festival of the passover (11·49) 820

פֶּסַח 5 festival of the passover (11·49) 820

פֶּסַח 6 festival of the passover (11·49) 820

נִגְרַע 7 to be restrained (5·7·22) 175

פֶּסַח 10 festival of the passover (11·49) 820

מָרֹר 11 bitter herb (1·5) 601

פֶּסַח 12 festival of the passover (11·49) 820

פֶּסַח 13 festival of the passover (11·49) 820

עַם kinsman (4·34) 769

חֵטְא punishment for sin (4·33) 307

פֶּסַח 14 festival of the passover (11·49) 820

אֶזְרָח native (4·17) 280

הֶאֱרִיךְ 19 to tarry long, be long (2·31·34) 73

הֶאֱרִיךְ 22 to tarry long, be long (2·31·34) 73

Chapter 10

חֲצֹצְרָה 2 clarion (5·29) 348

מִקְשָׁה perh. hammered work (3·9) 904

מִקְרָא convocation (7·22) 896

מַסַּע breaking camp (7·12) 652

נוֹעַד 3 to assemble by appointment (6·18·28) 416

אֶלֶף 4 thousand (4·12[?]) 48

תְּרוּעָה 5 blast [for march] (6·36) 929

קֵדֶם eastward (8·26) 870

תְּרוּעָה 6 blast [for march] (6·36) 929

תֵּימָן toward the south (3·24) 412

מַסַּע setting out (7·12) 652

הִקְהִיל 7 to summon an assembly (6·20·39) 874

הֵרִיעַ sound signal for war, march (2·40·44) 929

חֲצֹצְרָה 8 clarion (5·29) 348

צרר 9 to show hostility towards, vex (4·10·10) 865

הֵרִיעַ to sound signal for war, march (2·40·44) 929

חֲצֹצְרָה clarion (5·29) 348

חֲצֹצְרָה 10 clarion (5·29) 348

זִכָּרוֹן memorial (5·24) 272

מַסַּע 12 journey (7·12) 652

דֶּגֶל 14 standard, banner (13·14) 186

דֶּגֶל 18 standard, banner (13·14) 186

דֶּגֶל 22 standard, banner (13·14) 186

דֶּגֶל 25 standard, banner (13·14) 186

מַסַּע 28 setting out (7·12) 652

חֹתֵן 29 wife's father (1·21) 368

מוֹלֶדֶת 30 kindred (1·22) 409

תוּר 33 to seek out, select (14·19·22) 1064

מְנוּחָה resting-place (1·21) 629

רְבָבָה 36 multitude, myriad (1·16) 914

אֶלֶף thousand (4·12[?]) 12

Chapter 11

הִתְאַנֵּן 1 to complain, murmer (1·2·2) 59

שׁקע 2 to sink, sink down (1·3·6) 1054

אֲסַפְסֻף 4 collection, rabble (1·1) 63

הִתְאַוָּה to desire, lust after (3·16·27) 16

תַּאֲוָה desire (1·21) 16

דָּגָה 5 fish [coll.] (1·15) 185

חִנָּם for naught (1·32) 336

קִשֻּׁאָה cucumber (1·1) 903

אֲבַטִּיחַ watermelons (1·1) 105

חָצִיר green grass, herbage (1·1[?]) 348

בָּצָל onion (1·1) 130

שׁוּם garlic (1·1) 1002

בִּלְתִּי 6 except (3·24) 116

מָן manna (3·14) 577

מָן 7 manna (3·14) 577

גַּד coriander (1·2) 151

בְּדֹלַח bdellium (1·2) 95

שׁוּט 8 to go, rove about (1·7·13) 1001

לָקַט to gather (1·14·36) 544

טחן to grind (1·7·7) 377

רֵחַיִם [hand] mill (1·5) 932

דוּך to pound, beat (1·1) 188

מְדֹכָה mortar (1·1) 189

בשׁל to boil, cook (1·20·27) 143

פָּרוּר pot (1·3) 807

עֻגָה disk or cake of bread (1·7) 728

טַעַם taste (2·13) 381

לָשָׁד dainty bit (1·2) 545

טַל 9 dew (1·31) 378

מָן manna (3·14) 577

הָרָה 12 to conceive (1·38·40) 247

חֵיק bosom (1·38) 300

אֹמֵן foster father (1·7[?]) 52

יוֹנֵק suckling (1·11) 413

מֵאַיִן 13 whence? (1·48) 32

כָּבֵד 14 heavy (2·39) 458

כָּכָה 15 thus (5·34) 462

שֹׁטֵר 16 official, officer (1·25) 1009

הִתְיַצֵּב to station oneself, take one's stand (4·48·48) 426

אצל 17 to set apart (2·4·5) 69

טוֹב 18 to be well, good (3·18·21) 373

זָרָא 20 loathsome thing (1·1) 266

רַגְלִי 21 on foot (1·12) 920

דָּג 22 fish (1·19) 185

קָצֵר 23 to be short (2·11·13) 894

קרה to befall (1·13·27) 889

אצל 25 to set apart (2·4·5[?]) 69

מְשָׁרֵת 28 servant (1·20) 1058

בְּחוּרִים youth (1·3) 104

כלא to withhold (1·14·17) 476

קָנָא 29 to be jealous of (6·30·34) 888

גוז 31 to bring over (1·2·2) 156

שְׂלָו quail (2·4) 969

נָטַשׁ to leave alone (1·33·40) 643

מָחֳרָת 32 the morrow (4·32) 564

שְׂלָו quail (2·4) 969

הִמְעִיט to make small (4·13·22) 589

חֹמֶר heap (1·12) 330

שטח to spread, spread abroad (1·4·5) 1008

טֶרֶם 33 not yet (1·16) 382

91

הִתְאַוָּה 34 to desire, lust after (3·16·27) 16

Chapter 12

אֹדֹת 1 cause; 'א = על־ = because of (2·11) 15

עָנָו 3 humble, lowly, meek (1·21) 776

פִּתְאֹם 4 suddenly (2·25) 837

חִידָה 8 riddle, enigmatic saying (1·17) 295

תְּמוּנָה form, semblance (1·10) 568

מְצֹרָע 10 leprous (2·15) 863

שֶׁלֶג snow (1·20) 1017

בִּי 11 I pray, excuse me (1·12) 106

נואל to be foolish (1·4·4) 383

רֶחֶם 12 womb (4·33) 933

יָרַק 14 to spit (1·2·2) 439

בִּפְנֵי in the face of (1·17) 816

Chapter 13

תור 2 to spy out, explore (14·19·22) 1064

תור 16 to spy out, explore (14·19·22) 1064

תור 17 to spy out, explore (14·19·22) 1064

רָפֶה 18 slack (1·4) 952

מִבְצָר 19 fortification (3·37) 131

שָׁמֵן 20 fertile (1·10) 1032

רָזֶה lean [as in barren] (1·2) 931

בִּכּוּרִים firstfruits (3·17) 114

עֵנָב grape[s] (4·19) 772

תור 21 to spy out, explore (14·19·22) 1064

יָלִיד 22 born (2·12) 409

אֶשְׁכּוֹל 23 cluster (2·9) 79

זְמוֹרָה branch (1·5) 274

עֵנָב grape[s] (4·19) 772

מוֹט pole (3·4) 557

רִמּוֹן pomegranate (2·32) 941

תְּאֵנָה fig tree, fig (2·25·39) 1061

אֶשְׁכּוֹל 24 cluster (2·9) 79

אֹדֹת cause; 'א = על־ = because of (2·11) 15

תור 25 to spy out, explore (14·19·22) 1064

זוב 27 to flow (4·29·29[?]) 264

חָלָב milk (4·44) 316

אֶפֶס 28 א 'כי = save that, howbeit (3·43) 67

עַז strong, mighty, fierce (2·22) 738

בָּצוּר fortified (1·25[?]) 130

יָלִיד born (2·12) 409

ההסה 30 to still (1·1·1[?]) 245

דִּבָּה 32 evil report (3·9) 179

תור to spy out, explore (14·19·22) 1064

נְפִילִים 33 giants (1·3) 658

חָגָב locust, grasshopper (1·5) 290

Chapter 14

נלון 2 to murmur (4·8·18) 534

לוּ if only! O that! (4·19) 530

טַף 3 children (10·41) 381

בַּז spoil, plunder (3·27) 103

תור 6 to spy out, explore (14·19·22) 1064

תור 7 to spy out, explore (14·19·22) 1064

זוב 8 to flow (4·29·29[?]) 264

חָלָב milk (4·44) 316

מרד 9 to rebel (1·25·25) 597

רגם 10 to kill by stoning, to stone (3·15·15) 920

אָנָה 11 with עַד = to what point, how long? (2·39) 33

נאץ perh. to abhor, spurn (3·15·24) 611

דֶּבֶר 12 plague, pestilence (1·46) 184

עָצוּם mighty [strong] (3·31) 783

שֵׁמַע 15 hearing, report (1·17) 1034

מִבִּלְתִּי 16 on account of not (1·2) 116

אֶרֶךְ 18 long; אַפַּיִם 'א = slow to anger (1·15) 74

נקה to leave unpunished (2·13·37) 667

שִׁלֵּשִׁים those of the third generation (1·5) 1026

רִבֵּעַ pertaining to the fourth (1·4) 918

סלח 19 to pardon (5·33·46) 699

גֹּדֶל greatness (1·14) 152

הֵנָּה hither (1·49) 244

סְלַח 20 to pardon (5·33·46) 699

אוּלָם 21 but, but indeed (1·19) 19

נִסָּה 22 to test (1·36·36) 650

נִאֵץ 23 perh. to abhor, spurn (3·15·24) 611

עֵקֶב 24 because of (1·15) 784

מָתַי 27 when? (1·42) 607

נלין to murmur (4·8·18) 534

תְּלֻנָּה murmuring (3·8) 534

פֶּגֶר 29 corpse, carcass (3·22) 803

הלין to murmur (6·10·18) 534

טַף 31 children (10·41) 381

בַּז spoil, plunder (3·27) 103

פֶּגֶר 32 corpse, carcass (3·22) 803

זְנוּת 33 fornication (1·9) 276

פֶּגֶר corpse, carcass (3·22) 803

תור 34 to spy out, explore (14·19·22) 1064

תְּנוּאָ opposition (1·2) 626

נועד 35 to assemble by appointment (6·18·28) 416

תור 36 to spy out, explore (14·19·22) 1064

נלין to murmur (4·8·18) 534

דִּבָּה evil report (3·9) 179

דִּבָּה 37 evil report (3·9) 179

מַגֵּפָה plague (9·26) 620

תור 38 to spy out, explore (14·19·22) 1064

הִתְאַבֵּל 39 to mourn (1·19·38) 5

נַגַף 42 to be struck (1·23·48) 619

הֶעְפִּי 44 to be needless (1·1·2) 779

מוש to depart (1·20[?]·20) 559

הכתי 45 to beat in pieces (1·2·17) 510

Chapter 15

מוֹשָׁב 2 dwelling place (4·43) 444

פלא 3 inf. only; to make a special votive offering (2·3·5) 810

נְדָבָה freewill offering (3·27) 621

נִיחֹחַ soothing (18·43) 629

עִשָּׂרוֹן 4 tenth part (27·33) 798

בָּלַל to mix (26·42·42[?]) 117

הִין hin, a liquid measure (11·22) 228

הִין 5 hin, a liquid measure (11·22) 228

עִשָּׂרוֹן 6 tenth part (27·33) 798

בָּלַל to mix (26·42·42[?]) 117

הִין hin, a liquid measure (11·22) 228

הִין 7 hin, a liquid measure (11·22) 228

נִיחֹחַ soothing (18·43) 629

פלא 8 to make a special votive offering (2·3·5) 810

עִשָּׂרוֹן 9 tenth part (27·33) 798

בָּלַל to mix (26·42·42[?]) 117

הִין hin, a liquid measure (11·22) 228

הִין 10 hin, a liquid measure (11·22) 228

נִיחֹחַ soothing (18·43) 629

כָּכָה 11 thus (5·34) 462

שֶׂה sheep, goat (1·44) 961

כָּכָה 12 thus (5·34) 462

אֶזְרָח 13 native (4·17) 280

כָּכָה thus (5·34) 462

נִיחֹחַ soothing (18·43) 629

נִיחֹחַ 14 soothing (18·43) 629

עֲרִיסָה 20 coarse meal [dub.] (2·4) 791

חַלָּה a kind of cake (3·14) 319

גֹּרֶן treshing floor (3·34) 175

עֲרִיסָה 21 coarse meal [dub.] (2·4) 791

שגה 22 to commit sin of ignorance (1·17·21) 993

הָלְאָה 23 onwards (3·13) 229

שְׁגָגָה 24 sin of error, inadvertence (9·19) 993

נִיחֹחַ soothing (18·43) 629

נִסְלַח 25 to be forgiven (3·13·46) 699

שְׁגָגָה sin of error, inadvertence (9·19) 993

נִסְלַח 26 to be forgiven (3·13·46) 699

שְׁגָגָה sin of error, inadvertence (9·19) 993

שְׁגָגָה 27 sin of error, inadvertence (9·19) 993

שָׁגַג 28 to sin, go astray (1·5·5) 992

חֲטָאָה fault, sin (1·1[?]) 306

שְׁגָגָה sin of error, inadvertence (9·19) 993

נִסְלַח to be forgiven (3·13·46) 699

אֶזְרָח 29 native (4·17) 280

שְׁגָגָה sin of error, inadvertence (9·19) 993

רָם 30 high, lifted, exalted (2·31[?]) 926

אֶזְרָח native (4·17) 280

גִּדֵּף to revile, blaspheme (1·7·7) 154

בָּזָה 31 to despise (6·31·42) 102

הֵפֵר to break, frustrate (6·41·44) 830

קֹשֵׁשׁ 32 to gather stubble (2·6·8) 905

קֹשֵׁשׁ 33 to gather stubble (2·6·8) 905

מִשְׁמָר 34 prison (1·20) 1038

פֹּרַשׁ to be declared distinctly, made distinct (1·2·5) 831

רגם 35 to kill by stoning, to stone (3·15·15) 920

רגם 36 to kill by stoning, to stone (3·15·15) 920

צִיצִת 38 tassel (3·4) 851

פָּתִיל cord, thread (2·11) 836

תְּכֵלֶת violet thread (6·49) 1067

צִיצִת 39 tassel (3·4) 851

תּוּר to go about (14·19·22) 1064

Chapter 16

קָרִיא 2 called, summoned (2·2) 896

נִקְהַל 3 to assemble (3·19·39) 874

מַחְתָּה 6 censer (11·21) 367

הִבְדִּיל 9 separate (2·32·42) 95

כְּהֻנָּה 10 priesthood (6·13) 464

נוֹעַד 11 to assemble by appointment (6·18·28) 416

הִלִּין to murmur (6·10·18) 534

זוּב 13 to flow (4·29·29) 264

חָלָב milk (4·44) 316

הִשְׂתָּרֵר to play the prince over one (1·1·7) 979

זוּב 14 to flow (4·29·29) 264

חָלָב milk (4·44) 316

נִקֵּר to bore out (1·3·6) 669

מַחְתָּה 17 censer (11·21) 367

מַחְתָּה 18 censer (11·21) 367

הִקְהִיל 19 to summon an assembly 6·20·39) 874

נִבְדַּל 21 to be separated (1·10·42) 95

רֶגַע moment (2·22) 921

קָצַף 22 to be wroth (2·28·34) 893

נִסְפָּה 26 to be swept away (1·9·18) 705

טַף 27 children (10·41) 381

פְּקֻדָּה 29 visitation (5·32) 824

בְּרִיאָה 30 a creation, thing created (1·1) 135

בָּרָא to create, fashion (1·38·48) 135

פָּצָה to part, open (1·15·15) 822

בָּלַע to swallow up (4·20·41) 118

נָאֵץ perh. to abhor, spurn (3·15·24) 611

בָּלַע 32 to swallow up (4·20·41) 118

רְכוּשׁ property, goods (2·28) 940

בָּלַע 34 to swallow up (4·20·41) 118

Chapter 17

מַחְתָּה 2 censer (11·21) 367

מִבֵּין out of the midst of (2·21) 107

שְׂרֵפָה burning (3·13) 977

זָרָה to scatter (1·9·38) 279

הָלְאָה yonder, out there (3·13) 229

מַחְתָּה 3 censer (11·21) 367

חַטָּא sinner, sinful (2·19) 308

רִקּוּעַ expansion (1·1) 956

פַּח plate [of metal] (1·2) 809

צִפּוּי metal plating (2·5) 860

מַחְתָּה 4 censer (11·21) 367

רִקַּע to beat out (1·3·11) 955

צִפּוּי metal plating (2·5) 860

זִכָּרוֹן 5 memorial (5·24) 272

נלין 6 to murmur (4·8·18) 534

מָחֳרָת the morrow (4·32) 564

נקהל 7 to assemble (3·19·39) 874

נרמם 10 to arise (1·4·5) 942

רֶגַע moment (2·22) 921

מַחְתָּה 11 censer (11·21) 367

קֶצֶף wrath (3·29) 893

נֶגֶף plague (3·7) 620

נֶגֶף 12 plague (3·7) 620

נעצר 13 to be restrained, be retained (3·10·46) 783

מַגֵּפָה pestilence (9·26) 620

מַגֵּפָה 14 pestilence (9·26) 620

מִלְּבַד besides (15·33) 94

מַגֵּפָה 15 pestilence (9·26) 620

נעצר to be restrained, be retained (3·10·46) 783

נועד 19 to meet at an appointed place (6·18·28) 416

פָּרַח 20 to bud, sprout, shoot (2·29·34) 827

שכה to allay, cause to abate (1·1·5) 1013

תְּלֻנָּה murmuring (3·8) 534

הלין to murmur (6·10·18) 534

מָחֳרָת 23 the morrow (4·32) 564

פָּרַח to bud, sprout, shoot (2·29·34) 827

פֶּרַח bud, sprout (2·17) 827

צִיץ to put forth blossoms (1·7·8) 847

צִיץ blossom, flower (1·15) 847

גָּמַל to ripen, bear ripe [fruits] (1·34·37) 168

שָׁקֵד almond [tree] (1·4) 1052

מְרִי 25 rebellion (1·22) 598

תְּלֻנָּה murmuring (3·8) 534

גוע 27 to expire, perish (4·23·23) 157

קָרֵב 28 approaching (5·11) 898

גוע to expire, perish (4·23·23) 157

Chapter 18

כְּהֻנָּה 1 priesthood (6·13) 464

נִלְוָה 2 to be joined (2·11·12) 530

נִלְוָה 4 to be joined (2·11·12) 530

קֶצֶף 5 wrath (3·29) 893

מַתָּנָה 6 gift (4·18) 682

כְּהֻנָּה 7 priesthood (6·13) 464

פָּרֹכֶת curtain (2·25) 827

מַתָּנָה gift (4·18) 682

קָרֵב approaching (5·11) 898

מָשְׁחָה 8 consecrated portion (1·1) 603

אָשָׁם 9 trespass offering (4·42) 79

מַתָּנָה 11 gift (4·18) 682

תְּנוּפָה wave offering, wave breast (8·30) 632

יִצְהָר 12 fresh oil (1·23) 844

תִּירוֹשׁ must, fresh or new wine (1·38) 440

דָּגָן grain (2·40) 186

בִּכּוּרִים 13 firstfruits (3·17) 114

חֵרֶם 14 devoted (1·29) 356

פֶּטֶר 15 "first opens", i.e., firstborn (2·11) 809

רֶחֶם womb (4·33) 933

פְּדוּיִם 16 ransom (5·5) 804

עֵרֶךְ estimate, valuation (1·33) 789

גֵּרָה gerah, one-twentieth of a shekel (2·5) 176

זָרַק 17 to throw or scatter abundantly (1·32·34[?]) 284

נִיחֹחַ soothing (18·43) 629

חָזֶה 18 breast (2·13) 303

תְּנוּפָה wave offering, wave breast (8·30) 632

שׁוֹק leg (2·19) 1003

מֶלַח 19 salt (3·28) 571

מַעֲשֵׂר 21 tithe (5·31) 798

חֵלֶף exchange = in return for (2·2) 322

חֵטְא 22 punishment for sin (4·33) 307
מַעֲשֵׂר 24 tithe (5·31) 798
מַעֲשֵׂר 26 tithe (5·31) 798
דָּגָן 27 grain (2·40) 186
גֹּרֶן treshing floor (3·34) 175
יֶקֶב wine vat (2·16) 428
מַעֲשֵׂר 28 tithe (5·31) 798
מַתָּנָה 29 gift (4·18) 682
תְּבוּאָה 30 product, yield (2·43) 100
גֹּרֶן treshing floor (3·34) 175
יֶקֶב wine vat (2·16) 428
שָׂכָר 31 hire, wages (1·29) 969
חֵלֶף exchange =in return for (2·2) 322
חֵטְא 32 punishment for sin (4·33) 307

Chapter 19

פָּרָה 2 heifer (5·26) 831
אָדֹם red (1·9) 10
מוּם defect (1·21) 548
עֹל yoke (1·40) 760
אֶצְבַּע 4 finger (1·31) 840
הִזָּה to sprinkle (5·20·24) 633
נֹכַח front of (1·22) 647
פָּרָה 5 heifer (5·26) 831
פֶּרֶשׁ offal, refuse (1·7) 831
אֵזוֹב 6 hyssop (2·10) 23
שָׁנִי scarlet (2·42) 1040
תּוֹלֵעָה coccus ilicius [yielding scarlet color] (2·41) 1069
שְׂרֵפָה burning (3·13) 977
פָּרָה heifer (5·26) 831
אֵפֶר 9 ashes (2·22) 68
פָּרָה heifer (5·26) 831
נִדָּה impurity (6·30) 622
אֵפֶר 10 ashes (2·22) 68
פָּרָה heifer (5·26) 831
נִדָּה 13 impurity (6·30) 622
זָרַק to be poured (2·2·34[?]) 284

טְמְאָה uncleanness (2·37) 380
צָמִיד 15 cover (1·1) 855
פָּתִיל cord, thread (2·11) 836
שְׂרֵפָה 17 burning (3·13) 977
אֵזוֹב 18 hyssop (2·10) 23
טָבַל to dip (1·15·16) 371
הִזָּה to sprinkle (5·20·24) 633
הִזָּה 19 to sprinkle (5·20·24) 633
נִדָּה 20 impurity (6·30) 622
זָרַק to be poured (2·2·34[?]) 284
הִזָּה 21 to sprinkle (5·20·24) 633
נִדָּה impurity (6·30) 622

Chapter 20

נקהל 2 to assemble (3·19·39) 874
לוּ 3 if only! O that! (3·19) 530
גָּוַע to perish, die (4·23·23) 157
בְּעִיר 4 beasts, cattle (3·6) 129
תְּאֵנָה 5 fig tree, fig (2·25·39) 1061
הִקְהִיל 8 to summon an assembly (6·20·39) 874
בְּעִיר beasts, cattle (3·6) 129
הִקְהִיל 10 to summon an assembly (6·20·39) 874
מָרָה to be stubborn (3·21·43) 598
בְּעִיר 11 beasts, cattle (3·6) 129
מְרִיבָה 13 strife, contention (1·2) 937
תְּלָאָה 14 weariness, hardship (1·5) 521
בְּאֵר 17 well (5·36) 91
מְסִלָּה 19 highway (1·27) 700
כָּבֵד 20 heavy (2·39) 458
מֵאֵן 21 to refuse (3·45·45) 549
עַם 24 kinsman (4·34) 769
מָרָה to be stubborn (3·21·43) 598
הִפְשִׁיט 26 to strip (2·15·43) 832
הִפְשִׁיט 28 to strip (2·15·43) 832
גָּוַע 29 to perish, die (4·23·23) 157

Chapter 21

שָׁבָה	1	to take captive (3·29·37) 985
שְׁבִי		captivity, captives (4·46) 985
נָדַר	2	to vow (7·30·30) 623
הֶחֱרִים		to devote to destruction (2·46·49) 355
הֶחֱרִים	3	to devote to destruction (2·46·49) 355
קָצַר	4	to be short (2·11·13) 894
קוּץ	5	to feel a loathing, abhor (2·8·8) 880
קְלֹקֵל		contemptible, worthless (1·1) 887
נָחָשׁ	6	serpent (5·31) 638
שָׂרָף		fiery serpent (2·7) 977
נשׁךְ		to bite fatally (1·2·12) 675
נָחָשׁ	7	serpent (5·31) 638
שָׂרָף	8	fiery serpent (2·7) 977
נֵס		standard (3·21) 651
נָשַׁךְ		to bite (2·10·12) 675
נָחָשׁ	9	serpent (5·31) 638
נֵס		standard (3·21) 651
נָשַׁךְ		to bite (2·10·12) 675
אֶשֶׁד	15	lower part, bottom (1·7) 78
נִשְׁעַן		to lean, support oneself (1·22·22) 1043
בְּאֵר	16	well (5·36) 91
שִׁירָה	17	song (1·13) 1010
בְּאֵר		well (5·36) 91
עָנָה		to sing (1·13·16) 777
בְּאֵר	18	well (5·36) 91
חָפַר		to dig, search for (1·22·22) 343
כָּרָה		to dig (1·13·14) 500
נָדִיב		noble (1·27) 622
מְחֹקֵק		commander's staff (1·7) 349
מִשְׁעֶנֶת		staff (1·12) 1044
גַּיְא	20	valley (1·47) 161
נשׁקף		to overhang, look out and down (2·10·22) 1054

יְשִׁימוֹן		wilderness (2·13) 445
בְּאֵר	22	well (5·36) 91
עַז	24	strong, mighty, fierce (2·22) 738
מֹשֵׁל	27	one who uses a proverb (1·2[?]) 605
לֶהָבָה	28	flame (1·19) 529
קִרְיָה		town, city (1·30) 900
אוֹי	29	Woe! Alas! (2·24) 17
פָּלִיט		escaped one, fugitive (1·5) 812
שְׁבִית		captivity, captives (1·6) 986
יָרָה	30	to throw (1·13·25[?]) 434
רגל	32	go about as explorer, spy (1·14·16) 920
בִּלְתִּי	35	not, except (3·24) 116
שָׂרִיד		survivor (2·28) 975

Chapter 22

גוּר	3	to be afraid of (1·10·10) 158
קוּץ		to feel a sickening dread (2·8·8) 880
לחך	4	Pi. = to lick up (1·5·6) 535
לחך		Qal = to lick (1·1·6) 535
יֶרֶק		green (1·8) 438
מִמּוּל	5	close in front of (1·9) 660
עָצוּם	6	mighty [strong] (3·31) 783
אוּלַי		perhaps (5·45) 19
גרשׁ		to drive out (2·33·47) 176
קֶסֶם	7	divination (2·11) 890
פֹּה	8	here, hither (3·44) 805
קבב	11	to utter a curse against, curse (10·14·14) 866
אוּלַי		perhaps (5·45) 19
גרשׁ		to drive out (2·33·47) 176
מֵאֵן	13	to be recusant (3·45·45) 549
מֵאֵן	14	to refuse (3·45·45) 549
נִמְנַע	16	to be withheld (1·4·29) 586
קבב	17	to utter a curse against, curse (10·14·14) 866
מְלֹא	18	fulness (2·38) 571
קָטֹן		small (1·47) 881

בָּזֶה	19 in this [place], here (5·19) 261	
חבש	21 to bind up, i.e., equip for riding (1·27·31) 289	
אָתוֹן	she-ass (15·35) 87	
הִתְיַצֵּב	22 to station oneself, take one's stand (4·48·48) 426	
שָׂטָן	adversary (2·27) 966	
אָתוֹן	she-ass (15·35) 87	
שָׁלַף	23 to draw out (2·25·25) 1025	
אָתוֹן	she-ass (15·35) 87	
מִשְׁעוֹל	24 hollow way (1·1) 1043	
גָּדֵר	wall, fence (1·13) 154	
אָתוֹן	25 she-ass (15·35) 87	
נִלְחַץ	to squeeze oneself (1·1·15) 537	
לָחַץ	to squeeze (1·14·15) 537	
צַר	26 narrow, tight (1·20) 865	
אָתוֹן	27 she-ass (15·35) 87	
רָבַץ	to lie down, lie (1·24·30) 918	
מַקֵּל	staff (1·18) 596	
אָתוֹן	28 she-ass (15·35) 87	
אָתוֹן	29 she-ass (15·35) 87	
הִתְעַלֵּל	to deal wantonly, ruthlessly (1·7·17) 759	
לוּ	If only! O that! (4·19) 530	
אָתוֹן	30 she-ass (15·35) 87	
מֵעוֹד	ever since (1·2) 728	
הַסְכֵּין	to exhibit use or habit (2·4·11) 698	
שָׁלַף	31 to draw out (2·25·25) 1025	
קָדַד	to bow down (1·15·15) 869	
אָתוֹן	32 she-ass (15·35) 87	
שָׂטָן	adversary (2·27) 966	
יָרַט	to precipitate (1·2·2) 437	
לְנֶגֶד	in front of, before (1·32) 617	
אָתוֹן	33 she-ass (15·35) 87	
אוּלַי	perhaps (5·45) 19	
אֶפֶס	35 only (3·43) 67	
אָמְנָם	37 truly, indeed (1·5) 53	
מְאוּמָה	38 anything (1·32) 548	

Chapter 23

בָּזֶה	1 in this [place], here (5·19) 261	
הִתְיַצֵּב	3 to station oneself, take one's stand (4·48·48) 426	
אוּלַי	perhaps (5·45) 19	
נִקְרָה	to encounter, meet (4·6·27) 899	
שְׁפִי	bare place, height (1·10) 1046	
נִקְרָה	4 to encounter, meet (4·6·27) 899	
מָשָׁל	7 proverb (7·39) 605	
הַנְחָיה	to lead (1·26·40) 634	
זָעַם	to denounce (2·10·11) 276	
קבב	8 to utter a cruse against, curse (10·14·14) 866	
זָעַם	to denounce (2·10·11) 276	
שׁוּר	9 to behold (2·16·16) 1003	
בָּדָד	isolation (1·11) 94	
מָנָה	10 to count (1·12·28) 584	
רֹבַע	fourth part (1·1) 917	
קבב	11 to utter a curse against, curse (10·14·14) 866	
אֶפֶס	13 only (3·43) 67	
קבב	to utter a cruse against, curse (10·14·14) 866	
צֹפֶה	14 watchman (1·19) 859	
הִתְיַצֵּב	15 to station oneself, take one's stand (4·48·48) 426	
נִקְרָה	to encounter, meet (4·6·27) 899	
נִקְרָה	16 to encounter, meet (4·6·27) 899	
מָשָׁל	18 proverb (7·39) 605	
הַאֲזִין	to listen (1·41·41) 24	
כזב	19 to lie (1·12·16) 469	
תְּרוּעָה	21 battle cry (6·36) 929	
תּוֹעָפָה	22 eminence (2·4) 419	
רְאֵם	wild ox (2·9) 910	
נַחַשׁ	23 divination (2·2) 638	
קֶסֶם	divination (2·11) 890	
לָבִיא	24 lioness (2·11) 522	

אֲרִי lion (2·35) 71

טֶרֶף prey (1·17) 383

קבב 25 to utter a curse against, curse (10·14·14) 866

אוּלַי 27 perhaps (5·45) 19

יָשַׁר to be pleasing, right, agreeable (1·13·25) 448

קבב to utter a curse against, curse (10·14·14) 866

נשקף 28 to overhang, look out and down (2·10·22) 1054

יְשִׁימוֹ wilderness (2·13) 445

בָּזֶה 29 in this [place], here (5·19) 261

Chapter 24

טוֹב 1 to be pleasing (3·18·21) 373

נַחַשׁ divination (2·2) 638

מָשָׁל 3 proverb (7·39) 605

שׁתם to open [dub.] (2·2·2) 1060

אֹמֶר 4 word (2·48) 56

מַחֲזֶה vision (2·4) 303

שַׁדַּי name of God (2·48) 994

טוֹב 5 to be pleasant, delightful (3·18·21) 373

גַּנָּה 6 garden (1·16) 171

אֲהָלִים odoriferous trees, perh. aloes (1·4) 14

נזל 7 to flow (1·8·9) 633

דְּלִי bucket (1·2) 194

תּוֹעָפֹת 8 eminence (2·4) 419

רְאֵם wild ox (2·9) 910

גרם to break bones, break (1·2·3[?]) 175

מָחַץ to shatter (2·14·14) 563

כָּרַע 9 to bow down (1·29·35) 502

אֲרִי lion (2·35) 71

לָבִיא lioness (2·11) 522

סָפַק 10 to clap (1·6·6[?]) 706

קבב to utter a curse against, curse (10·14·14) 866

מָנַע 11 to hold back (1·25·29) 586

מְלֹא 13 fulness (2·38) 571

מָשָׁל 15 proverb (7·39) 605

שׁתם to open [dub.] (2·2·2) 1060

אֹמֶר 16 word (2·48) 56

מַחֲזֶה vision (2·4) 303

שַׁדַּי name of God (2·48) 994

שׁוּר 17 to behold (2·16·16) 1003

כּוֹכָב star (1·37) 456

מָחַץ to shatter (2·14·14) 563

קָרְקַר hairy crown, scalp (1·1) 903

שֵׁת [battle] din (1·1) 981

יְרֵשָׁה 18 possession (2·2) 440

רדה 19 to have dominion, rule, dominate (1·22·23) 921

שָׂרִיד survivor (2·28) 975

מָשָׁל 20 proverb (7·39) 605

אֹבֵד destruction (2·2) 2

עֲדִי even to (2·11) 723

מָשָׁל 21 proverb (7·39) 605

עֲדִי even to (2·11) 723

אֵיתָן enduring, firm (1·14) 450

מוֹשָׁב dwelling place (4·43) 444

קֵן nest (1·13) 890

בָּעֵר 22 to devour, burn (1·26·28[?]) 129

שׁבה to take captive (3·29·37) 985

מָשָׁל 23 proverb (7·39) 605

אוֹי Woe! Alas! (2·24) 17

אֵל these (1·10[?]) 41

צִי 24 ship (1·4) 850

עֲדִי even to (2·11) 723

אֹבֵד destruction (2·2) 2

Chapter 25

צמד 3 to join or attach oneself (2·3·5) 855

הוֹקִיע 4 to crucify [dub.]; some solemn form of execution (1·3·8) 429

חָרוֹן [burning of] anger (2·41) 354

צמד	5 to join or attach oneself (2·3·5) 855		מָרָה	14 to be stubborn (3·21·43) 598
רֹמַח	7 spear, lance (1·15) 942		מְרִיבָה	strife, contention (1·2) 937
קֻבָּה	8 large vaulted tent (1·1) 866		סָמַךְ	18 to lay (4·41·48) 701
דקר	to pierce, pierce through (1·7·11) 201		הוֹד	20 majesty, splendor (1·24) 217
קֵבָה	stomach, belly (1·2) 867		אוּר	21 Urim (1·7) 22
נעצר	to be restrained, be retained (3·10·46) 783		סָמַךְ	23 to lay (4·41·48) 701

Num 25:5–28:26

מַגֵּפָה plague (9·26) 620

מַגֵּפָה 9 plague (9·26) 620

קִנֵּא 11 to be jealous of (6·30·34) 888

קִנְאָה jealousy (9·43) 888

כְּהֻנָּה 13 priesthood (6·13) 464

קִנֵּא to be jealous of (6·30·34) 888

אֻמָּה 15 tribe, people (1·3) 52

צרר 17 to show hostility towards, vex (4·10·10) 865

צרר 18 to show hostility towards, vex (4·10·10) 865

נֵכֶל knavery (1·1) 647

נכל to beguile (1·1·4) 647

מַגֵּפָה plague (9·26) 620

מַגֵּפָה 19 plague (9·26) 620

Chapter 26

קָרִיא 9 called, summoned (2·2) 896

הַצֵּיה to engage in a struggle (2·3·8) 663

בָּלַע 10 to swallow up (4·20·41) 118

נֵס warning (3·21) 651

הִמְעִיט 54 to make small (4·13·22) 589

Chapter 27

נוֹעד 3 to assemble by appointment (6·18·18) 416

חֵטְא guilt of sin, sin (4·33) 307

נִגְרַע 4 to be withdrawn (5·7·22) 175

שְׁאֵר 11 flesh relation (1·17) 984

עָם 13 kinsman (4·34) 769

Chapter 28

נִיחֹחַ 2 soothing (18·43) 629

אֵיפָה 5 ephah, quantity of wheat, barley = 10 omers (2·38) 35

בָּלַל to mix (26·42·42[?]) 117

כָּתִית beaten (1·5) 510

הִין hin, a liquid measure (11·22) 228

נִיחֹחַ 6 soothing (18·43) 629

הִין 7 hin, a liquid measure (11·22) 228

הִסִּיךְ to pour out (1·13·24) 650

שֵׁכָר intoxicating drink, strong drink (3·23) 1016

נִיחֹחַ 8 soothing (18·43) 629

עִשָּׂרוֹן 9 tenth part (27·33) 798

בָּלַל to mix (26·42·42[?]) 117

עִשָּׂרוֹן 12 tenth part (27·33) 798

בָּלַל to mix (26·42·42[?]) 117

עִשָּׂרוֹן 13 tenth part (27·33) 798

בָּלַל to mix (26·42·42[?]) 117

נִיחֹחַ soothing (18·43) 629

הִין 14 hin, a liquid measure (11·22) 228

פֶּסַח 16 festival of the passover (11·49) 820

מִקְרָא 18 convocation (7·22) 896

בָּלַל 20 to mix (26·42·42[?]) 117

עִשָּׂרוֹן tenth part (27·33) 798

עִשָּׂרוֹן 21 tenth part (27·33) 798

מִלְּבַד 23 besides (15·33) 94

נִיחֹחַ 24 soothing (18·43) 629

מִקְרָא 25 convocation (7·22) 896

בִּכּוּרִים 26 firstfruits (3·17) 114

שָׁבוּעַ week (1·20) 988

מִקְרָא convocation (7·22) 896
נִיחֹחַ 27 soothing (18·43) 629
בָּלַל 28 to mix (26·42·42[?]) 117
עִשָּׂרוֹן tenth part (27·33) 798
עִשָּׂרוֹן 29 tenth part (27·33) 798
מִלְּבַד 31 besides (15·33) 94

Chapter 29

מִקְרָא 1 convocation (7·22) 896
תְּרוּעָה blast [for march] (6·36) 929
נִיחֹחַ 2 soothing (18·43) 629
בָּלַל 3 to mix (26·42·42[?]) 117
עִשָּׂרוֹן tenth part (27·33) 798
עִשָּׂרוֹן 4 tenth part (27·33) 798
מִלְּבַד 6 besides (15·33) 94
נִיחֹחַ soothing (18·43) 629
עָשׂוֹר 7 tenth day (1·15) 797
מִקְרָא convocation (7·22) 896
נִיחֹחַ 8 soothing (18·43) 629
בָּלַל 9 to mix (26·42·42[?]) 117
עִשָּׂרוֹן tenth part (27·33) 798
עִשָּׂרוֹן 10 tenth part (27·33) 798
מִלְּבַד 11 besides (15·33) 94
כִּפֻּרִים atonement (2·8) 498
מִקְרָא 12 convocation (7·22) 896
חגג to keep a pilgrim feast (1·16·16) 290
נִיחֹחַ 13 soothing (18·43) 629
בָּלַל 14 to mix (26·42·42[?]) 117
עִשָּׂרוֹן tenth part (27·33) 798
עִשָּׂרוֹן 15 tenth part (27·33) 798
מִלְּבַד 16 besides (15·33) 94
מִלְּבַד 19 besides (15·33) 94
מִלְּבַד 22 besides (15·33) 94
מִלְּבַד 25 besides (15·33) 94
מִלְּבַד 28 besides (15·33) 94
מִלְּבַד 31 besides (15·33) 94
מִלְּבַד 34 besides (15·33) 94

עֲצֶרֶת 35 assembly (1·11) 783
נִיחֹחַ 36 soothing (18·43) 629
מִלְּבַד 38 besides (15·33) 94
נְדָבָה 39 freewill offering (3·27) 621

Chapter 30

נדר 3 to vow (7·30·30) 623
שְׁבוּעָה oath (5·30) 989
אִסָּר binding obligation (11·11) 64
נדר 4 to vow (7·30·30) 623
אִסָּר binding obligation (11·11) 64
נְעוּרִים youth (2·46) 655
הֶחֱרִישׁ 5 to be silent (6·38·46) 361
אִסָּר binding obligation (11·11) 64
הֵנִיא 6 to restrain (6·8·8) 626
אִסָּר binding obligation (11·11) 64
סלח to forgive (5·33·46) 699
מִבְטָא 7 rash utterance (2·2) 105
הֶחֱרִישׁ 8 to be silent (6·38·46) 361
אִסָּר binding obligation (11·11) 64
הֵנִיא 9 to restrain (6·8·8) 626
הֵפֵר to make ineffectual, annul (6·41·44) 830
מִבְטָא rash utterance (2·2) 105
סלח to forgive (5·33·46) 699
גרש 10 to drive out (1·8·47) 176
נָדַר 11 to vow (7·30·30) 623
אִסָּר binding obligation (11·11) 64
שְׁבוּעָה oath (5·30) 989
הֶחֱרִישׁ 12 to be silent (6·38·46) 361
הֵנִיא to restrain (6·8·8) 626
אִסָּר binding obligation (11·11) 64
הֵפֵר 13 to make ineffectual, annul (6·41·44) 830
מוֹצָא that which goes forth (3·37) 425
אִסָּר binding obligation (11·11) 64
סלח to forgive (5·33·46) 699
שְׁבוּעָה 14 oath (5·30) 989

אִסָּר   binding obligation (11·11) 64

הֵפֵר   to make ineffectual, annul (6·41·44) 830

הֶחֱרִישׁ   15 to be silent (5·38·46) 361

אִסָּר   binding obligation (11·11) 64

הֵפֵר   16 to make ineffectual, annul (6·41·44) 830

נְעוּרִים   17 youth (2·46) 655

Chapter 31

נקם   2 to avenge (1·13·34) 667

נְקָמָה   vengence (2·27) 668

עַם   kinsman (4·34) 769

נֶחֱלַץ   3 to be equipped (3·7·27) 323

נְקָמָה   vengence (2·27) 668

נמסר   5 to be delivered over (1·1·2) 588

אֶלֶף   thousand (4·12[?]) 48

חָלוּץ   equipped (6·17[?]) 323

חֲצֹצְרָה   6 clarion (5·29) 348

תְּרוּעָה   blast [for march] (6·36) 929

צבא   7 to wage war, fight (4·12·14) 838

שׁבה   9 to take captive (3·29·37) 985

טַף   children (10·41) 381

בָּזַז   to spoil, plunder (3·37·40) 102

מוֹשָׁב   10 dwelling place (4·43) 444

טִירָה   encampment (1·7) 377

מַלְקוֹחַ   11 booty (5·7) 544

שְׁבִי   12 captivity, captives (4·46) 985

מַלְקוֹחַ   booty (5·7) 544

קָצַף   14 to be wroth (2·28·34) 893

נְקֵבָה   15 female (2·22) 666

מסר   16 to offer (1·1·2) 588

מַגֵּפָה   plague (9·26) 620

טַף   17 children (10·41) 381

מִשְׁכָּב   act of lying [sexually] (3·46) 1012

טַף   18 children (10·41) 381

מִשְׁכָּב   act of lying [sexually] (3·46) 1012

שְׁבִי   19 captivity, captives (4·46) 985

בְּדִיל   22 tin, alloy (1·5) 95

עֹפֶרֶת   lead (1·9) 780

נִדָּה   23 impurity (6·30) 622

מַלְקוֹחַ   26 booty (5·7) 544

שְׁבִי   captivity, captives (4·46) 985

חָצָה   27 to divide (2·11·15) 345

מַלְקוֹחַ   booty (5·7) 544

מֶכֶס   28 tax (6·6) 493

מַחֲצִית   29 half (4·16) 345

מַחֲצִית   30 half (4·16) 345

מַלְקוֹחַ   32 booty (5·7) 544

בַּז   spoil, plunder (3·27) 103

בָּזַז   to spoil, plunder (3·37·40) 102

מִשְׁכָּב   35 act of lying [sexually] (3·46) 1012

מֶחֱצָה   36 half (2·2) 345

מֶכֶס   37 tax (6·6) 493

מֶכֶס   38 tax (6·6) 493

מֶכֶס   39 tax (6·6) 493

מֶכֶס   40 tax (6·6) 493

מֶכֶס   41 tax (6·6) 493

מַחֲצִית   42 half (4·16) 345

חָצָה   to divide (2·11·15) 345

צבא   to wage war, fight (4·12·14) 838

מֶחֱצָה   43 half (2·2) 345

מֶחֱצִית   47 half (4·16) 345

אֶצְעָדָה   50 armlet band clasping upper arm (1·2) 858

צָמִיד   bracelet (1·6) 855

טַבַּעַת   ring (1·44) 371

עָגִיל   hoop, ring (1·2) 722

כּוּמָז   name of a golden ornament (1·2) 484

בָּזַז   53 to spoil, plunder (3·37·40) 102

זִכָּרוֹן   54 memorial, reminder (5·24) 272

Chapter 32

עָצוּם   1 mighty [strong] (3·31) 783

פֹּה   6 here, hither (3·44) 805

הֵנִיא 7 to restrain (6·8·8) 626

הֵנִיא 9 to restrain (6·8·8) 626

בִּלְתִּי 12 except (3·24) 116

הִנִיע 13 to cause to wander (1·14·36) 631

תַּרְבּוּת 14 increase, brood (1·1) 916

חַטָּא sinner, sinful (3·19) 308

ספה to add (1·8·18) 705

חָרוֹן anger (2·41) 354

גְּדֵרָה 16 wall, hedge (3·8) 155

פֹּה here, hither (3·44) 805

טַף children (10·41) 381

נֶחֱלַץ 17 to be equipped (3·7·22) 323

חוש to make haste (1·15·21) 301

טַף children (10·41) 381

מִבְצָר fortification (3·37) 131

הָלְאָה 19 forwards (3·13) 229

נֶחֱלָץ 20 to be equipped (3·7·27) 323

חָלוּץ 21 warrior, equipped one (6·17[?]) 323

נכבש 22 to be subdued (2·5·14) 461

נָקִי exempt (1·43) 667

טַף 24 children (10·41) 381

גְּדֵרָה wall, hedge (3·8) 155

צֹנֶה flocks, sf. צנאכם (1·2) 856

טַף 26 children (10·41) 381

חָלוּץ 27 warrior, equipped one (6·17[?]) 323

חָלוּץ 29 warrior, equipped one (6·17[?]) 323

נכבש to be subdued (2·5·14) 461

חָלוּץ 30 warrior, equipped one (6·17[?]) 323

חָלוּץ 32 warrior, equipped one (6·17[?]) 323

גְּבוּלָה 33 border, boundary (3·10) 148

מִבְצָר 36 fortification (3·37) 131

גְּדֵרָה wall, hedge (3·8) 155

חַוָּה 41 tent village (2·7) 295

Chapter 33

מַסָּע 1 journey (7·12) 652

מַסָּע 2 journey (7·12) 652

מוֹצָא place of going forth (3·27) 425

מָחֳרָת 3 the morrow (4·32) 564

פֶּסַח festival of the passover (11·49) 820

רָם high, lifted, exalted (2·31[?]) 926

שֶׁפֶט 4 judgement (1·16) 1048

תָּמָר 9 palm tree, date palm (1·12) 1071

מַשְׂכִּית 52 carved figure (1·6) 967

צֶלֶם image (1·17) 853

מַסֵּכָה molten image (1·25) 651

הֵמְעִיט 54 to make diminish (4·13·22) 589

שֵׂךְ 55 thorn (1·1) 968

צְנִין thorn, prick (1·2) 856

צַד side (1·31) 841

צרר to show hostility towards, vex (4·10·10) 865

דמה 56 to intend, think (1·13·27) 197

Chapter 34

גְּבוּלָה 2 border, boundary (3·10) 148

מֶלַח 3 salt (3·28) 571

קֶדֶם eastward (8·26) 870

מַעֲלֶה 4 ascent (1·19) 751

עַקְרָב scorpion (1·9) 785

תּוֹצָאָה outgoing, extremity (5·23) 426

תּוֹצָאָה 5 outgoing, extremity (5·23) 426

תאה 7 to mark out (2·2·2) 1060

תאה 8 to mark out (2·2·2) 1060

תּוֹצָאָה outgoing, extremity (5·23) 426

תּוֹצָאָה 9 outgoing, extremity (5·23) 426

הִתְאַוָּה 10 to desire (3·16·27) 16

קֶדֶם eastward (8·26) 870

מָחָה 11 to strike (1·1·1) 562

קֶדֶם eastward (8·26) 870

תּוֹצָאָה 12 outgoing, extremity (5·23) 426

מֶלַח salt (3·28) 571

גְּבוּלָה border, boundary (3·10) 148

קֶדֶם 15 eastward (8·26) 870

Chapter 35

רְכוּשׁ 3 property, goods (2·28) 940

קֶדֶם 5 eastward (8·26) 870

מִקְלָט 6 refuge (11·20) 886

רָצַח to murder, slay (18·38·43) 953

הֶמְעִיט 8 to make diminish (4·13·22) 589

כְּפִי according to (5·16) 804

הִקְרָה 11 to select as suitable (1·3·27) 899

מִקְלָט refuge (11·20) 886

רָצַח to murder, slay (18·38·43) 953

שְׁגָגָה sin of error, inadvertence (9·19) 993

מִקְלָט 12 refuge (11·20) 886

גֹּאֵל kinsman (8·44[?]) 145

רָצַח to murder, slay (18·38·43) 953

מִקְלָט 13 refuge (11·20) 886

מִקְלָט 14 refuge (11·20) 886

תּוֹשָׁב 15 sojourner (1·14) 444

מִקְלָט refuge (11·20) 886

שְׁגָגָה sin of error, inadvertence (9·19) 993

רָצַח 16 to murder, slay (18·38·43) 953

רָצַח 17 to murder, slay (18·38·43) 953

רָצַח 18 to murder, slay (18·38·43) 953

גֹּאֵל 19 kinsman (8·44[?]) 145

רָצַח to murder, slay (18·38·43) 953

פָּגַע to meet, light upon (2·40·46) 803

שֹׂנְאָה 20 hating, hatred (1·17) 971

הֲדָף to push, thrust (2·11·11) 213

צְדִיָּה lying-in-wait (2·2) 841

אֵיבָה 21 personal hostility (2·5) 33

רָצַח to murder, slay (18·38·43) 953

גֹּאֵל kinsman (8·44[?]) 145

פָּגַע to meet, light upon (2·40·46) 803

פֶּתַע 22 suddenness (2·7) 837

בְּלֹא without (3·29) 518

אֵיבָה personal hostility (2·5) 33

הֲדָף to push, thrust (2·11·11) 213

צְדִיָּה lying-in-wait (2·2) 841

בְּלֹא 23 without (3·29) 518

גֹּאֵל 24 kinsman (8·44[?]) 145

רָצַח 25 to murder, slay (18·38·43) 953

גֹּאֵל kinsman (8·44[?]) 145

מִקְלָט refuge (11·20) 886

רָצַח 26 to murder, slay (18·38·43) 953

מִקְלָט refuge (11·20) 886

גֹּאֵל 27 kinsman (8·44[?]) 145

מִקְלָט refuge (11·20) 886

רָצַח to murder, slay (18·38·43) 953

מִקְלָט 28 refuge (11·20) 886

רָצַח to murder, slay (18·38·43) 953

מוֹשָׁב 29 dwelling place (4·43) 444

רָצַח 30 to murder, slay (18·38·43) 953

כֹּפֶר 31 ransom (2·13) 497

רָצַח to murder, slay (18·38·43) 953

כֹּפֶר 32 ransom (2·13) 497

מִקְלָט refuge (11·20) 886

הֶחֱנִיף 33 to pollute (2·4·10) 337

Chapter 36

נִגְרַע 3 to be withdrawn (5·7·22) 175

יֹבֵל 4 ram (1·27) 385

נִגְרַע to be withdrawn (5·7·22) 175

DEUTERONOMY

Chapter 1

מוֹל — 1 in front of (1·1) 557
הוֹאִיל — 5 to undertake to do (1·18·18) 383
בֵּאֵר — to make plain (2·3·3) 91
שָׁכֵן — 7 neighbor (1·20) 1015
שְׁפֵלָה — lowland (1·20) 1050
חוֹף — shore, coast (1·7) 342
כּוֹכָב — 10 star (4·37) 456
אֵיכָה — 12 in what manner (5·18) 32
טֹרַח — burden (1·2) 382
יהב — 13 to give, provide (2·31·31) 396
נָבוֹן — discerning (2·21) 106
שֹׁטֵר — 15 official, officer (7·25) 1009
הִכִּיר — 17 to regard (4·37·40) 647
גּוּר — to dread, be afraid of (3·10·10) 158
קשה — to be hard, difficult (2·5·28) 904
נוֹרָא — 19 dreadful (6·44) 431
חָפַר — 22 to search out (2·22·22) 343
רגל — 24 to go about as explorer, spy (1·14·16) 920
המרה — 26 to show rebelliousness (6·22·43) 598
נרגן — 27 to murmur (1·2·3) 920
שְׂנְאָה — hating, hatred (2·17) 971
אָנָה — 28 whence? whither? (1·39) 33
המסיס — to cause to melt (1·1·20) 587
רָם — high, i.e., tall (7·31[?]) 926
בָּצוּר — made inaccessible, fortified (4·25) 130
ערץ — 29 to tremble (4·11·14) 792
תּוּר — 33 to seek out, select (1·19·22) 1064
קָצַף — 34 to be wroth (2·28·34) 893
זוּלָה — 36 with the exception of (2·16) 265
הִתְאַנַּף — 37 be angry (4·6·14) 60
בִּגְלַל — on account of (3·10) 164

טַף — 39 children (7·41) 381
בַּז — spoil, plunder (1·27) 103
חָגַר — 41 to gird on (1·44·44) 291
ההין — to be easy (1·1·1) 223
נֶגֶּף — 42 to be smitten (3·23·48) 619
המרה — 43 to show rebelliousness (6·22·43) 598
הזיד — to act presumptuously (3·8·10) 267
דְּבוֹרָה — 44 bee (1·4) 184
הכתית — to beat in pieces (1·2·17) 510
הַאֲזִין — 45 to give ear, listen (2·41·41) 24

Chapter 2

התגרה — 5 to excite oneself, engage in strife with (4·11·14) 173
יְרֻשָׁה — possession, inheritance (7·14) 440
אֹכֶל — 6 food (3·44) 38
שבר — to buy grain (1·16·21) 991
כרה — to get by trade (1·4·4) 500
חָסֵר — 7 to lack, decrease (3·20·24) 341
צוּר — 9 to show hostility, to treat as foe (2·5·5) 849
התגרה — to excite oneself, engage in strife with (4·11·14) 173
יְרֻשָׁה — possession, inheritance (7·14) 440
רָם — 10 high, i.e., tall (7·31[?]) 926
יְרֻשָׁה — 12 possession, inheritance (7·14) 440
הָמַם — 15 to confuse, discomfit (1·13·13) 243
מוּל — 19 in front of (5·25) 557
צוּר — to show hostility to, to treat as foe (2·5·5) 849
התגרה — to excite oneself, engage in strife with (4·11·14) 173
יְרֻשָׁה — possession, inheritance (7·14) 440
התגרה — 24 to excite oneself, engage in strife with (4·11·14) 173
פַּחַד — 25 dread (3·49) 808
שֵׁמַע — hearing, report (1·17) 1034

רָגַז to quake (1·30·41) 919
חִיל to writhe (1·29·46) 296
הִשְׁבִּיר 28 to sell grain (1·5·21) 991
הִקְשָׁה 30 to make stiff, stubborn (2·21·28) 904
אמץ to harden, make obstinate (3·19·41) 54
הֶחֱרִים 34 to devote to destruction (6·46·49) 355
מַת man (6·21) 607
טַף children (7·41) 381
שָׂרִיד survivor (2·28) 975
בָּזַז 35 to plunder (3·37·40) 102
קִרְיָה 36 town, city (2·30) 900
שָׂגַב to be high (1·2·20) 960
אֹכֶל 38 food (3·44) 38

Chapter 3

בִּלְתִּי 3 except, besides that[?] (1·24) 116
שָׂרִיד survivor (2·28) 975
קִרְיָה 4 town, city (2·30) 900
חֶבֶל lot, region (4·49) 286
בָּצוּר 5 made inaccessible, fortified (4·25) 130
גָּבֹהַּ high (2·41) 147
בְּרִיחַ bar (1·41) 138
פְּרָזִי hamlet dweller (1·3) 826
הֶחֱרִים 6 to devote to destruction (6·46·49) 355
מַת man (6·21) 607
טַף children (7·41) 381
בָּזַז 7 to plunder (3·37·40) 102
מִישׁוֹר 10 tableland (2·23) 449
עֶרֶשׂ 11 couch, divan (2·10) 793
חֶבֶל 13 region, lot (4·49) 286
חֶבֶל 14 region, lot (4·49) 286
חַוָּה tent village (1·7) 295
מֶלַח 17 salt (2·28) 571

אֲשֵׁד mountain slope (2·7) 78
חָלוּץ 18 equipped (1·17[?]) 323
טַף 19 children (7·41) 381
יְרֻשָּׁה 20 possession, inheritance (7·14) 440
גֹּדֶל 24 greatness, magnificence (6·14) 152
הִתְעַבֵּר 26 to put oneself in a fury, become furious (1·8·8) 720
תֵּימָן 27 south, southern quarter (1·24) 412
אמץ 28 to make firm, strengthen, harden (3·19·41) 54
גַּיְא 29 valley (3·47) 161
מוּל in front of (5·25) 557

Chapter 4

גרע 2 to diminish (2·14·22) 175
דָּבֵק 4 clinging (1·3) 180
בִּינָה 6 understanding (1·37) 108
נָבוֹן discerning (2·21) 106
הִקְהִיל 10 to summon an assembly (3·20·39) 874
עֲרָפֶל 11 heavy cloud (2·15) 791
תְּמוּנָה 12 form, semblance (6·10) 568
זוּלָה except, only (2·16) 265
לוּחַ 13 tablet (16·40) 531
תְּמוּנָה 15 form, semblance (6·10) 568
פֶּסֶל 16 idol, image (5·31) 820
תְּמוּנָה form, semblance (6·10) 568
סֶמֶל image (1·5) 702
תַּבְנִית figure, image (5·20) 125
נְקֵבָה female (1·22) 666
תַּבְנִית 17 figure, image (5·20) 125
צִפּוֹר bird[s] (3·40) 861
עוֹף to fly (1·18·25) 733
תַּבְנִית 18 figure, image (5·20) 125
רמשׂ to creep (1·16·16) 942
דָּגָה fish [coll.] (1·15) 185
יָרֵחַ 19 moon (2·27) 437
כּוֹכָב star (4·37) 456

נדּח   to be thrust aside (4·13·43) 623

כּוּר   20 furnace (1·8) 468

הִתְאַנַּ 21 to be angry (4·6·14) 60

פֶּסֶל 23 idol, image (5·31) 820

תְּמוּנַ   likeness, representation (6·10) 568

קַנָּא 24 jealous (3·6) 888

נוֹשֵׁן 25 to be old (1·3·3[?]) 445

פֶּסֶל   idol, image (5·31) 820

תְּמוּנַ   likeness, representation (6·10) 568

הֵעִיד 26 to call as witness (5·39·44) 729

הַאֲרִי   to prolong (11·31·34) 73

מַת 27 man (6·21) 607

נָהַג   to lead off (2·10·30) 624

הֵרִיחַ 28 to smell (1·11·14) 926

רַחוּם 31 compassionate (1·13) 933

הִרְפָּה   to abandon, forsake (4·21·44) 951

לְמִן 32 from (2·14) 583

בָּרָא   to create (1·38·48) 135

נִסָּה 34 to try (8·36·36) 650

מַסָּה   trial (3·3) 650

מוֹפֵת   sign (9·36) 68

מוֹרָא   awe-inspiring spectacular deed (4·12) 432

מִלְּבַד 35 besides (2·33) 94

יִסַּר 36 to discipline (5·30·41) 415

בִּפְנֵי 37 in the face of (4·17) 816

עָצוּם 38 mighty [strong] (6·31) 783

מִמַּעַל 39 above, on the top of (2·29) 751

הַאֲרִי 40 to prolong (11·31·34) 73

הִבְדִּי 41 to separate, make a division between (6·32·42) 95

רָצַח 42 to murder, slay (7·38·43) 953

בִּבְלִי   without (2·5) 115

שֹׂנֵא   enemy (9·41) 971

תְּמוֹל   aforetime (3·23) 1069

שִׁלְשֹׁו   aforetime, previously (3·25) 1026

אֵל   these (3·10) 41

מִישׁוֹ 43 tableland (2·23) 449

עֵדָה 45 testimony (3·32) 730

גַּיְא 46 valley (3·47) 161

מוּל   in front of (5·25) 557

אַשֵׁד 49 mountain slope (2·7) 78

Chapter 5

פֹּה   3 here, hither (4·44) 805

בִּפְנֵי   4 in the face of (5·17) 816

פֶּסֶל   8 idol, image (5·31) 820

תְּמוּנָה   likeness, representation (6·10) 568

מִמַּעַל   8 above, on the top of (2·29) 751

קַנָּא   9 jealous (3·6) 888

שִׁלֵּשִׁים   pertaining to the third (1·5) 1026

רִבֵּעַ   pertaining to the fourth (1·4) 918

אֹהֵב 10 friend (2·36[?]) 12

נקה 11 to leave unpunished (1·12·36) 667

הַאֲרִיךְ 16 to prolong (11·31·34) 73

רָצַח 17 to murder, slay (7·38·43) 953

נאף 18 to commit adultery (1·16·30) 610

גנב 19 to steal, take by stealth (2·30·39) 170

חָמַד 21 to desire (2·16·21) 326

הִתְאַוָּה   to desire, long for (1·16·27) 16

עֲרָפֶל 22 heavy cloud (2·15) 791

לוּחַ   tablet (16·40) 531

גֹּדֶל 24 greatness (6·24) 152

פֹּה 31 here, hither (4·44) 805

הַאֲרִיךְ 33 to prolong (11·31·34) 73

Chapter 6

הַאֲרִיךְ   2 to prolong (11·31·34) 73

זָב   3 to flow (6·29·29) 264

חָלָב   milk (8·44) 316

שנן   7 to teach incisively (1·1·9) 1041

קָשַׁר   8 to bind, confine (2·36·44) 905

טוֹטָפֹת   bands (2·3) 377

מְזוּזָה   9 doorpost (2·20) 265

טוֹב 11 good things, goods, property (2·32) 375

חָצֵב to hew out, dig (3·14·17) 345

זַיִת olive, olive tree (5·38) 268

קַנָּא 15 jealous (3·6) 888

נִסָּה 16 to test (8·36·36) 650

עֵדָה 17 testimony (3·32) 730

הָדַף 19 to thrust out (2·11·11) 213

עֵדָה 20 testimony (3·32) 730

מוֹפֵת 22 sign (9·36) 68

פֹּה 28 here, hither (4·44) 805

Chapter 7

נָשַׁל 1 to clear away (4·6·7) 675

עָצוּם mighty [strong] (6·31) 783

הֶחֱרִים 2 to devote to destruction (6·46·49) 355

הִתְחַתֵּן 3 to form a marriage alliance with (1·11·11) 368

נָתַץ 5 to tear down (1·31·42) 683

מַצֵּבָה pillar (3·35) 663

אֲשֵׁרָה a sacred pole, symbol of Canaanite goddess (3·40) 81

גִּדֵּעַ to hew down (2·9·22) 154

פָּסִיל idol, image (3·23) 820

סְגֻלָּה 6 property (3·8) 688

רבב 7 to be, become many (1·23·24) 912

חָשַׁק to love (3·8·11) 365

שְׁבוּעָה 8 oath (1·30) 989

אֹהֵב 9 friend (2·36[?]) 36

שֹׂנֵא 10 enemy (9·41) 971

אָחַר keep back, bring late (2·15·17) 29

עֵקֶב 12 because of (2·15) 784

דָּגָן 13 grain (7·40) 186

תִּירוֹשׁ fresh or new wine (7·38) 440

יִצְהָר fresh oil (6·23) 844

שֶׁגֶר offspring, young [of beasts] (4·5) 993

אֶלֶף cattle (4·8) 48

עַשְׁתָּרוֹת ewes, young (4·4) 300

עָקָר 14 barren (1·11) 785

חֳלִי 15 sickness (3·24) 318

מַדְוֶה sickness (2·2) 188

שֹׂנֵא enemy (9·41) 971

חוס 16 to pity (5·24·24) 299

מוֹקֵשׁ lure (1·27) 430

אֵיכָה 17 in what manner (5·18) 32

מַסָּה 19 trial (3·3) 650

מוֹפֵת sign (9·36) 68

צִרְעָה 20 hornets (1·3) 864

ערץ 21 to tremble (4·11·14) 792

נוֹרָא dreadful (6·44) 431

נָשַׁל 22 to clear away (4·6·7) 675

אֵל these (3·10) 41

הום to discomfit (1·1·6) 223

מְהוּמָה 23 discomfiture (2·12) 223

הִתְיַצֵּב 24 to hold one's ground, to take one's stand (5·48·48) 426

בִּפְנֵי in the face of (5·17) 816

פָּסִיל 25 idol, image (3·23) 820

חמד to desire (2·16·21) 326

נוקש to be ensnared (1·4·8) 430

חֵרֶם 26 ban, devoted thing (3·29) 356

שִׁקֵּץ to detest (1·6·6) 1055

תעב to regard as an abomination, abhor (3·14·21) 1073

Chapter 8

נִסָּה 2 to test (8·36·36) 650

הִרְעִיב 3 to allow to be hungry (1·2·14) 944

מָן manna (2·14) 577

מוֹצָא that which goes forth [of mouth, i.e., utterance] (2·27) 425

שִׂמְלָה 4 wrapper, mantle (6·29) 971

בלה become old and worn out (3·11·16) 115

בָּצֵק to swell, blister (1·2·2) 130

יָסַר 5 to discipline (5·30·41) 415

תְּהוֹם 7 deep, sea, abyss (2·36) 1062

בִּקְעָה valley, plain (3·19) 132

חִטָּה 8 wheat (2·30) 334

שְׂעֹרָה barley (1·34) 972

תְּאֵנָה fig tree, fig (1·39) 1061

רִמּוֹן pomegranate (1·32) 941

זַיִת olive, olive tree (5·38) 268

מִסְכֵּן 9 poverty (1·1) 587

חָסֵר to lack, decrease (3·20·24) 341

חָצֵב to hew out, dig (3·14·17) 345

נוֹרָא 15 dreadful (6·44) 431

נָחָשׁ serpent (1·31) 638

שָׂרָף fiery serpent (1·7) 977

עַקְרָב scorpion (1·9) 785

צִמָּאוֹ thirsty ground (1·3) 855

חַלָּמִישׁ flint (2·5) 321

מָן 16 manna (2·14) 577

נָסָה to test (8·36·36) 650

עֹצֶם might (1·4) 782

הֵעִיד 19 to testify (5·39·44) 729

עֵקֶב 20 because of (2·15) 784

Chapter 9

עָצוּם 1 mighty [strong] (6·31) 783

בָּצוּר made inaccessible, fortified (4·25) 130

רָם 2 high, i.e., tall (7·31[?]) 926

הִתִיצֵּב to hold one's ground, take one's stand (3·48·48) 426

הִכְנִיעַ 3 to subdue (1·11·36) 488

הָדַף 4 to thrust out (2·11·11) 213

רִשְׁעָה wickedness (3·15) 958

יֹשֶׁר rightness, uprightness (1·14) 449

רִשְׁעָה wickedness (3·15) 958

קָשֶׁה 6 stiff, stubborn (4·36) 904

עֹרֶף neck (4·33) 791

הִקְצִיף 7 to provoke to wrath (3·5·34) 893

לְמִן from (2·14) 583

הִמְרָה to show rebelliousness (6·22·43) 598

הִקְצִיף 8 to provoke to wrath (3·5·34) 893

הִתְאַנַּף to be angry (4·6·14) 60

לוּחַ 9 tablet (16·40) 531

לוּחַ 10 tablet (16·40) 531

אֶצְבַּע finger (1·31) 840

לוּחַ 11 tablet (16·40) 531

מַסֵּכָה 12 molten image (3·25) 651

קָשֶׁה 13 stiff, stubborn (4·36) 904

עֹרֶף neck (4·33) 791

הַרְפֵּה 14 to refrain, let alone (4·21·44) 951

מָחָה to blot out (3·22·25) 562

עָצוּם mighty [strong] (6·31) 783

לוּחַ 15 tablet (16·40) 531

עֵגֶל 16 calf (2·35) 722

מַסֵּכָה molten metal (3·25) 651

לוּחַ 17 tablet (16·40) 531

יָגֹר 19 to be afraid (2·5·5) 388

קָצַף to be wroth (2·28·34) 893

הִתְאַנַּף 20 be angry (4·6·14) 60

עֵגֶל 21 calf (2·35) 722

כָּתַת to crush (1·5·17) 510

טָחַן to grind (1·7·7) 377

דָּקַק to crush, thresh (1·4·13) 200

הִקְצִיף 22 to provoke to wrath (3·5·34) 893

הִמְרָה 23 to show rebelliousness (6·22·43) 598

הִמְרָה 24 to show rebelliousness (6·22·43) 598

גֹּדֶל 26 greatness (6·14) 152

קְשִׁי 27 stubborness (1·1) 904

רֶשַׁע wickedness (1·30) 957

מִבְּלִי 28 from want of (2·25) 115

שִׂנְאָה hating, hatred (2·17) 971

Chapter 10

פֶּסֶל	1 to hew out (2·6·6) 820	
לוּחַ	tablet (16·40) 531	
לוּחַ	2 tablet (16·40) 531	
שִׁטִּים	3 acacia (1·28) 1008	
פֶּסֶל	to hew out (2·6·6) 820	
לוּחַ	tablet (16·40) 531	
לוּחַ	4 tablet (16·40) 531	
מִכְתָּב	writing (3·9) 508	
לוּחַ	5 tablet (16·40) 531	
כֹּהֵן	6 to act as priest (1·23·23) 464	
הִבְדִּיל	8 to separate, make a distinction between (6·32·42) 95	
מַסָּע	11 journey (1·12) 652	
הֵנָּה = הֵן	14	
חָשַׁק	15 to love (3·8·11) 365	
מוּל	16 to circumcise (2·12·29) 557	
עָרְלָה	foreskin (1·16) 790	
עֹרֶף	16 neck (4·33) 791	
הִקְשָׁה	to make stiff, stubborn (2·21·28) 904	
נוֹרָא	17 dreadful (6·44) 431	
שֹׁחַד	bribe (4·23) 1005	
יָתוֹם	18 orphan (11·42) 450	
שִׂמְלָה	wrapper, mantle (6·29) 971	
נוֹרָא	21 dreadful, wonderful thing (6·44) 431	
כּוֹכָב	22 star (4·37) 456	

Chapter 11

מוּסָר	2 correction (1·50) 416	
גֹּדֶל	greatness (6·14) 152	
הֵצִיף	4 to cause to overflow (1·2·3) 847	
פָּצָה	6 to part, open (1·15·15) 822	
בָּלַע	to swallow up, engulf (1·20·41) 118	
יְקוּם	substance (1·3) 879	
הֶאֱרִיךְ	9 to prolong (11·31·34) 73	

זָב	to flow (6·29·29) 264	
חָלָב	milk (8·44) 316	
גַּן	10 garden, enclosure (1·41) 171	
יָרָק	herbage (1·3) 438	
בִּקְעָה	11 valley, plain (3·19) 132	
מָטָר	rain (6·37) 564	
מָטָר	14 rain (6·37) 564	
יוֹרֶה	early rain (1·2) 435	
מַלְקוֹשׁ	later rain (1·8) 545	
דָּגָן	grain (7·40) 186	
תִּירוֹשׁ	fresh or new wine (7·38) 440	
יִצְהָר	fresh oil (6·23) 844	
עֵשֶׂב	15 herb, herbage (3·33) 793	
פָּתָה	16 to be enticed, deceived (1·5·27) 834	
עָצַר	17 to restrain, refrain (2·36·46) 783	
מָטָר	rain (6·37) 564	
יְבוּל	produce (2·13) 385	
מְהֵרָה	quickly, hastily (1·20) 555	
קָשַׁר	18 to bind, confine (2·36·44) 905	
טוֹטָפוֹת	bands (2·3) 377	
מְזוּזָה	20 doorpost (2·20) 265	
עָצוּם	23 mighty [strong] (6·31) 783	
הִתְיַצֵּב	25 to hold one's ground, take one's stand (5·48·48) 426	
בִּפְנֵי	in the face of (5·17) 816	
פַּחַד	dread (3·49) 808	
מוֹרָא	fear (4·12) 432	
קְלָלָה	26 curse (11·33) 887	
קְלָלָה	28 curse (11·33) 887	
קְלָלָה	29 curse (11·33) 887	
מוּל	30 in front of (5·25) 557	
אֵלוֹן	terebinth, tall tree (1·10) 18	
מוֹרֶה	teacher (1·9) 435	

Chapter 12

רָם	2 high, lifted, exalted (7·31[?]) 926	
רַעֲנָן	luxuriant, fresh (1·19) 947	

נָתַץ 3 to tear down (1·6·42) 683

מַצֵּב pillar (3·35) 663

אֲשֵׁר a tree, symbol of Canaanite goddess (3·40) 81

פְּסִיל idol, image (3·23) 820

גָּדַע to hew down (2·9·22) 154

מַעֲשֵׂר 6 tithe (7·31) 798

נְדָבָה freewill offering (4·27) 621

מִשְׁל 7 outstretching (6·7) 1020

פֹּה 8 here, hither (4·44) 805

מָנוֹחַ 9 resting-place (1·21) 629

בֶּטַח 10 securely (3·43) 105

מַעֲשֵׂר 11 tithe (7·31) 798

מִבְחָר choicest, best (1·12) 104

נָדַר to vow (5·30·30) 623

אַוָּה 15 desire, will (4·7) 16

צְבִי gazelle (4·11) 840

אַיָּל hart, deer (4·11) 19

מַעֲשֵׂר 17 tithe (7·31) 798

דָּגָן grain (7·40) 186

תִּירוֹשׁ fresh or new wine (7·38) 440

יִצְהָר fresh oil (6·23) 844

נָדַר to vow (5·30·30) 623

נְדָבָה freewill offering (4·27) 621

מִשְׁל 18 outstretching (6·7) 1020

הִרְחִיב 20 to enlarge (3·21·25) 931

אַוָּה to desire (2·11·27) 16

אַוָּה desire, will (4·7) 16

אַוָּה 21 desire, will (4·7) 16

צְבִי 22 gazelle (4·11) 840

אַיָּל hart, deer (4·11) 19

נקשׁ 30 to be thrust (1·1·5) 669

אֵיכָה in what manner (5·18) 32

Chapter 13

גרע 1 to diminish (2·14·22) 175

חלם 2 to dream (3·26·28) 321

מוֹפֵת sign (9·36) 68

מוֹפֵת 3 sign (9·36) 68

חלם 4 to dream (3·26·28) 321

נִסָּה to test (8·36·36) 650

חלם 6 to dream (3·26·28) 321

סָרָה apostasy (2·7) 694

הִדִּיחַ to thrust away (4·27·43) 623

הֵסִית 7 to instigate (1·18·18) 694

בֵּעֵר to consume (12·26·28[?]) 129

חֵיק fold of garment at breast (5·38) 300

סֵתֶר 7 secrecy (4·35) 712

חוּס 9 to pity (5·24·24) 299

חָמַל to spare (1·40·40) 328

בִּגְלַל 10 on account of (3·10) 164

סקל 11 to stone (4·12·22) 709

הִדִּיחַ to thrust away (4·27·43) 623

בְּלִיַּעַל 14 worthlessness (2·27) 116

הִדִּיחַ to thrust away (4·27·43) 623

חקר 15 to search [for] (1·22·27) 350

הֶחֱרִים 16 to devote to destruction (6·46·49) 355

רְחוֹב 17 broad open place, plaza (1·43) 932

כָּלִיל whole offering (2·15) 483

תֵּל mound (1·5) 1068

מְאוּמָה 18 anything (2·32) 548

חֵרֶם ban, devoted thing (3·29) 356

חָרוֹן [burning of] anger (1·41) 354

רַחֲמִים compassion (1·38) 933

רְחַם to have compassion (2·41·46) 933

Chapter 14

הִתְגֹּדֵד 1 to cut oneself (1·7·8) 151

קָרְחָה baldness, bald spot [made in mourning] (1·11) 901

סְגֻלָּה 2 property (3·8) 688

שֶׂה 4 sheep, goat (5·44) 961

כֶּשֶׂב lamb (1·13) 461

אַיָּל 5 hart, deer (4·11) 19

צְבִי gazelle (4·11) 840

יַחְמוּר	roebuck (1 · 2) 331	
אַקּוֹ	wild goat (1 · 1) 70	
דִּישֹׁן	a clean animal, antelope[?] (1 · 1) 190	
תְּאוֹ	antelope (1 · 2) 1060	
זֶמֶר	an animal allowed as food, probably mountain sheep (1 · 1) 275	
הִפְרִיס	6 to divide (4 · 12 · 14) 828	
פַּרְסָה	hoof (5 · 21) 828	
שׁסע	to divide, cleave (2 · 5 · 8) 1042	
שֶׁסַע	cleft (1 · 4) 1043	
גֵּרָה	cud (4 · 11) 176	
גֵּרָה	7 cud (4 · 11) 176	
הִפְרִיס	to divide (4 · 12 · 14) 828	
פַּרְסָה	hoof (5 · 21) 828	
שׁסע	to divide, cleave (2 · 5 · 8) 1042	
אַרְנֶבֶת	hare (1 · 2) 58	
שָׁפָן	rock badger (1 · 4) 1050	
חֲזִיר	8 swine (1 · 7) 306	
הִפְרִיס	to divide (4 · 12 · 14) 828	
פַּרְסָה	hoof (5 · 21) 828	
גֵּרָה	cud (4 · 11) 176	
נְבֵלָה	corpse (4 · 48) 615	
סְנַפִּיר	9 fin (2 · 5) 703	
קַשְׂקֶשֶׂת	scale [of fish] (2 · 8) 903	
סְנַפִּיר	10 fin (2 · 5) 703	
קַשְׂקֶשֶׂת	scale [of fish] (2 · 8) 903	
צִפּוֹר	11 bird[s] (3 · 40) 861	
נֶשֶׁר	12 eagle (3 · 26) 676	
פֶּרֶס	bearded vulture (1 · 2) 828	
עָזְנִיָּה	unclean bird of prey (1 · 2) 740	
רָאָה	13 bird of prey, perhaps kite (1 · 1) 178	
אַיָּה	hawk, falcon, kite (1 · 3) 17	
דַּיָּה	a bird of prey (1 · 1) 178	
מִין	species (4 · 31) 568	
עֹרֵב	14 raven (1 · 12) 788	
מִין	species (4 · 31) 568	
יַעֲנָה	15 ostrich (1 · 8) 419	

תַּחְמָס	male ostrich (1 · 2) 329	
שַׁחַף	sea mew, gull (1 · 2) 1006	
נֵץ	bird of prey (1 · 3) 665	
מִין	species (4 · 31) 568	
כּוֹס	16 a kind of owl (1 · 3) 468	
יַנְשׁוּף	a bird (1 · 3) 676	
תִּנְשֶׁמֶת	unclean bird (1 · 2) 675	
קָאָת	17 bird, usually a pelican (1 · 5) 866	
רָחָמָה	carrion vulture (1 · 2) 934	
שָׁלָךְ	cormorant (1 · 2) 1021	
חֲסִידָה	18 stork (1 · 6) 339	
אֲנָפָה	an unclean bird (1 · 2) 60	
מִין	species (4 · 31) 568	
דּוּכִיפַת	an unclean bird (1 · 2) 189	
עֲטַלֵּף	bat (1 · 3) 742	
שֶׁרֶץ	19 swarmers, swarming things (1 · 15) 1056	
נְבֵלָה	21 corpse (4 · 48) 615	
נָכְרִי	foreigner (5 · 45) 648	
בִּשֵּׁל	to boil (2 · 20 · 27) 143	
גְּדִי	kid (1 · 16) 152	
חָלָב	milk (8 · 44) 316	
עִשֵּׂר	22 to give tithe (2 · 5 · 9) 797	
תְּבוּאָה	product, yield (6 · 43) 100	
מַעֲשֵׂר	23 tithe (7 · 31) 798	
דָּגָן	grain (7 · 40) 186	
תִּירוֹשׁ	fresh or new wine (7 · 38) 440	
יִצְהָר	fresh oil (6 · 23) 844	
צוּר	25 to confine, secure (3 · 31 · 31) 848	
אִוָּה	26 to desire (2 · 11 · 27) 16	
שֵׁכָר	intoxicating drink, strong drink (2 · 23) 1016	
מַעֲשֵׂר	28 tithe (7 · 31) 798	
תְּבוּאָה	product, yield (6 · 43) 100	
יָתוֹם	29 orphan (11 · 42) 450	

Chapter 15

שְׁמִטָּה	1 a letting drop [of exactions], a remitting (5 · 5) 1030	

שֶׁמֶט	2	a letting drop [of exactions], a remitting (5·5) 1030
שמט		to let drop, fall (1·7·9) 1030
מַשֵּׁה		loan (1·1) 674
נגשׂ		to exact (2·4·7) 620
נָכְרִי	3	foreigner (5·45) 648
נגשׂ		to exact (2·4·7) 620
השׁמ		to cause to let drop (1·1·9) 1030
אֶפֶס	4	אֶפֶס כִּי save that, howbeit (3·43) 67
העבי	6	to cause to give pledge (3·3·5) 716
עבט		to give pledge (2·2·5) 716
אמץ	7	to harden, make obstinate (3·19·41) 54
קָפַץ		to draw together, shut (1·5·7) 891
העבי	8	to lend (3·3·5) 716
דַּי		sufficiency, enough for (1·12) 191
מַחְסֹ		need (1·13) 341
חָסֵר		to lack, decrease (3·20·24) 341
בְּלִיַּע	9	worthlesness (2·27) 116
שְׁמִטָּ		a letting drop [of exactions], a remitting (5·5) 1030
חֵטְא		sin, guilt of sin (8·33) 307
בִּגְלַל	10	on account of (3·10) 164
מִשְׁלַ		outstretching (6·7) 1020
חָפְשִׁי	12	free (3·17) 344
חָפְשׁ	13	free (3·17) 344
רֵיקָם		in empty condition, empty (2·16) 938
הַעֲנִי	14	to make a necklace (2·2·3) 778
גֹּרֶן		threshing floor (2·34) 175
יֶקֶב		wine vat (2·16) 248
מַרְצֵעַ	17	awl (1·2) 954
קשׁה	18	to be hard, severe (2·5·28) 904
חָפְשִׁי		free (3·17) 344
מִשְׁנֶה		double (2·35) 1041
שָׂכָר		hire, wages (2·29) 969
שָׂכִיר		hireling, hired laborer (2·18) 969
גָּזַז	19	to shear (1·14·15) 159

מוּם	21	defect (4·21[?]) 548
פִּסֵּחַ		lame (1·14) 820
עִוֵּר		blind (3·25) 734
צְבִי	22	gazelle (4·11) 840
אַיָּל		hart, deer (4·11) 19

Chapter 16

אָבִיב	1	month of ear forming or growing (2·8) 1
פֶּסַח		passover (4·49) 820
פֶּסַח	2	passover (4·49) 820
חָמֵץ	3	that which is leavened (1·11) 329
עֳנִי		affliction (2·36) 777
חִפָּזוֹן		hurried flight (1·3) 342
שְׂאֹר	4	leaven (1·5) 959
פֶּסַח	5	passover (4·49) 820
פֶּסַח	6	passover (4·49) 820
בּשׁל	7	to boil (2·20·27) 143
עֲצֶרֶת	8	assembly (1·11) 783
שָׁבוּעַ	9	week (4·20) 988
חֶרְמֵשׁ		sickle (2·2) 357
קָמָה		standing grain (3·10) 879
שָׁבוּעַ	10	week (4·20) 988
מִסָּה		sufficiency (1·1) 588
נְדָבָה		freewill offering (4·27) 621
יָתוֹם	11	orphan (11·42) 450
סֻכָּה	13	booth (3·31) 697
גֹּרֶן		threshing floor (2·34) 175
יֶקֶב		wine vat (2·16) 428
יָתוֹם	14	orphan (11·42) 450
חגג	15	to keep a pilgrim feast (1·16·16) 290
תְּבוּאָה		product, yield (6·43) 100
שָׂמֵחַ		glad, joyful, merry (1·21) 970
זָכוּר	16	male (2·4) 271
שָׁבוּעַ		week (4·20) 988
סֻכָּה		booth (3·31) 697
רֵיקָם		empty (2·16) 938

מַתָּנָה 17 gift (1·17) 682

שֹׁטֵר 18 official, officer (7·25) 1009

הִכִּיר 19 to regard (4·37·40) 647

שֹׁחַד bribe (4·23) 1005

עִוֵּר to make blind (1·5·5) 734

סלף to pervert (1·7·7) 701

אֲשֵׁרָה 21 a sacred tree, pole symbol of
Canaanite goddess (3·40) 81

מַצֵּבָה 22 pillar (3·35) 663

Chapter 17

שֶׂה 1 sheep, goat (5·44) 961

מוּם defect (4·21[?]) 548

יָרֵחַ 3 moon (2·27) 437

סקל 5 to stone (4·12·22) 509

בָּעַר 7 to consume (12·26·28) 129

נפלא 8 to be too difficult for (2·13·24) 810

דִּין judgement (1·19) 192

הורה 10 to teach (4·45[?]·45[?]) 434

הורה 11 to teach (4·45[?]·45[?]) 434

זָדוֹן 12 proudly, pride (2·20) 267

בָּעַר 13 to consume (12·26·28) 129

הזיד to act presumptuously (3·8·10) 267

נָכְרִי 15 foreign (5·48) 648

מִשְׁנֶה 18 copy (2·35) 1041

הֶאֱרִיךְ 20 to prolong (11·31·34) 73

Chapter 18

שֶׂה 3 sheep, goat (5·44) 961

קֵבָה stomach, belly (1·2) 867

דָּגָן 4 grain (7·40) 186

תִּירוֹשׁ fresh or new wine (7·38) 440

יִצְהָר fresh oil (6·23) 844

גֵּז shearing (1·4) 159

אַוָּה 6 desire, will (4·7) 16

מִמְכָּר 8 sale (7·10) 569

קֹסֵם 10 to practice divination (1·11·11) 890

קֶסֶם divination (1·11) 890

עוֹנֵן to practice soothsaying (2·10·11) 778

נחֵשׁ to practice divination (1·9·9) 638

כִּשֵּׁף to practice sorcery (1·6·6) 506

חבר 11 to tie magic knots, charm (1·11·28) 287

חֶבֶר spell, company (1·7) 288

אוֹב necromancer (1·6) 15

יִדְּעֹנִי familiar spirit (1·11) 396

בִּגְלַל 12 on account of (2·9) 164

עוֹנֵן 14 to practice soothsaying (2·10·11) 778

קֹסֵם false prophet (1·9) 890

הזיד 20 to act presumptuously (3·8·10) 267

אֵיכָה 21 in what manner (5·18) 32

זָדוֹן 22 proudly, pride (2·10[?]) 267

יגר to be afraid (2·5·5) 388

or

גור to dread, be afraid of (3·10·10) 158

Chapter 19

הִבְדִּיל 2 to separate, make a distinction between (6·32·42) 95

שִׁלֵּשׁ 3 to do a third time, divide into three parts (1·4·9) 1026

רָצַח to murder, slay (7·38·43) 953

רָצַח 4 to murder, slay (7·38·43) 953

בִּבְלִי without (2·5) 115

שֹׂנֵא enemy (9·41) 971

תְּמוֹל aforetime (3·23) 1069

שִׁלְשׁוֹם aforetime, previously (3·25) 1026

חטב 5 to cut or gather wood (1·2·3) 310

נדח to be impelled (4·13·43) 623

גַּרְזֶן axe (2·4) 173

נָשַׁל to drop off (4·6·7) 675

גֹּאֵל 6 kinsman (2·44[?]) 145

רָצַח to murder, slay (7·38·43) 953

חמם to be or grow warm (1·23·26) 328

114

הִשִּׂיג	to overtake (4·48·48) 673	
שׂנֵא	enemy (9·41) 971	
תְּמוֹל	aforetime (3·23) 1069	
שִׁלְשׁ	aforetime, previously (3·25) 1026	
הִבְדִּיל	7 to separate, make a distinction between (6·32·42) 95	
הִרְחִ	to enlarge (3·21·25) 931	
נָקִי	10 exempt (6·43) 667	
שׂנֵא	11 enemy (9·41) 971	
אָרַב	to lie in wait (1·20·23) 70	
גֹּאֵל	12 kinsman (2·44[?]) 145	
אֵל	these (3·10) 41	
חוס	13 to pity (5·24·24) 299	
נָקִי	exempt (6·43) 667	
בָּעֵר	to consume (12·26·28) 129	
הִסִּיג	14 to displace (2·7·19) 690	
גְּבֻל	to bound, border (1·3·5) 148	
חֵטְא	15 sin, guilt of sin (8·33) 307	
סָרָה	16 defection (2·7[?]) 694	
זָמַם	19 to purpose, devise (1·13·13) 273	
בָּעֵר	to consume (12·26·28) 129	
חוס	21 to pity (5·24·24) 299	

Chapter 20

קָרֵב	3 approaching (1·11) 898	
רכך	to be timid, fearful (1·6·8) 939	
חפז	to be alarmed (1·6·10) 342	
ערץ	to tremble (4·11·14) 792	
שׁטֵר	5 official, officer (7·25) 1009	
חנך	to dedicate (2·5·5) 335	
אֵרַשׂ	7 to betroth (2·6·11) 76	
שׁטֵר	8 official, officer (7·25) 1009	
יָרֵא	fearing (1·45) 431	
רַך	tender, delicate, soft (3·16) 940	
נָמֵס	to melt (1·19·21) 587	
שׁטֵר	9 official, officer (7·25) 1009	
מַס	11 slave gangs (1·23) 586	
צור	12 to shut in, besiege (3·31·31) 848	

זָכוּר	13 male (2·4) 271	
טַף	14 children (7·41) 381	
בָּזַז	to plunder (3·37·40) 102	
נְשָׁמָה	16 breathing things (1·24) 675	
הֶחֱרִים	17 to devote to destruction (6·46·49) 355	
צור	19 to shut in, besiege (3·31·31) 848	
נדח	to impel (1·1·43) 623	
גַּרְזֶן	axe (2·4) 173	
מָצוֹר	siege (5·25) 848	
מַאֲכָל	20 food (2·30) 38	
מָצוֹר	siege works (5·25) 848	

Chapter 21

עֶגְלָה	3 heifer (4·12) 722	
מָשַׁךְ	to draw (1·30·36) 604	
עֹל	yoke (2·40) 760	
עֶגְלָה	4 heifer (4·12) 722	
אֵיתָן	ever-flowing, permanent (1·14) 450	
ערף	to break the neck (2·6·6) 791	
עֶגְלָה	heifer (4·12) 722	
ערף	to break the neck (2·6·6) 791	
נָקִי	8 exempt (6·43) 667	
בָּעֵר	9 to consume (12·26·28) 129	
נָקִי	exempt (6·43) 667	
שָׁבָה	10 to take captive (1·29·37) 985	
שְׁבִי	captive (3·46) 985	
שִׁבְיָה	11 captives (2·9) 986	
יָפֶה	beautiful (1·40) 421	
תֹּאַר	outline, form (1·15) 1061	
חָשַׁק	to love (3·8·11) 365	
גִּלַּח	12 to shave (1·18·23) 164	
צִפֹּרֶן	fingernail (1·2) 862	
שִׂמְלָה	13 wrapper, mantle (6·29) 971	
שְׁבִי	captivity, captive (3·46) 985	
יֶרַח	month (2·12) 437	
בָּעַל	to marry (2·10·12) 127	
הִתְעַמֵּר	14 to deal tyrannically (2·2·2) 771	

שָׂנִיא	15 hated, held in aversion (1·1) 971
בכר	16 to constitute as firstborn (1·2·4) 114
הִכִּיר	17 to acknowledge (4·37·40) 647
אוֹן	manly vigour (1·10) 20
בְּכֹרָה	right of first-born (1·10) 114
סרר	18 to be stubborn (2·16·16) 710
מָרָה	to be rebellious (2·21·43) 598
יִסֵּר	to discipline (5·30·41) 415
סרר	20 to be stubborn (2·16·16) 710
מָרָה	to be rebellious (2·21·43) 598
זָלַל	squandering (1·6[?]) 272
סֹבֵא	drunkard (1·3) 684
רגם	21 to kill by stoning, to stone (1·15·15) 920
בָּעֵר	to consume (12·26·28) 129
חֵטְא	22 sin, guilt of sin (8·33) 307
תָּלָה	22 to execute by hanging (2·23·27) 1067
נְבֵלָה	23 corpse (4·48) 615
תָּלָה	to execute by hanging (2·23·27) 1067
קְלָלָה	curse (11·33) 887

Chapter 22

שֶׂה	1 sheep, goat (5·44) 961
נדח	to be driven away (4·13·43) 623
הִתְעַלֵּם	to hide oneself (3·6·29) 761
שִׂמְלָה	3 wrapper, mantle (6·29) 971
אֲבֵדָה	a lost thing (1·4) 2
הִתְעַלֵּם	to hide oneself (3·6·29) 761
הִתְעַלֵּם	4 to hide oneself (3·6·29) 761
שִׂמְלָה	5 wrapper, mantle (6·29) 971
קַן	6 nest (2·13) 890
צִפּוֹר	bird[s] (3·40) 861
אֶפְרֹחַ	young one (2·4) 827
בֵּיצָה	egg (2·6) 101
רָבַץ	to stretch oneself out, lie down (3·24·30) 918

הַאֲרִיךְ	7 to prolong (11·31·34) 73
מַעֲקֶה	8 parapet (1·1) 785
גָּג	roof (1·29) 150
כִּלְאַיִם	9 two kinds (1·4) 476
תְּבוּאָה	product, yield (6·43) 100
חרש	10 to plow (1·21·24) 360
שַׁעַטְנֵז	11 mixed stuff (1·2) 1043
צֶמֶר	wool (1·16) 856
פֵּשֶׁת	flax, linen (1·16) 833
גָּדִל	12 tassel (1·2) 153
כְּסוּת	covering (1·8) 492
עֲלִילָה	14 wantonness (2·24) 760
בְּתוּלִים	tokens of virginity (5·10) 144
בְּתוּלִים	15 tokens of virginity (5·10) 144
עֲלִילָה	17 wantonness (2·24) 760
בְּתוּלִים	tokens of virginity (5·10) 144
שִׂמְלָה	[bed]covering (6·29) 971
יִסֵּר	18 to discipline (5·30·41) 415
עָנַשׁ	19 to fine, punish (1·6·9) 778
בְּתוּלָה	virgin (4·50) 143
בְּתוּלִים	20 tokens of virginity (5·10) 144
סקל	21 to stone (4·12·22) 709
נְבָלָה	disgraceful folly (1·13) 615
בָּעֵר	to consume (12·26·28) 129
בְּעוּלָה	22 married woman (1·4[?]) 127
בָּעֵר	to consume (12·26·28) 129
בְּתוּלָה	23 virgin (4·50) 143
ארש	to be betrothed (4·5·11) 76
סקל	24 to stone (4·12·12) 709
בָּעֵר	to consume (12·26·28) 129
ארש	25 to be betrothed (4·5·11) 76
חֵטְא	26 sin, guilt of sin (8·33) 307
רָצַח	to murder, slay (7·38·43) 953
ארש	27 to be betrothed (4·5·11) 76
מוֹשִׁיעַ	savior (3·27) 446
בְּתוּלָה	28 virgin (4·50) 143
ארש	to be betrothed (4·5·11) 76

Chapter 23

פָּצַ֫ 2 to wound, wound by bruising (1·3·3) 822

דַּכָּ crushing (1·1) 194

שָׁפְכָ male organ (1·1) 1050

מַמְזֵ 3 bastard (1·2) 561

קִדֵּ 5 to come to meet (1·24·26) 869

שָׂכַ to live (1·17·20) 968

קָלַל 6 curse (11·33) 887

תָּעַ 8 to regard as an abomination, abhor (3·14·21) 1073

קָרֶ 11 chance, accident (1·1) 899

יָתֵד 14 peg (1·24) 450

אָזֵן tools, implements (1·1) 24

חָפַ to search for (2·22·22) 343

צֵאָה filth, excrement (1·2) 844

הוֹנָ 17 oppress (1·14·18) 413

קָדֵשׁ 18 temple prostitute (2·11) 873

אֶתְנַ 19 hire of harlot (1·11) 1072

זוֹנָה harlot (1·33[?]) 275

מְחִיר hire (1·15) 564

כֶּ֫לֶב dog (1·32) 476

הִשָּׁ 20 to make one give interest (3·3·4) 675

נֶ֫שֶׁ interest (3·12) 675

אֹכֶל food (3·44) 38

נֶ֫שֶׁךְ אֹכֶל = usuary of food 38

נשׁך to give interest (1·1·4) 675

נָכְרִ 21 foreigner (5·45) 648

הַשֵּׁ to make one give interest (3·3·4) 675

מִשְׁ outstretching (6·7) 1020

נָדַר 22 to vow (5·30·30) 623

אָחַ to keep back, bring late (2·15·17) 29

חֵטְ sin, guilt of sin (8·33) 307

נָדַר 23 to vow (5·30·30) 623

חֵטְ sin, guilt of sin (8·33) 307

מוֹצָ 24 that which goes forth (2·27) 425

נָדַר to vow (5·30·30) 623

נְדָבָה voluntariness (4·27) 621

עֵנָב 25 grapes (4·19) 772

שֹׂבַע appetite, fill (1·8) 959

קָמָה 26 standing grain (3·10) 879

קָטַף to pluck off (1·4·5) 882

מְלִילָה ear of wheat (1·1) 576

חֶרְמֵשׁ sickle (2·2) 357

הֵנִיף to wield (2·32·34[?]) 631

Chapter 24

בָּעַל 1 to marry (2·10·12) 127

כְּרִיתוּת divorcement (2·4) 504

כְּרִיתוּת 3 divorcement (2·4) 504

נָקִי 5 exempt (6·43) 667

חבל 6 to bind by a pledge (3·11·12) 286

רֵחַיִם |hand|mill (1·5) 932

גנב 7 to steal, take by stealth (2·30·39) 170

הִתְעַמֵּר to deal tyrannically (2·2·2) 771

גַּנָּב thief (1·17) 170

בִּעֵר to consume (12·26·28) 129

צָרַ֫עַת 8 leprosy (1·35) 863

הוֹרָה to teach (4·45[?]·45[?]) 434

הִשָּׁה 10 to lend (2·2·11[?]) 674

מְאוּמָה anything (2·32) 548

עבט to take pledge [the thing pledged] (2·2·5) 716

עֲבוֹט pledge, article pledged (4·4) 716

נשׁה 11 to lend (1·9·11[?]) 674

עֲבוֹט pledge, article pledged (4·4) 716

עֲבוֹט 12 pledge, article pledged (4·4) 716

עֲבוֹט 13 pledge, article pledged (4·4) 716

שַׂלְמָה outer garment (2·16) 971

עָשַׁק 14 to oppress, wrong (3·36·37) 798

שָׂכִיר hireling, hired laborer (2·18) 969

שָׂכָר 15 hire, wages (2·29) 969

חֵטְא guilt of sin (8·33) 307

חֵטְא	16 guilt of sin (8·33) 307	

חֵטְא 16 guilt of sin (8·33) 307

יָתוֹם 17 orphan (11·42) 450

חבל to bind by a pledge (3·11·12) 286

קצר 19 to reap, harvest (1·24·24) 894

קָצִיר harvest (1·49) 894

עֹמֶר sheaf (1·8) 771

יָתוֹם orphan (11·12) 450

חבט 20 to beat off (1·4·5) 286

זַיִת olive, olive tree (5·38) 268

פאר to go over the boughs, glean (1·1·1) 802

יָתוֹם orphan (11·42) 450

בצר 21 to cut off |grapes| (1·7·7[?]) 130

עולל to glean (1·8·17) 760

יָתוֹם orphan (11·42) 450

Chapter 25

הצדיק to declare righteous, justify (1·12·41) 842

הרְשִׁיעַ to condemn as guilty (1·25·34) 957

כְּדֵי 2 according to the sufficiency, as much as it demands (1·5) 191

מַכָּה 3 plague (6·48) 642

נקְלָה to be lightly esteemed, dishonored (1·5·6) 885

חסם 4 to muzzle (1·2·2) 340

דָּשׁ to tread, thresh (1·12·15) 190

יָבָם 5 husband's brother (2·2) 386

יבם to do the duty of a husband's brother (2·3·3) 386

נמחה 6 to be blotted out (1·9·35) 562

יְבָמָה 7 sister in law (2·4) 386

מֵאֵן to refuse (1·45·45) 549

יָבָם husband's brother (2·2) 386

יבם to do the duty of a husband's brother (2·3·3) 386

בֵּאֵר 8 to make plain (2·3) 91

יְבָמָה 9 sister-in-law (2·4) 386

חָלַץ to draw, draw off (2·5·27) 322

יָרַק to spit (1·2·2) 439

בִּפְנֵי in the face of (5·17) 816

כָּכָה thus (2·34) 462

חָלַץ 10 to draw, draw off (2·5·27) 322

נַעַל sandal (3·22) 653

נצה 11 to struggle with each other (1·5· 663

מְבוּשִׁים privates (1·1) 102

קצץ 12 to cut off (1·4·14) 893

חוס to pity (5·24·24) 299

כִּיס 13 bag (1·5) 476

קָטָן small, small things (2·47) 881

אֵיפָה 14 ephah, measure or receptacle holdi an ephah (3·38) 35

קָטָן small, small things (2·47) 881

שָׁלֵם 15 complete, full, perfect (3·28) 1023

אֵיפָה ephah, measure or receptacle holdi an ephah (3·38) 35

הֶאֱרִיךְ to prolong (11·31·34) 73

עָוֶל 16 injustice, unrighteousness (2·21) 7

קרה 18 to encounter, meet (1·13·27) 899

זנב to cut off the tail, attack the rear (1·2·2) 275

נחשל to shatter (1·1·1) 365

עָיֵף faint, weary (1·17) 746

יָגֵעַ weary, warisome (1·3) 388

מחה 19 to blot out (3·22·35) 562

זֵכֶר remembrance (2·23) 271

Chapter 26

טֶנֶא 2 basket (4·4) 380

טֶנֶא 4 basket (4·4) 380

מַת 5 man (6·21) 607

עָצוּם 5 mighty |strong| (6·31) 783

קָשֶׁה 6 severe (4·36) 904

עֳנִי 7 affliction (2·36) 777

לַחַץ oppression (1·11) 537

מוֹרָא 8 awe-inspiring spectacle (4·12) 432

מוֹפֵת wonder (9·36) 68

זָב 9 to flow (6·29·29) 264

חָלָב milk (8·44) 316

הֶעְשִׂיר 12 to tithe (1·2·9) 797

מַעֲשֵׂר tithe (7·31) 798

תְּבוּאָה product, yield (6·43) 100

יָתוֹם orphan (11·42) 450

בָּעֵר 13 to consume (12·26·28) 129

יָתוֹם orphan (11·42) 450

אֹנִי 14 mourning[?] not in BDB (1·2)

בָּעֵר to consume (12·26·28) 129

הִשְׁקִיף 15 to over hang, look out and
down (1·12·22) 1054

מָעוֹן dwelling (1·18) 732

זָב to flow (6·29·29) 264

חָלָב milk (8·44) 316

סְגֻלָּה 18 property (3·8) 688

Chapter 27

שִׂיד 2 to whitewash (2·2·2) 966

שִׂיד lime, whitewash (2·4) 966

זָב 3 to flow (6·29·29) 264

חָלָב milk (8·44) 316

שִׂיד 4 to whitewash (2·2·2) 966

שִׂיד lime, whitewash (2·4) 966

הֵנִיף 5 to wield (2·32·34[?]) 631

שָׁלֵם 6 complete, full, perfect (3·28) 1023

בָּאֵר 8 to make plain (2·3·3) 91

הַסְכֵּת 9 to keep silence (1·1·1) 698

קְלָלָה 13 curse (11·33) 887

רָם 14 uplifted (7·31[?]) 926

פֶּסֶל 15 idol, image (5·31) 820

מַסֵּכָה molten image (3·25) 651

חָרָשׁ graver, artificer (1·38) 360

סֵתֶר secrecy (4·35) 712

אָמֵן truly (12·26) 53

הַקְלֶה 16 to treat with contempt, dishonor

(1·1·16) 885

אָמֵן truly (12·26) 53

הִסִּיג 17 to displace (2·7·19) 690

אָמֵן truly (12·26) 53

הִשְׁגָּה 18 to lead astray (1·4·21) 993

עִוֵּר blind (3·25) 734

אָמֵן truly (12·26) 53

יָתוֹם 19 orphan (11·42) 450

אָמֵן truly (12·26) 53

אָמֵן 20 truly (12·26) 53

אָמֵן 21 truly (12·26) 53

אָמֵן 22 truly (12·26) 53

חֹתֶנֶת 23 wife's mother (1·1[?]) 368

אָמֵן truly (12·26) 53

סֵתֶר 24 secrecy (4·35) 712

אָמֵן truly (12·26) 53

שֹׁחַד 25 bribe (4·23) 1005

נָקִי exempt (6·43) 667

אָמֵן truly (12·26) 53

אָמֵן 26 truly (12·26) 53

Chapter 28

הִשִּׂיג 2 to overtake (4·48·48) 673

שֶׁגֶר 4 offspring, young [of beasts] (4·5) 993

אֶלֶף cattle (4·8) 48

עַשְׁתָּרוֹת ewes, young (4·4) 800

טֶנֶא 5 basket (4·4) 380

מִשְׁאֶרֶת kneading trough (2·4) 602

נִגַּף 7 to be smitten (3·23·48) 619

אָסָם 8 storehouse (1·2) 62

מִשְׁלַח outstretching (6·7) 1020

מָטָר 12 rain (6·37) 564

הִלְוָה to lend (3·9·14) 531

לֹוה to borrow (1·5·14) 531

זָנָב 13 tail, end (2·11) 275

לְמַעְלָה upwards (1·34) 751

לְמַטָּה downwards (1·10) 641

קְלָלָה 15 curse (11·33) 887

הִשִּׂיג	to overtake (4·48·48) 673
טֶנֶא	17 basket (4·4) 380
מִשְׁאֶרֶת	kneading trough (2·4) 602
שֶׁגֶר	18 offspring, young [of beasts] (4·5) 993
אֶלֶף	cattle (4·8) 48
עַשְׁתְּרוֹת	ewes, young (4·4) 800
מְאֵרָה	20 curse (1·5) 73
מְהוּמָה	discomfiture (2·12) 223
מִגְעֶרֶת	rebuke (1·1) 172
מִשְׁלַח	outstretching (6·7) 1020
רֹעַ	evil, badness (1·19) 947
מַעֲלָל	practice (1·41) 760
דֶּבֶר	21 pestilence, plague (1·46) 184
שַׁחֶפֶת	22 consumption (1·2) 1006
קַדַּחַת	fever (1·2) 869
דַּלֶּקֶת	inflamation (1·1) 196
חַרְחֻר	violent heat, fever (1·1) 359
שִׁדָּפוֹן	smut (1·5) 995
יֵרָקוֹן	rust (1·6) 439
מָטָר	24 rain (6·37) 564
אָבָק	dust (1·6) 7
נִגָּף	25 to be smitten (3·23·48) 619
זַעֲוָה	terror, object of trembling (1·7) 266
נְבֵלָה	26 carcass (4·48) 615
מַאֲכָל	food (2·30) 38
הֶחֱרִיד	to drive in terror, rout an army (1·16·39) 353
שְׁחִין	27 boil (2·13) 1006
עֹפֶל	hemorrhoid (1·6) 779
גָּרָב	itch, scab (1·3) 173
חֶרֶס	an eruptive disease (1·1) 360
שִׁגָּעוֹן	28 madness (1·3) 993
עִוָּרוֹן	blindness (1·2) 734
תִּמָּהוֹן	bewilderment (1·2) 1069
מְשַׁשׁ	29 to grope (2·6·8[?]) 606
צָהֳרַיִם	midday, noon (1·23) 843
עִוֵּר	blind (3·25) 734
אֲפֵלָה	darkness (1·10) 66
עָשַׁק	to oppress, wrong (3·36·37) 798
גָּזַל	to seize, tear away (2·29·30) 159
מוֹשִׁיעַ	savior (3·27) 446
אָרַשׂ	30 to betroth (2·6·11) 76
שָׁגַל	to violate, ravish (1·1·4) 993
טָבַח	31 to slaughter (1·11·11) 370
גָּזַל	to seize, tear away (2·29·30) 159
מוֹשִׁיעַ	savior (3·27) 446
אֵל	32 strength, power (1·5) 43
יְגִיעַ	33 produce (1·16) 388
עָשַׁק	to oppress, wrong (3·36·37) 798
רָצַץ	to crush (1·11·19) 954
שֻׁגָּע	34 to be maddened (1·5·7) 993
שְׁחִין	35 boil (2·13) 1006
בֶּרֶךְ	knee (1·25) 139
שׁוֹק	leg (1·19) 1003
קָדְקֹד	scalp, hairy crown (3·11) 869
שַׁמָּה	37 appalment, horror (1·39) 1031
מָשָׁל	byword (1·39) 605
שְׁנִינָה	sharp [cutting] word, taunt (1·4) 1042
נָהַג	to lead off (2·10·30) 624
הֶחָסִיל	38 to consume (1·1·1) 340
אַרְבֶּה	locust (1·24) 916
אָגַר	39 to gather [food] (1·3·3) 8
תּוֹלֵעָה	worm, grub (1·41) 1069
זַיִת	40 olive, olive tree (5·38) 268
סוּךְ	to annoint oneself (1·8·9) 691
נָשַׁל	to drop off (4·6·7) 675
שְׁבִי	41 captivity (3·46) 985
צְלָצַל	42 whirring locust (1·2) 852
מַטָּה	43 downwards (2·3) 641
לוה	44 to borrow (1·5·14) 531
הלוה	to lend (3·9·14) 531
זָנָב	tail, end (2·11) 275
קְלָלָה	45 curse (11·33) 887
הִשִּׂיג	to overtake (4·48·48) 673
מוֹפֵת	46 wonder (9·36) 68

טוֹב 47 goodness [of heart], joy (2·32) 375

צָמָא 48 thirst (1·17) 854

עֵירֹם nakedness (1·10) 735

חֹסֶר want, lack (2·3) 341

עֹל yoke (2·40) 760

צַוָּאר neck, back of the neck (1·41) 848

דָּאָה 49 to fly swiftly (1·4·4) 178

נֶשֶׁר eagle (3·26) 676

עַז 50 strong, mighty, fierce (1·22) 738

דָּגָן 51 grain (7·40) 186

תִּירוֹשׁ fresh or new wine (7·38) 440

יִצְהָר fresh oil (6·23) 844

שֶׁגֶר offspring, young [of beasts] (4·5) 993

אֶלֶף cattle (4·8) 48

עַשְׁתְּ ewes, young (4·4) 800

גָּבֹהַ 52 high (2·41) 147

בָּצוּר made inaccessible, fortified (4·25) 130

מָצוֹר 53 siege (5·25) 848

מָצוֹק stress (3·6) 848

הֵצִיק to constrain, bring into straits (3·11·11) 847

רַךְ 54 tender, delicate, soft (3·16) 940

עָנֹג dainty (2·3) 772

חֵיק fold of the garment at the breast (3·38) 300

מִבְּלִי 55 from want of (2·25) 115

מָצוֹר siege (5·25) 848

מָצוֹק stress (3·6) 848

הֵצִיק to constrain, bring into straits (3·11·11) 847

רַךְ 56 tender, delicate, soft (3·16) 940

עָנֹג dainty (2·3) 772

נִסָּה to try (8·36·36) 650

הַצִּיג to set (1·5·16) 426

התע to be of dainty habit (1·9·10) 772

רֹךְ tenderness, delicacy (1·1) 940

חֵיק fold of the garment at the breast (3·38) 300

שִׁלְיָה 57 after birth (1·1) 1017

מִבֵּין from between (1·21) 107

חֹסֶר want, lack (2·3) 341

סֵתֶר secrecy (4·35) 712

מָצוֹר siege (5·25) 848

מָצוֹק stress (3·6) 848

הֵצִיק to constrain, bring into straits (3·11·11) 847

נוֹרָא 58 fearful (6·44) 431

הִפְלִיא 59 to do something exceptional, wonderful (1·10·24) 810

מַכָּה plague (6·48) 642

חֳלִי sickness (3·24) 318

מַדְוֶה 60 sickness (2·2) 188

יגר to be afraid (2·5·5) 388

חֳלִי 61 sickness (3·24) 318

מַכָּה plague (6·48) 642

הֶעֱלִים to conceal, hide (1·11·29) 761

מֵת 62 man (6·21) 607

כּוֹכָב star (4·37) 456

שׂוֹשׂ 63 to exult, display joy (4·26·26) 965

נסח to be torn away (1·1·4) 650

הִרְגִּיעַ 65 to rest, repose (1·8·13) 921

מָנוֹחַ resting place (1·7) 629

רֹגֶז quivering, quaking (1·1) 919

כִּלְיוֹן failing (1·2) 479

דְּאָבוֹן faintness (1·1) 178

תלא 66 to hang (1·3·3) 1067

מִנֶּגֶד in front (2·26) 617

פָּחַד to be in dread (2·23·26) 808

פַּחַד 67 dread (3·49) 808

פָּחַד to be in dread (2·23·26) 808

אֳנִיָּה 68 a ship (1·31) 58

קָנָה owner [as purchaser] (1·7) 888

מִלְּבַד 69 besides (2·33) 94

Chapter 29

מַסָּה	2 trial (3·3) 650
מוֹפֵת	wonder (9·36) 68
בלה	4 to become old and worn out (3·11·16) 115
שַׂלְמָה	clothes (2·16) 971
נַעַל	sandal (3·22) 653
שֵׁכָר	5 intoxicating drink, strong drink (2·23) 1016
שֹׁטֵר	9 official, officer (7·25) 1009
טַף	10 children (7·41) 381
חֹטֵב	cutter of wood (1·6[?]) 310
שֹׁאֵב	water drawer (1·5) 980
אָלָה	11 oath, curse (6·36) 46
אָלָה	13 oath, curse (6·36) 46
פֹּה	14 here, hither (4·44) 805
שִׁקּוּץ	16 detested thing (1·28) 1055
גִּלּוּל	idol (1·48) 165
שֹׁרֶשׁ	17 root (1·33) 1057
פרה	to be fruitful, bear fruit (1·22·29) 826
רֹאשׁ	bitter and poisonous herb (3·12) 912
לַעֲנָה	wormwood (1·8) 542
אָלָה	18 curse, oath (6·36) 46
שְׁרִירוּת	stubborness (1·10) 1057
ספה	18 to snatch away (1·8·18) 705
רָוֶה	watered (1·3) 924
צָמֵא	thirsty (1·9) 854
סלח	19 to forgive (1·33·46) 699
עָשַׁן	to smoke (1·6·6) 798
קִנְאָה	anger (1·43) 888
רָבַץ	to stretch oneself out, lie down (3·24·30) 918
אָלָה	curse, oath (6·36) 46
מָחָה	to blot out (3·22·35) 562
הִבְדִּיל	20 to separate, make a distinction

	between (6·32·42) 95
אָלָה	curse, oath (6·36) 46
נָכְרִי	21 foreigner (5·45) 648
מַכָּה	plague (6·48) 646
תַּחֲלֻאִים	diseases (1·5) 316
גָּפְרִית	22 brimstone, pitch (1·7) 172
מֶלַח	salt (2·28) 571
שְׂרֵפָה	burning (1·13) 977
הִצְמִיחַ	to cause to grow (1·14·33) 855
עֵשֶׂב	herb, herbage (3·33) 793
מַהְפֵּכָה	overthrow (1·6) 246
כָּכָה	23 thus (2·34) 462
חֳרִי	burning (1·6) 354
קְלָלָה	26 curse (11·33) 887
נָתַשׁ	27 to pull up (1·17·22) 684
קֶצֶף	wrath (1·29) 893

Chapter 30

קְלָלָה	1 curse (11·33) 887
הִדִּיחַ	to thrust out (4·27·43) 623
שְׁבוּת	3 captivity (1·26) 986
רִחַם	to have compassion (2·41·46) 933
נדח	4 to be thrust out (4·13·43) 623
מול	6 to circumcise (2·12·29) 557
אָלָה	7 curse, oath (6·36) 46
שֹׂנֵא	enemy (9·41) 971
שׂושׂ	9 to exult, display joy (4·26·26) 965
נפלא	11 to be too difficult for (2·13·24) 810
נדח	17 to be thrust aside (4·13·43) 623
הֶאֱרִיךְ	18 to prolong (11·31·34) 73
הֵעִיד	19 to call as witness (5·39·44) 729
קְלָלָה	curse (11·33) 887

Chapter 31

אמץ	6 to be strong (3·16·41) 54
ערץ	to tremble (4·11·14) 792
הרפה	to abandon, forsake (4·21·44) 951
אמץ	7 to be strong (3·16·41) 54

הרפה 8 to abandon, forsake (4·22·44) 951

שְׁמִטָּה 10 a letting drop of exactions, a remitting (5·5) 1030

סֻכָּה booth (3·31) 697

נפלא 11 to be too difficult for (2·13·24) 810

הקהי 12 to summon as assembly (3·20·39) 874

טַף children (7·41) 381

התיצ 14 to hold one's ground, take one's stand (5·48·48) 426

נֵכָר 16 that which is foreign (2·36) 648

הֵפֵר to break, frustrate (2·41·44) 830

שִׁירָה 19 song (6·13) 1010

זָב 20 to flow (6·29·29) 264

חָלָב milk (8·44) 316

דָּשֵׁן to be fat, grow fat (1·1·11) 206

נאֵץ to spurn (1·15·24) 610

הֵפֵר to break, frustrate (2·41·44) 830

שִׁירָה 21 song (6·13) 1010

יֵצֶר imagination (1·9) 428

בְּטֶרֶם before (1·39) 382

שִׁירָה 22 song (6·13) 1010

אמץ 23 to be strong (3·16·41) 54

צַד 26 side (1·31) 841

מְרִי 27 rebellion (1·22) 598

מָרָה to be rebellious (2·21·43) 598

עֹרֶף neck (4·33) 791

קָשֶׁה stiff, stubborn (4·36) 904

בְּעוֹד while, yet (1·20) 728

המרד to show rebelliousness (6·22·43) 698

הקהי 28 to summon an assembly (3·20·39) 874

שֹׁטֵר official, officer (7·25) 1009

הֵעִיד to call as witness (5·39·44) 729

שִׁירָה 30 song (6·13) 1010

Chapter 32

הַאֲזִין 1 to give ear, hear (2·41·41[?]) 24

אֹמֶר speech, word (1·48) 56

ערף 2 to drip, drop (2·2·2) 791

מָטָר rain (6·37) 564

לֶקַח teaching (1·9) 544

נזל to distil (1·8·9) 633

טַל dew (3·31) 378

אִמְרָה speech, word (2·30) 57

שְׂעִירִים rain|drops| (1·1) 973

דֶּשֶׁא grass (1·14) 206

רְבִיבִים copious showers (1·6) 914

עֵשֶׂב herbage, herb (3·33) 793

יהב 3 to give, ascribe (2·31·31) 396

גֹּדֶל greatness (6·14) 152

פֹּעַל 4 deed, thing done (2·37) 821

עָוֶל injustice, unrighteousness (2·21) 732

מוּם 5 defect (4·21[?]) 541

עִקֵּשׁ twisted, perverted (1·11) 786

פְּתַלְתֹּל tortuous (1·1) 836

גמל 6 to repay (2·34·37) 168

נָבָל foolish (2·18) 614

קָנָה to get, acquire (1·5·5) 888

הִפְרִיד 8 to divide (1·7·26) 828

גְּבוּלָה border, boundary (1·10) 148

חֶבֶל 9 lot, region (4·49) 286

תֹּהוּ 10 nothingness, waste (1·20) 1062

יְלֵל howling (1·1) 410

יְשִׁימוֹן wilderness (1·13) 445

אִישׁוֹן pupil |of eye| (1·4) 36

נֶשֶׁר eagle (3·26) 676

קֵן nestlings (2·13) 890

גּוֹזָל young of a bird (1·2) 160

רחף to hover (1·3·3) 934

אֶבְרָה pinion (1·4) 7

בָּדָד 12 isolation, alone (2·11) 94

נֵכָר that which is foreign (2·36) 648

הנחה to lead, guide (1·26·40) 634

תְּנוּבָה 13 fruit, produce (1·5) 626

שָׂדַי	field, land (1·13) 961		מוֹסָד	foundation (1·13) 414
הֵינִיק	to nurse, give suck (1·10·18) 413		הָסְפָה	23 to catch up, or perhaps read אסף, to gather (1·1·18) 705
חַלָּמִישׁ	flint (2·5) 321			
חֶמְאָה	14 curd (1·10) 326		מָזֶה	24 empty (1·1) 561
חָלָב	milk (8·44) 316		לחם	to eat (1·6·6) 536
כַּר	he-lamb (1·11) 503		רֶשֶׁף	firebolt (1·7) 958
עַתּוּד	he-goat (1·29) 800		קֶטֶב	destruction (1·4) 881
כִּלְיָה	kidney (1·30) 480		מְרִירִי	bitter (1·1) 601
חִטָּה	wheat (2·30) 334		זחל	to crawl (1·3·3[?]) 267
עֵנָב	grapes (4·19) 772		שׁכל	25 to make childless (1·18·24) 1013
חֶמֶר	wine (1·2) 330		חֶדֶר	chamber, room (1·34) 293
שמן	15 to grow fat (2·3·5) 1031		אֵימָה	terror, dread (1·16·17) 33
בעט	to kick (1·2·2) 127		בָּחוּר	young man (1·45) 104
עָבָה	15 to be thick, gross (of rebellion) (1·3·3) 716		בְּתוּלָה	virgin (4·50) 143
כשׂה	to be sated (1·1·1) 505		יוֹנֵק	suckling (1·11) 413
נטשׁ	to abandon (1·33·40) 643		שֵׂיבָה	gray hair, hoary head (1·20[?]) 966
נבל	to be foolish (1·4·24[?]) 614		הִפְאָה	26 to cleave in pieces (1·1·1) 802
הִקְנִיא	16 to provoke to jealous anger (2·4·34) 888		אֱנוֹשׁ	man, mankind (1·42) 60
שֵׁד	17 demon (1·2) 993		זֵכֶר	remembrance (2·23) 271
שׁער	to be acquainted with (1·1·1) 973		לוּלֵי	27 if not, unless (1·10) 530
שׁיה	18 read נשׁה, to forget (1·1·1) 1009		כַּעַס	vexation, anger (2·25) 495
נָאַץ	19 to spurn (1·8·24) 610		יגר	to be afraid of (2·5·5) 388
כַּעַס	vexation, anger (2·25) 495			or
תַּהְפֻּכָה	20 perversity, perverse thing (1·10) 246		גור	to be afraid of (3·10·10) 158
אֵמוּן	trusting (1·1[?]) 53		נכר	to misconstrue (1·4·8) 649
קִנֵּא	21 to excite to jealous anger (1·30·34) 88		רָם	high, lifted, exalted (7·31[?]) 926
הִקְנִיא	to provoke to jealous anger (2·4·34) 888		תְּבוּנָה	28 understanding (1·42) 108
נָבָל	foolish (2·18) 614		לוּ	29 if (1·19) 530
קדח	22 to be kindled (1·5·5) 869		חכם	to be wise (1·18·26) 314
יקד	to be kindled (1·3·8) 428		אֵיכָה	30 in what manner (5·18) 32
תַּחְתִּי	lower, lowest (1·19) 1066		רְבָבָה	myriad (3·16) 914
יְבוּל	produce (2·13) 385		פָּלִיל	31 judge (1·3) 813
לָהַט	to set ablaze (1·9·11) 529		שְׂדֵמָה	32 field (1·6) 995
			עֵנָב	grapes (4·19) 772
			רוֹשׁ	bitter and poisonous herb (3·12) 912
			אֶשְׁכֹּל	cluster (1·9) 79
			מְרֹר	bitter thing, bitter herb (1·5) 601
			תַּנִּין	33 serpent (1·15) 1072

רֹאשׁ venom (3 · 12) 912

פֶּתֶן venemous serpent, perhaps the cobra (1 · 6) 837

אַכְזָר cruel fierce (1 · 4) 470

כמס 34 to store up (1 · 1 · 1) 485

חתם to seal (1 · 23 · 27) 367

נָקָם 35 vengeance (3 · 17) 668

שִׁלֵּם recompense (1 · 1) 1024

מוֹט to slip (1 · 15 · 39) 556

אֵיד distress, calamity (1 · 24) 15

חָשׁ to make haste (1 · 15 · 21) 301

עָתִיד prepared (1 · 5) 800

דִּין 36 to judge (1 · 23 · 24) 192

אזל to be gone, used up (1 · 6 · 6) 23

אֶפֶס end, i.e., extreme limit (3 · 43) 67

עָצֻר to restrain, refrain (2 · 36 · 46) 783

אֵי 37 where (1 · 39) 32

חָסָה to seek refuge (1 · 37 · 37) 340

נָסִיךְ 38 drink offering, libation (1 · 6) 651

סִתְרָה shelter (1 · 1) 7!2

מָחַץ 39 to shatter (2 · 14 · 14) 563

שָׁנַן 41 to whet, sharpen (1 · 7 · 9) 1041

בָּרָק lightning, flashing (1 · 20) 140

נָקָם vengeance (3 · 17) 668

הִשְׁכִּיר 42 to make drunk (1 · 6 · 20) 1016

שִׁבְיָה captives (2 · 9) 986

פֶּרַע leader [perh.] (1 · 2) 828

נקם 43 to avenge (1 · 13 · 34) 667

נָקָם vengeance (3 · 17) 668

שִׁירָה 44 song (3 · 13) 1010

הֵעִיד 46 to enjoin solemnly (5 · 39 · 44) 729

רֵיק 47 empty, idle, worthless (1 · 14) 938

הֶאֱרִיךְ to prolong (11 · 31 · 34) 73

בְּעֶצֶם 48 selfsame, itself (1 · 17) 782

עַם 50 kinsman (2 · 34) 769

מעל 51 to act unfaithfully (1 · 35 · 35) 591

מִנֶּגֶד 52 some way off from, at a distance (2 · 26) 617

Chapter 33

זָרַח 2 to rise, come forth (1 · 18 · 18) 280

הוֹפִיעַ to shine forth (1 · 8 · 8) 422

אָתָה to come (2 · 19 · 21) 87

רְבָבָה myriad (3 · 16) 914

אשדת = אש דת , (1 · 1) דת law decree (1 · 22) 206

חבב 3 to love (1 · 1 · 1) 285

תֻּכָּה to be lead[dub.?], to be assembled [dub.?] (1 · 1 · 1) 1067

דַּבְּרֹת word (1 · 1) 184

מוֹרָשָׁה 4 possession (1 · 9) 440

קְהִלָּה assembly, congregation (1 · 2) 875

מַת 6 man (6 · 21) 607

עֵזֶר help, succour (3 · 21) 740

תֻּמִּים 8 Thummin [dub.] (1 · 5) 1070

אוּר Urim (1 · 7) 22

חָסִיד pious, godly (1 · 32) 339

נִסָּה to try (8 · 36 · 36) 650

הִכִּיר 9 to acknowledge (4 · 37 · 40) 647

אִמְרָה speech, word (2 · 30) 57

הוֹרָה 10 to teach (4 · 45[?] · 45[?]) 434

קְטוֹרָה smoke of sacrifice (1 · 1) 882

כָּלִיל whole offering (2 · 15) 483

פֹּעַל 11 deed, thing done (2 · 37) 821

מָחַץ to shatter (2 · 14 · 14) 563

קָם adversary (1 · 12) 878

יָדִיד 12 beloved (1 · 8) 391

בֶּטַח securely (3 · 43) 105

חפף to enclose, cover (1 · 1 · 1) 342

מֶגֶד 13 excellence (5 · 8) 550

טַל dew (3 · 31) 378

תְּהוֹם deep, sea, abys (2 · 36) 1062

רָבַץ to stretch oneself out, lie down (3 · 24 · 30) 918

מֶגֶד 14 excellence (5 · 8) 550

תְּבוּאָה	product, yield (6·43) 100	
גֶּרֶשׁ	yield (1·1) 177	
יֶרַח	calendar month (2·12) 437	
מֶגֶד	15 excellence (5·8) 550	
מֶגֶד	16 excellence (5·8) 550	
סְנֶה	blackberry bush (1·6) 702	
תְּבוּאָה	product, yield (6·43) 100	
קָדְקֹד	scalp, hairy crown (3·11) 869	
נָזִיר	one devoted (1·15) 634	
הָדָר	17 splendor, majesty (1·30) 214	
רְאֵם	wild ox (1·9) 910	
נגח	to thrust (1·6·11) 618	
אֶפֶס	end, extremity (3·43) 67	
רְבָבָה	myriad (3·16) 914	
שֶׁפַע	19 abundance (1·1) 1051	
ינק	to suck (1·8·18) 413	
שׂפן	to be hidden (1·1) 706	
טָמַן	to hide (1·28·31) 380	
חוֹל	sand (1·22) 297	
הִרְחִיב	20 to enlarge (3·21·25) 931	
לָבִיא	lioness (1·11) 522	
טָרַף	to tear (1·19·24) 382	
קָדְקֹד	scalp, hairy crown (3·11) 869	
חֶלְקָה	21 portion of ground (1·24) 324	
מְחֹקֵק	commander (1·7) 349	
ספן	to cover (1·6·6) 706	
אתה	to come (2·19·21) 87	
גּוּר	22 young, whelp (1·7) 158	
אַרְיֵה	lion (1·45) 71	
זנק	to leap (1·1·1) 276	
שָׂבֵעַ	23 abounding (1·10) 960	
דָּרוֹם	south (1·17) 204	

טָבַל	24 to dip (1·15·16) 371	
מִנְעָל	25 bolt (1·1) 653	
דֹּבֶא	rest[?] (1·1) 179	
עֵזֶר	26 help, succour (3·21) 740	
גַּאֲוָה	majesty (2·19) 144	
שַׁחַק	cloud (1·21) 1007	
מְעֹנָה	27 refuge (1·9) 733	
גרש	to drive out (1·34·48) 176	
בֶּטַח	28 securely (3·43) 105	
בָּדָד	isolation, alone (2·11) 94	
דָּגָן	grain (7·40) 186	
תִּירוֹשׁ	fresh or new wine (7·38) 440	
ערף	to drip, drop (2·2·2) 791	
טַל	dew (3·31) 378	
אֶשֶׁר	29 happiness, blessedness (1·44) 80	
עֵזֶר	help, succour (3·21) 740	
גַּאֲוָה	majesty (2·19) 144	
נכחש	to cringe (1·1·22) 471	

Chapter 34

בִּקְעָה	3 valley, plain (3·19) 132	
תָּמָר	palm tree, date palm (1·12) 1071	
גַּיְא	6 valley (3·47) 161	
מוּל	in front of (5·25) 557	
קְבֻרָה	grave (1·14) 869	
כהה	7 to grow faint (1·5·8[?]) 462	
לֵחַ	freshness (1·1) 535	
בְּכִי	8 weeping (1·30) 113	
אֵבֶל	mourning (1·24) 5	
סָמַךְ	9 to lay (1·41·48) 701	
מוֹפֵת	11 wonder (9·36) 68	
מוֹרָא	12 awe-inspiring spectacle (4·12) 432	

APPENDIX

Words occurring more than fifty times

CONCERNING THE APPENDIX

1. This list is keyed to BDB.
2. The forms are pointed as in BDB.
3. Verbs with nonextant GlO forms are not pointed.
4. If BDB lists two basic forms, both are listed unless one is obviously rare.
5. This list does not include proper nouns and numerals.
6. Verb meanings are listed by the stem. *Qal* always appears first unless otherwise noted.
7. Stem meanings are listed only if they differ from the following:

Niph.	= passive of *Qal*
Piel	= intensive of *Qal*
Pual	= passive intensive
Hiph.	= causative of *Qal*
Hoph.	= passive of *Hiph.*
Hithp.	= reflexive of *Qal*

8. However, stem meanings may be listed even though they fit the above stereotypes (see no. 7) when there are only three or fewer occurrences.
9. For stems that have both stereotyped and nonstereotyped meanings, only the nonstereotyped meanings are listed (unless the stereotyped meanings qualify for exception 8). The existence of other stereotyped meanings is noted by an asterisk (*).

אָב	father 3
אָבַד	to perish 1
	Pi. to cause to perish
	Hiph. to destroy, put to death
אָבָה	to be willing, consent 2
אֶבְיוֹן	in want, needy, poor 2
אֶבֶן	stone 6
אָדוֹן	lord (see BDB for explanation of
	(אֲדֹנָי, אֲדֹנָי, אֲדֹנִי) 10
אָדָם	man, mankind 9
אֲדָמָה	ground, land 9
אֶדֶן	base, pedestal 10
אָהֵב	to love 12
	Niph. ptc. =lovely, lovable 2 S 1:23
	Pi. ptc.=friends Zech. 13:6; lovers
אַהֲבָה	love 13
אֹהֶל	tent 13
אוֹ	or 14
אָוֶן	trouble, sorrow, wickedness 19
אוֹצָר	treasure, store, treasury, storehouse 69
אוֹר	light 21
אוֹת	sign 16
אָז	at that time, then 23
אֹזֶן	ear 23
אָח	brother 26
אָחוֹת	sister 27
אחז	to grasp, take hold, take possession 28
	Pi. to enclose, overlay Job 26:9
	Hoph. to be fastened to 2 Chron. 9:18
אֲחֻזָּה	possession 28
אַחַר	behind, after 29
אַחֵר	another 29
אַחֲרוֹן	coming after, behind 30
אַחֲרִית	after-part, end 31
אֹיֵב	(ptc. of איב) enemy 33
אֵיךְ	how? how! 32
אַיִל	ram 17
אַיִן	subst., nothing, naught 34
	part of negation, is not, are not
אִישׁ	man 35
אַךְ	surely, howbeit 36
אָכַל	to eat 37

אַל	Adv. of negation 39
אֵל	god, God; power (5t) 42
אֶל	to, towards 39
אֱלוֹהַּ	god, God 43
אַלּוּף	chief 49
אַלְמָנָה	widow 48
אֶלֶף	thousand 48
אִם	hypoth. part., interrog. part. 49
אֵם	mother 51
אָמָה	maid, hand maid 51
אַמָּה	cubit 52
אֱמוּנָה	firmness, steadfastness, fidelity 53
אמן	to confirm, support 52
	Hiph. to stand firm, to trust, believe
אָמַר	to utter, say 55
	Niph. to be called
	Hiph. to avow Deut. 26:17, 18
	Hithp. to act proudly, boast Ps. 94:4, Isa. 61:6
אֱמֶת	firmness, faithfulness, truth 54
אֲנַחְנוּ	we 59
אֲנִי	I 58
אָנֹכִי	I 59
אָסַף	to gather, remove 62
	**Pi.* ptc. as subst.=rearguard, rearward
אסר	to tie, bind, imprison, to harness 63
	Pu. to be taken prisoner Isa. 22:3
אַף	nose, nostril, face, anger 60
אַף	also, yea 64
אֵצֶל	in proximity to, beside 69
אֲרוֹן	chest, ark 75
אֶרֶז	cedar 72
אֹרַח	way, path 73
אֹרֶךְ	length 73
אֶרֶץ	earth, land 75
ארר	to curse 76
	Hoph. to be cursed Num. 22:6
אֵשׁ	fire 77
אִשָּׁה	woman, wife, female 61
אִשֶּׁה	an offering made by fire 77
אֲשֶׁר	part. of relation 81
אֵת	mark of the accusative 84
אֵת	with 85
אַתְּ	you (sing. fem.) 61
אַתָּה	you (sing. masc.) 61

אַתֶּם you (pl. masc.) 61

בְּ in, at, by, with 88

בֶּגֶד garment, covering 93

בְּהֵמָה beast, animal, cattle 96

בּוֹא to come in, come, go in, go 97

בּוֹר pit, cistern, well 92

בּוּשׁ to be ashamed 101

Po'lel to delay Exod. 32:1 Judg. 5:28

Hithpo'l to be ashamed before one another Gen. 2:25

בָּחַר to choose 103

Pu. to be chosen, selected Eccl. 9:4

בֶּטֶן belly, body, womb 105

בָּטַח to trust 105

בִּין to discern, understand 106

Niph. to be intelligent, discerning, have understanding

Po'l. to attentively consider Deut. 32:10

*Hiph. to understand

Hithpo'l. to show oneself attentive, consider diligently

to get understanding Jer. 23:20; Job 26:14; Ps. 119:104

to show oneself to have understanding Ps. 119:100

בֵּין in the interval of, between 107

בַּיִת house, מִבַּיִת = on the inside, מִבַּיִת = within 108

בָּכָה to weep, bewail 113

Pi. to lament Jer. 31:25

to bewail Ezek. 8:14

בְּכֹר, בְּכוֹר first born 114

בַּל Adv., not 115

בָּמָה high place 119

בֵּן son 119

בָּנָה to build 124

בַּעַד away from, behind, about, on behalf of 126

בַּעַל owner, lord, husband, citizens 127

בָּעַר to burn, consume 128

*Pi. to kindle, light

Pu. to burn Jer. 36:22

בָּקַע to cleave, break open or through 131

Pu. to be ripped open Josh. 9:4 Ezek. 26:10 Hos. 14:1

Hoph. to be broken into Jer. 39:2

Hithp. to burst (themselves) open Josh. 9:13

to cleave asunder Mic. 1:4

בָּקָר cattle, herd, ox 133

בֹּקֶר morning 133

בקשׁ *Pi.* to seek 134

Pu. to be sought Jer. 50:20 Esth. 2:23 Ezek. 26:21

בַּרְזֶל iron 137

בָּרַח to go through, flee 137

*Hiph. to pass through Ex. 26:28

בְּרִית covenant 136

ברך to kneel, bless 138

Niph. to bless oneself Gen. 12:3, 18:18, 28:14

Pi. to bless; to salute, greet

Pu. to be prospered

to have prosperity invoked Num. 22:6

Hiph. to cause to kneel Gen. 24:11

בְּרָכָה blessing 139

בָּשָׂר flesh 142

בַּת daughter 123

גָּאַל to redeem, act as kinsman 145

*Niph. to redeem oneself Lev. 25:49

גְּבוּל border, boundary, territory 147

גִּבּוֹר strong, mighty 150

גְּבוּרָה strength, might 150

גִּבְעָה hill 148

גֶּבֶר man 149

גָּדוֹל great 152

גָּדַל to grow up, become great 152

Pi. to cause to grow

to make great, powerful

to magnify

Pu. to be brought up Ps. 144:12

Hiph. to make great

to magnify

to do great things

Hithp. to magnify oneself Isa. 10:15 Ezek. 38:23 Dan. 11:36

גּוֹי nation, people 156

גּוּר to sojourn 157

Hithpo'l. to seek hospitality with 1 Kings 17:20 (Hos. 7:14 dub.)

גּוֹרָל lot 174

גָּלָה to uncover, remove 162
*Niph. to uncover oneself
*Pi. to disclose, lay bare
to make known, reveal
Hiph. to carry away into exile, take into exile
Hithp. to be uncovered Gen. 9:21
to reveal oneself Prov. 18:2

גַּם also, moreover, yea 168

גָּמָל camel 168

גֶּפֶן vine 172

גֵּר sojourner 158

דָּבֵק to cling, cleave, keep 179
Pu. to be joined together Job 38:38, 41:9
*Hiph. to pursue closely
to overtake
Hoph. to be made to cleave Ps. 22:16

דבר to speak 180
Niph. to speak with one another
Hiph. to lead, or put to flight Ps. 18:48, 47:4
Hithp. to speak

דָּבָר speech, word; saying, utterance; matter, affair 182

דְּבַשׁ honey 185

דּוֹד beloved, love, uncle 187

דּוֹר period, generation; dwelling Isa. 38:12 Ps. 49:20 189

דֶּלֶת door 195

דָּם blood 196

דַּעַת knowledge 395

דָּרַךְ to tread, march
*Hiph. to tread, tread down 201

דֶּרֶךְ way, road, distance, journey, manner 201

דָּרַשׁ to resort to, seek 205
Niph. to let oneself be inquired of
to be required Gen. 42:22
to be sought out 1 Chron. 26:31

הֲ, הַ, הַ (def. art.) the 206

הֲ, הַ, הַ interrog. part. 209

הֶבֶל vapor, breath 210

הוּא (3rd pers. sing. pron.) he, she (in Pent.), it; with art. = that 214–216

הוֹי ah, alas, ha 222

הִיא (3rd pers. sing. pron.) she, it; with art. = that 214–216

הָיָה to be, become, come to pass, fall out 224

הֵיכָל palace, temple 228

הָלַךְ to go, come, walk 229
Niph. to be gone Ps. 109:23
Hithp. to walk, walk about, move to and fro

הלל to be boastful 237
Pi. to praise
Hithpa. to make one's boast Ps. 10:3 44:9
Hithpa. to glory, boast, make one's boast
Po'el. to make fool of Isa. 44:25 Job 12:17 Eccl. 7:7
Po'al. to be mad Ps. 102:9, Eccl. 2:2
Hithpo. to act madly, like a madman

הֵם, הֵמָּה (3rd pers. pl. masc. pron.; as neuter, rarely) they; with art=those (not defined in BDB) 241

הָמוֹן sound, murmur, roar, crowd, abundance 242

הֵן lo! behold! 243

הֵנָּה fem. of הֵמָּה (see above) 241

הִנֵּה lo! behold! 243

הָפַךְ to turn, overturn 245
*Niph. to turn oneself, turn, turn back
Hithp. to turn this way and that Gen. 3:24 Judg. 7:13 Job 37:12
to transform oneself Job 38:14
Hoph. to be turned (upon) Job 30:15

הַר mountain, hill, hill country 249

הָרַג to kill, slay 246
Pu. to be slain Is. 27:7

וָ, וּ, וְ (adv., conj.) so, then, and, and also, but, both ... and (וְ ... וְ), consecutive verb formations, (cohort.) so that (introduces apodosis after כִּ, אִם) then 251–255

זֹאת fem, of זֶה (see below)

זָבַח to slaughter for sacrifice 256

זָבַח   *Pi.* to sacrifice
     sacrifice 257

זֶה   (demonstr. sing. masc. pron. [fem., זֹאת] and adv.) this, here; also used idiomatically with prepositions 260–262

זָהָב   gold 262

זָכַר   to remember 269

זָכָר   male 271

זָנָה   to commit fornication, to be a harlot 275
     Pu. Ezek. 16:34 לֹא ז'=fornication was not done
     Hiph. to cause to commit fornication
     to commit fornication

זעק   to cry, cry out, call 277
     Niph. to be called together.
     to assemble
     to join
     Hiph. to call, call out, or together
     to make a crying Job 35:9 (וי ז' ויאמר)
     to have proclamation made Jonah 3:7
     to call out to, or at Zech. 6:8

זָקֵן   old 278

זר   strange (adj.), stranger (noun) BDB under זור 266

זְרוֹעַ   arm, shoulder, strength 283

זָרַע   to sow, scatter seed 281
     Niph. to be made pregnant Num. 5:28
     Pu. to be sown Isa. 40:24
     Hiph. to produce seed Gen. 1:11, 12
     to bear a child Lev. 12:2

זֶרַע   sowing, seed, offspring 282

חַג   festive-gathering, feast 290

חָדַל   to cease 292
     Hoph. to be made to leave Judg. 9:9, 11, 13

חָדָשׁ   new 294

חֹדֶשׁ   new moon, month 294

חוֹמָה   wall 327

חוּץ   the outside, a street 299

חָזָה   to see, behold 302

חָזַק   to be or grow firm, strong, strengthen 304

     Pi. to make strong, firm, hard
     to strengthen
     Hiph. to prevail
     to take or keep hold, seize, grasp
     Hithp. to strengthen oneself
     to put forth strength
     to withstand 2 Chron. 13:7, 8
     to hold strongly with

חָזָק   strong, stout, mighty 305

חָטָא   to miss, go wrong, sin 306
     Hiph. to miss the mark Judg. 20:16
     to bring into guilt, condemnation
     Hithp. to miss or lose oneself Job 41:17
     to purify oneself

חַטָּאת   sin, sin offering 308

חַי   alive, living 311

חָיָה   to live 310
     Pi. to preserve alive, let live
     to give life Job 33:4
     to quicken, revive, refresh
     Hiph. to preserve alive, let live
     to quicken, revive

חַיָּה   living thing, animal; life (some poetry); appetite Job 38:39; revival, renewal Isa. 57:10, 312

חַיִּים   life 313

חַיִל   strength, efficiency, wealth, army 298

חָכָם   wise 314

חָכְמָה   widsom 315

חֵלֶב   fat 316

חָלָה   to be weak, sick 317
     Niph. to make oneself sick Jer. 12:13
     to be made sick Dan. 8:27 Amos 6:6; Ptc.=diseased
     Pi. to make sick Deut. 29:21 Ps. 77:11,
     to appease, entreat the favor of
     Pu. to be made weak Isa. 14:10
     Hithp. to make oneself sick 2 Sam. 13:2, 5, 6
     Hiph. to become sick Hos. 7:5

חֲלוֹם   dream 321

חלל   *Niph.* to pollute, defile oneself Lev. 21:4, 9, 320

to be polluted, defiled
Pi. to defile, pollute
to dishonor
to violate
to treat as common
Pu. to be profaned Ezek. 36:23
Hiph. to allow to be profaned Ezek. 39:7, 20:9
to begin
Hoph. to be begun Gen. 4:26
חָלָל pierced 319
חָלַק to divide, share 323
*Niph. to divide oneself Gen. 14:15
to assign, distribute 1 Chron. 23:6, 24:3 (see *Pi.*)
*Pi. to assign, distribute 1 Chron. 23:6, 24:3 (see Niph.)
to scatter Gen. 49:7 Lam. 4:16
Pu. to be divided Isa. 33:23 Amos 7:17 Zech. 14:1
Hiph. to receive a portion Jer. 37:12
Hithp. to divide among themselves Josh. 18:5
חֵלֶק portion, tract, territory 324
חֵמָה heat, rage 404
חֲמוֹר he-ass, male donkey 331
חָמָס violence, wrong 329
חֵן favor, grace 336
חָנָה to decline, bend down, encamp 333
חָנַן to show favor, be gracious 335
Niph. to be pitied Jer. 22:23
Pi. to make gracious Jer. 26:25
Po'el to direct favor to Ps. 102:15 Prov. 14:21
Hoph. to be shown favor Isa. 26:10 Prov. 21:10
Hithp. to seek or implore favor
חֶסֶד goodness, kindness 338
חָפֵץ to delight in 342
חֵץ arrow 346
חֲצִי half 345
חָצֵר enclosure, court 346
חֹק something prescribed, a statute, decree, ordinance 349

חֻקָּה something prescribed, enactment, statute 349
חֶרֶב sword 352
חָרָה to burn, be kindled (of anger) 354
Niph. to be angry Isa. 41:11, 45:24 Song of Sol. 1:6
Hiph. to be burned (?) Neh. 3:20
to cause to be kindled Job 19:11
Hithp. to heat oneself in vexation Ps. 37:1, 7, 8, Prov. 24:19
to hotly contend (dub.) Jer. 12:5
to strive eagerly (dub.) Jer. 22:15
הֶרְפָּה reproach 357
חָשַׁב to think, account, reckon 362
Hithp. to reckon oneself Num. 23:9
חֹשֶׁךְ darkness, obscurity 365
חָתַת to be shattered, dismayed 369
Niph. to be put in awe Mal. 2:5
Pi. to dismay, scare Job 7:14
to be shattered (?) Jer. 51:56
טָהוֹר clean, pure 373
טָהֵר to be clean, pure 372
Pi. to cleanse, purify
to pronounce clean *Pu.* to be cleansed 1 Sam. 20:26 Ezek. 22:24
Hithp. to purify oneself
to present oneself for purification
טוֹב pleasant, agreeable, good 373
טָמֵא to be, become unclean 379
Niph. to defile oneself, be defiled
to be regarded as unclean Job 18:3
Pi. to defile
to pronounce unclean
Hithp. to defile oneself
Hothp. to be defiled Deut. 24:4
טָמֵא unclean 379
יְאֹר stream, canal; stream of Nile 384
יָבֵשׁ to be dry, dried up, withered 386
Pi. to make dry, dry up
*Hiph. to exhibit dryness
יָד hand 388
ידה to shoot Jer. 50:14, 392
Pi. to cast Lam. 3:53 Zech. 2:4
Hiph. to give thanks, laud, praise

to confess

Hithp. to confess

to give thanks 2 Chron. 30:22

יָדַע to know 393

Niph. to make oneself known

to be perceived Gen. 41:21 Ps. 74:5

to be instructed Jer. 31:19

Pi. to cause to know Job 38:12 Ps. 104:19(?)

Po. to cause to know 1 Sam. 21:3

Pu. ptc: known Isa. 12:5 as subst.=acquaintance (remaining Pu.)

Hithp. to make oneself known Gen. 45:1 Num. 12:6

יוֹם day 398

יוֹמָם daytime, by day 401

יַחְדָּו together 403

יטב to be good, well, glad, pleasing 405

יַיִן wine 406

יכח *Hiph.* to decide, adjudge, prove 406

Hoph. to be chastened Job. 33:19

Niph. to reason together Isa. 1:18

to reason Job 23:7

to be set right, justified Gen. 20:16

Hithp. to argue Mic. 6:2

יָכֹל to be able, have power, prevail, endure 407

יָלַד to bear, bring forth, beget 408

Pi. to cause (or help) to bring forth Exod. 1:16

Ptc. as subst.=midwife

Pu. to be born

Hiph. to beget

Hithp. to declare pedigree Num. 1:18

יֶלֶד child, son, boy, youth 409

descendants Isa. 29:23

יָם sea, freq. indicates western point of compass, west 410

יָמִין right hand 411

יָסַף to add 414

Niph. to join oneself to Exod. 1:10

יַעַן on account of, because 774

יָעַץ to advise, counsel 419

Niph. to consult together, exchange

counsel

Hithp. to conspire Ps. 83:4

יַעַר wood, forest, thicket 420

יָצָא to go or come out 422

יָצַק to pour, cast, flow 427

Hiph. to pour out

Hoph. ptc.=cast, molten firmly established Job 11:15

יָרֵא to fear 431

Pi. to make afraid, terrify

יָרַד to come or go down, descend 432

יְרִיעָה curtain 438

יָרַשׁ take possession of, inherit, dispossess 439

Niph. to be impoverished

Pi. to take possession of, devour Deut. 28:42

Hiph. to take possession of Num. 14:24

יֵשׁ is, are 441

יָשַׁב to sit, remain, dwell 442

Pi. to set Ezek. 25:4

Hiph. to cause to be inhabited Ezek. 36:33 Isa. 54:3

to marry (only Ezra and Nehemiah)

Hoph. to be made to dwell Isa. 5:8

to be inhabited Isa. 44:26

יְשׁוּעָה salvation; victory 447

ישׁע *Hiph.* to deliver 446

Niph. to be liberated, saved

יָשָׁר straight, right 449

יתר *Qal* ptc.=remainder 1 Sam. 15:15, 4

Niph. to be left over, remain over

Hiph. to leave over, leave

to excel, show preeminence Gen. 49:4

to show excess=have more than enough Exod. 36:7

to make abundant Deut. 28:11; 30:9

יֶתֶר remainder, excess, preeminence 451

כְּ the like of, like, as 453

כַּאֲשֶׁר according as, as, when 455

כָּבֵד to be heavy, weighty, burdensome, honored 457

Niph. to be made heavy Prov. 8:24

to be honored, enjoy honor

to get oneself glory

Pi. to make heavy, insensible 1 Sam. 6:66

to make honorable

to honor, glorify

Pu. to be made honorable, honored Isa. 58:13 Pr. 13:18, 27:18

Hiph. to display honor

Hithp. to make oneself heavy Nah. 3:15

to honor oneself Prov. 12:9

כָּבוֹד abundance, honor, glory 458

כבס to wash, ptc. only = fuller, washer 460

Pu. to be washed Lev. 13:58, 15:17

Hothp. to be washed out Lev. 13:55, 56

כֶּבֶשׂ lamb 461

כֹּה thus, here 462

כֹּהֵן priest 463

כּוּן *Niph.* to be set up, established, fixed 465

to be directed aright

to be prepared, ready

Hiph. to establish, set up

to fix, make ready

to direct

to arrange, order 2 Chron. 29:19, 35:20

Po'lel to set up, establish

to constitute, make

to fix

to direct Job 8:8

Po'lal to be established Ps. 37:23

to be prepared Ezek. 28:13

Hithpo'l to be established

כֹּחַ strength, power 470

כִּי that, for, when, because, since 471

כִּכָּר a round; hence

1. a round district

2. a round loaf

3. a round weight, talent

כֹּל whole, all 481

כָּלָה to be complete, at an end, finished, accomplished, spent 477

Pi. to complete, bring to an end, finish

accomplish

to cause to cease Num. 17:25, Ps. 78:33

to exhaust, use up

to consume Lev. 26:16

to destroy

Pu. to be finished, ended Ps. 72:20

to be complete Gen. 2:1

כְּלִי article, utensil, vessel 479

כְּמוֹ like, as, when 455

כֵּן so, thus 485

כָּנָף wing, extremity 489

כִּסֵּא (כִּסֵּה) seat of honor, throne 490

כסה to conceal, cover, ptc. only: Act.=to conceal Prov. 12:16, 23 491

Pass.="covered" Ps. 32:1

Niph. to be covered Jer. 51:42 Ezek. 24:8

Pual to be clothed 1 Chron. 21:16 Eccl. 6:4

כְּסִיל stupid fellow, fool 493

כֶּסֶף silver, money 494

כָּעַס to be vexed, angry 494

Pi. to be angered 1 Sam. 1:6 Deut. 32:21

כַּף hollow, flat of hand, palm, sole, pan 496

כְּפִי according to the command of, according to the mouth of, in proportion to (of, that) 805

כִּפֶּר *Pi.* to cover over, pacify, make propitiation, atone 497

Hithp. to be covered 1 Sam. 3:14

Nithp. to be covered Deut. 21:8

כְּרוּב cherub 500

כֶּרֶם vineyard 501

כָּרַת to cut off, cut down 503

Niph. to be chewed Num. 11:33

Pual to be cut off Ezek. 16:4

to be cut down Judg. 6:28

Hiph. to take away 1 Sam. 20:15

to permit to perish 1 Kings 18:5

כָּשַׁל to stumble, stagger, totter 505

Niph. (= Qal)

to be tottering, feeble Isa. 40:30, 1 Sam.

Appendix

2:4. Zech. 12:8
Pi. Ezek. 36:14 only (but see BDB)
*Hiph. to make feeble, weak Lam. 1:14
Hoph. ptc. only=the ones who have stumbled Jer. 18:23 Ezek. 21:20(?)

כָּתַב to write 507
Pi. to write Isa. 10:1

כָּתֵף shoulder, shoulder-blade; side; support 1 Kings 7:30, 34 509
לְ to, for, in regard to 510
לֹא, לוֹא Adv., not 518
לֵב inner man, mind, will, heart 524
לֵבָב inner man, mind, will, heart 523
לְבַד in a state of separation, alone, by itself 94
לְבַד מִן besides, apart from 94
לְבִלְתִּי so as not, in order not (to) 116
לָבַשׁ to put on, wear, clothe, be clothed 527
Pu. ptc. only=arrayed

לחם to fight, do battle Ps. 35:1, 56:2, 3 535
Niph. to engage in battle, wage war
לֶחֶם bread, food 536
לַיִל, לַיְלָה night 538
לוּן, לִין to lodge, pass the night 533
Hiph. to cause to rest, lodge 2 Sam. 17:8
Hithpo'l to dwell, abide Job 39:28 Ps. 91:1
לָכַד to capture, seize, take 539
Hithp. to grasp each other Job 41:9
to compact Job 38:30
לָכֵן therefore 486
לָמַד to exercise in, learn 540
Pi. to teach
לָמָּה, לָמָה why? 554
לְמַעַן for the sake of, on account of, to the intent that, in order that 775
לְפִי according to (as) 805
לִפְנֵי at the face of or front of, in the presence of, before 816
לָקַח to take 542

Pu. to be taken Gen. 2:23 3:19, 23 Jer. 29:22
to be stolen Judg. 17:2
to be taken captive Jer. 48:46
to be taken away, removed 2 Kings 2:10 Isa. 53:8
Hoph. to be taken, brought
Hithp. to take hold of oneself Exod. 9:24 Ezek. 1:4

לָשׁוֹן tongue 546
מְאֹד muchness, force, abundance, exceedingly 547
מֵאַחַר from after 29
מָאַס to reject, refuse, despise 549
מָגֵן shield 171
מִגְרָשׁ common, common land, open land 177
מִדְבָּר wilderness 184
מָדַד to measure 551
Pi. to extend, continue Job 7:4
to measure, measure off 2 Sam. 8:2 Ps. 60:8, 108:8
Po. to be measured Hab. 3:6
Hithpo. to measure himself 1 Kings 17:21
מִדָּה measure, measurement 551
garment Ps. 133:2
size Jer. 22:14
stature 1 Chron. 11:23, 20:6
מַדּוּעַ wherefore? on what account? 396
מְדִינָה province 193
מַה, מָה what? how? aught? 552
מהר *Niph.* to be hurried, hasty 554
Pi. to hasten, make haste
Inf. Abs. מַהֵר quickly, speedily
מַהֵר quickly, speedily 555
מוֹעֵד appointed time, place, meeting 417
מוּת to die 559
Po'lel to kill, put to death
*Hoph. to die prematurely Prov. 19:16
מָוֶת death 560
מִזְבֵּחַ altar 258
מִזְמוֹר melody 274
מִזְרָח place of sunrise, east 280

מַחֲנֶה encampment, camp 334

מָחָר tomorrow, in time to come 563

מַחֲשָׁבָה thought, device 364

מַטֶּה staff, rod, shaft; tribe, branch Ezek. 19:11, 12, 14 641

מִי who? 566

מַיִם (pl. of מַי) pl. only; water, waters 565

מָכַר to sell 569
*Niph. to sell oneself

מָלֵא to be full, fill 569
*Niph. to be accomplished, ended Exod. 7:25 Job 15:32
*Pi. to confirm 1 Kings 1:14
Pu. ptc.=set Song of Sol. 5:14
Hithp. to mass oneself Job 16:10

מָלֵא full 570

מַלְאָךְ messenger 521

מְלָאכָה occupation, work; workmanship; property; service, use; public business 521

מִלְחָמָה battle, war 536

מלט Niph. to slip away 1 Sam. 20:29 2 Sam. 4:6 572
to escape
to be delivered
Pi. to lay (eggs) Isa. 34:15
to let escape 2 Kings 23:18
to deliver
Hiph. to give birth to Isa. 66:7
to deliver Isa. 31:5
Hithp. to slip forth, escape Job 41:11
to escape Job 19:20

מָלַךְ to be, become, king or queen, to reign 573
Hoph. to be made king Dan. 9:1

מֶלֶךְ king 572

מַלְכוּת royalty, royal power, reign, kingdom 574

מִלִּפְנֵי from before, because 817

מַמְלָכָה kingdom, sovereignty, dominion, reign 575

מִן out of, from, on account of, off, on the side of, since, above, than, so that not 577

מִנְחָה gift, tribute, offering 585

מְנַצֵּחַ Pi. ptc. of נצח; in Psalms=perh. musical director, choir master; elsewhere=director 663

מִסְפָּר number; recounting Judg. 7:15 708

מְעַט a little, fewness, a few 589

מַעַל above, upwards 751

מֵעַל from upon, from over, from by (beside) 758–759

מַעֲלָה upwards 751

מֵעִם from with or beside; away from, from 768

מַעֲשֶׂה deed, work 795

מִפְּנֵי from the face or presence of, from before, because 818

מָצָא to attain to, find 592
to learn, devise Eccl. 7:27, 27, 29
to experience Ps. 116:3 Eccl. 7:14
to find out
to come upon, light upon
to hit Deut. 19:5 1 Sam. 31:3 1 Chron. 10:3
*Niph. to be gained; secured Ho. 14:9
to be left
to be present
to prove to be 1 Chron. 24:4 2 Chron. 2:16
to be sufficient Josh. 17:16
*Hiph. to cause to encounter 2 Sam. 3:8 Zech. 11:6
to present Lev. 9:12, 13, 18

מַצָּה unleavened bread or cake(s) 595

מִצְוָה commandment 846

מִקְדָּשׁ sacred place, sanctuary 874

מָקוֹם standing place, place 879

מִקְנֶה cattle 889

מַרְאֶה sight, appearance, vision 909

מָרוֹם height 928

מָשַׁח to smear, anoint 602

מִשְׁכָּן dwelling place, 'tabernacle' 1015

מָשַׁל to rule, have dominion, reign 605
Hiph. to cause to rule Ps. 8:7 Dan. 11:39
to exercise dominion Job 25:2

מִשְׁמֶרֶת guard, watch; charge, function 1038

מִשְׁפָּחָה clan 1046

מִשְׁפָּט judgment, justice, right manner, fitting 1 Kings 5:8; fitness Isa. 28:26; 40:14 1048

מֵת dead one, corpse 559 (מוּת)

מִתַּחַת from under, from beneath, from 1066

נָא part. of entreaty of exhortation, I pray, now 609

נְאֻם utterance, declaration 610

נבא Niph. to prophesy 612

Hithp. to prophesy

נבט Pi. to look Isa. 5:30 613

Hiph. to look

to regard, show regard

נָבִיא spokesman, speaker, prophet 611

נֶגֶב south country, Negeb, south 616

נגד Hiph. to declare, tell 616

to avow, acknowledge, confess Isa. 3:9 Ps. 38:19

Hoph. to be told, announced, reported

נֶגֶד in front of, in sight of, opposite to 617

נָגַע to touch, reach, strike 619

Niph. to be stricken, defeated Josh. 8:15

Pi. to strike Gen. 12:17 2 Kings 15:5 2 Chron. 26:20

Pu. to be stricken Ps. 73:5

*Hiph. to reach, extend

to approach

to befall

נֶגַע stroke, plague, mark 619

נגש to draw near, approach 620

Niph. (as Qal)

Hoph. to be brought near 2 Sam. 3:34 Mal. 1:11

Hithp. to draw near Isa. 45:20

נֶדֶר vow 623

נָהָר stream, river 625

נוּחַ to rest 628

*Hiph. to leave

to abandon Jer. 14:9 Ps. 119:121

to permit

Hoph. to be caused to rest La. 5:5 Zech. 5:11

ptc. as subst=space left, open space Ezek. 41:9, 11

נוס to flee, escape 630

Po'lel to cause to flee, to drive Isa. 59:19

Hithpo'l to take flight Ps. 60:6

Hiph. to put to flight Deut. 32:30

to drive hastily Exod. 9:20

to cause to disappear, hide Judg. 6:11

נָחַל to get or take as a possession 635

Pi. to divide for a possession

נַחַל torrent, torrent valley, wady 636

נַחֲלָה possession, property, inheritance 635

נחם Niph. to be sorry 636

to comfort oneself

Pi. to comfort, console

Pual to be relieved, consoled Isa. 54:11, 66:13

Hithp. to be sorry, have compassion Deut. 32:36 Ps. 135:14

to rue Num. 23:19

to comfort oneself, be relieved Gen. 37:35 Ps. 119:52

to ease oneself Ezek. 5:13 Gen. 27:42

נְחֹשֶׁת copper, bronze, (dual) fetter of copper or bronze 638

נָטָה to stretch out, spread out, extend incline, bend 639

Niph. to be stretched out Num. 24:6 Zech. 1:16

to stretch themselves out Jer. 6:4

Hiph. to stretch out Isa. 31:3 Jer. 6:12 15:6

to spread out 2 Sam. 16:22, 21:10 Isa 54:2

to turn, incline

נטע to plant 642

Niph. to be planted Isa. 40:24

נכה Niph. to be smitten 2 Sam. 11:1 645

Pu. to be smitten Exod. 9:31, 32

Hiph. to smite, strike

נֶסֶךְ drink-offering; molten images 651

נָסַע to pull out or up, set out, journey 652

Niph. to be pulled up Isa. 38:12 Job 4:21

נַעַר boy, lad, youth; servant 654

נַעֲרָה girl, damsel 655

נָפַל to fall, lie 656

Pi'lel Ezek. 28:23 But BDB="rd. וְנָפַל"

נֶפֶשׁ soul, living being, life, self, person, desire, appetite, emotion, passion 659

נצב *Niph.* to take one's stand, stand 662

Hiph. to station, set, set up

Hoph. to be fixed, determined Gen. 28:12 Judg. 9:6 Nah. 2:8

נצל *Niph.* to deliver oneself, be delivered 664

*Pi.*to strip off, spoil 2 Chron. 20:25 Exod. 3:22, 12:36

to deliver Ezek. 14:14

Hiph. to snatch away, deliver

Hoph. to be plucked out Amos. 4:11 Zech. 3:2

Hithp. to strip oneself Exod. 33:6

נצר to watch, guard, keep 665

נָשָׂא to lift, carry, take 669

נָשִׂיא a chief, prince 672

נָתַן to give, put, set 678

Hoph. (as *Niph.*)

סָבַב to turn about, go around, surround 685

Niph. to turn oneself

to be turned over Jer. 6:12

Pi. to change 2 Sam. 14:20

Po. to encompass, surround

סָבִיב circuit, round about 686

סָגַר to shut, close 688

Pi. to deliver up

Pu. to be shut up

Hiph. to deliver up

to shut up

סוּס horse 692

סוֹפֵר secretary, muster officer, scribe 708

סוּר to turn aside 693

Po'lel to turn aside Lam. 3:11

*Hiph. to put aside

סֶלָה (a benediction[?]) see BDB 699

סֶלַע crag, cliff 700

סֹלֶת fine flour 701

סָפַר to count 707

Pi. to recount, rehearse, declare

סֵפֶר document, writing, book 706

סָתַר *Niph.* to hide oneself 711

to be hid, concealed

Pi. to carefully hide Isa. 16:3

Pu. to be carefully concealed Prov. 27:5

Hithp. to hide oneself

Hiph. to conceal, hide

עָבַד to work, serve 712

Niph. to be tilled Deut. 21:4 Ezek. 36:9, 34

ptc.=cultivated Eccl. 5:8 (dub.)

Pu. to be worked Deut. 21:3 Isa. 14:3

עֶבֶד servant, slave, subject 713

עֲבֹדָה labor, service 715

עָבַר to pass over, through, by, on 716

Niph. to be forded Ezek. 47:5

Pi. to impregnate Job 21:10

to cause to pass across 1 Kings 6:21

עֵבֶר region across or beyond, side 719

עַד as far as, even to, up to, until, while 723

עֵד witness 729

עֵדָה congregation 417

עֵדוּת testimony 730

עוֹד still, yet, again, besides 728

עוֹלָם forever, always, everlasting; ancient, old; age 761

עָוֹן iniquity, guilt; punishment of iniquity 730

עוֹף coll. birds, fowl; flying insects 733

עוּר to rouse oneself, awake 734

Po'l to rouse, incite

Pilp. to rouse, (raise?) Isa. 15:5

Hithpo'l to be excited Job 31:29, 17:8

to rouse oneself Isa. 64:6

Hiph. to rouse

to act aroused Ps. 35:23, 73:20

עוֹר   skin, hide 736

עֵז   she-goat; pl. subst.=goat's hair 777

עֹז   strength, might 738

עָזַב   to leave, forsake, loose 736
Pu. to be deserted Isa. 32:14 Jer. 49:25

עָזַר   to help 740
Hiph. (dub.) as Qal 2 Sam. 18:3 2 Chron. 28:23

עַיִן   eye; surface Exod. 10:5, 15 Num. 22:5, 11
appearance Lev. 13:5, 37, 55 Num. 11:7 1 Sam. 16:7(?), gleam, sparkle Ezek. 1 (5t), 8:2, 10:9 Dan. 10:6 Prov. 23:31 744

עִיר   city, town; fortress 746

עַל   on, on the ground of, according to, on account of, on behalf of, concerning, besides, in addition to, together with, beyond, above, over, by, onto, toward, to, against 752–759

עָלָה   to go up, ascend, climb 748
Niph. to take oneself away 2 Sam. 2:27
to be exalted Ps. 47:10, 97:9
Hiph. to take away Ps. 102:25 Job 36:20
Hoph. to be carried away Nah. 2:8
to be taken up 2 Chron. 20:34
to be offered Judg. 6:23
Hithp. to lift oneself Jer. 51:3

עֹלָה   whole burnt offering 750

עֶלְיוֹן   upper, high, highest 751

עַם, עָם   people, nation 766

עִם   with 767

עָמַד   to take one's stand, stand; to arise, appear
to be appointed Ezek. 10:14
to grow flat, insipid Jer. 48:11 763
Hiph. to station, set
to have a fixed look אֶת-פָּנָיו ע' 2 Kings 8:11
to restore Ezra 9.9
to raise Dan. 11:11, 13

עַמּוּד   pillar, column 765

עָמָל   trouble, mischief, toil 765

עֵמֶק   valley, lowland 770

עָנָה   to answer, respond 772
Niph. to make answer Ezra 14:4, 7
Hiph. ptc. Eccl. 5:19 (dub.) See BDB

ענה   to be put down or become low Isa. 25:5 776
to be depressed, down cast Isa. 31:4
to be afflicted Ps. 116:10, 119:67 Zech. 10:2
Niph. to humble oneself Exod. 10:3
to be afflicted Isa. 53:7, 58:10 Ps. 119:107
Pi. to humble, afflict
Pu. to be afflicted Ps. 119:71, 132:1 Isa. 53:4
to be humbled Lev. 23:29
Hiph. to afflict 1 Kings 8:35 2 Chon. 6:26
Hithp. to humble oneself Gen. 16:9 Ezek. 8:21 Dan. 10:12
to be afflicted 1 Kings 2:26 Ps. 107:17

עָנִי   poor, afflicted, humble 776

עָנָן   cloudmass, cloud 777

עָפָר   dry earth, dust; ore Job 28:2 779

עֵץ   tree, trees, wood 781

עֵצָה   counsel, advice 420

עֶצֶם   bone, substance; self (same) 782

עֶרֶב   evening; night Job 7:4 787

עֲרָבָה   desert plain, steppe 787

עֶרְוָה   nakedness, pudenda 788

עָרַךְ   to arrange, set in order
to compare Isa. 40:18 Ps. 40:6
to be comparable Ps. 89:7 Job 28:17, 19 789
Hiph. to value, tax

עָשָׂה   to do, work
to make
to acquire
to use 1 Sam. 8:16 Exod. 38:24
to spend, pass. Eccl. 6:12 793
Pu. to be made Ps. 139:15

עֵת   time; experiences, fortunes Isa. 33:6 Ps. 31:16 1 Chron. 29:30 773

עַתָּה now 773

פֵּאָה corner, side 802

פָּדָה to ransom 804

פֶּה mouth; end 2 Kings 10:21, 21:16
Ezra. 9:11
portion Deut. 21:17 2 Kings 2:9 Zech.
13:8 804

פוּץ to be dispersed, scattered 806
Niph. (as Qal)

פלל *Pi.* to mediate, arbitrate, interpose
813
Hithp. to pray, intercede

פֶּן lest 814

פָּנָה to turn, turn and look, look 815
Pi. to turn away, put out of the way
Hiph. to turn Judg. 15:4 1 Sam. 10:9
Jer. 48:39
to make a turn
Hoph. to be turned Jer. 49:8 Ezek. 9:2

פָּנֶה face 815

פָּעַל to do, make 821

פַּעַם once, time, step, now; anvil 821

פָּקַד to attend to, visit, muster, appoint
823
Niph. to be missed, lacking
Pi. to muster Isa. 13:4
Pu. to be passed in review Exod. 38:21
to be caused to miss Isa. 38:10
Hithp. to be mustered Judg. 20:15, 17,
21:9
Hothp. (as Hithp.)
Hiph. to set, make overseer
to commit, entrust
to deposit
Hoph. to be visited Jer. 6:6
to be deposited Lev. 5:23
to be made overseer

פַּר young bull, steer 830

פְּרִי fruit 826

פַּרְעֹ Pharaoh 829

פָּרַשׂ to spread out, spread 831
Niph. to be scattered Ezek. 17:21,
34:12

פָּרָשׁ horseman; horse 832

פֶּשַׁע transgression; guilt of transgression;
punishment for transgression; Dan.
8:12, 13, 9:24; offering for transgression Mic. 6:7 833

פתח to open 834

פֶּתַח doorway, opening, entrance 835

צֹאן (coll.) small cattle, sheep and goats,
flock, flocks 838

צָבָא army, host; war, warfare, service
838

צַדִּיק just, righteous 843

צֶדֶק rightness, righteousness 841

צְדָקָה righteousness 842

צוה *Pi.* to lay charge (upon), give charge
(to), charge, command, order 845

צוּר rock, cliff 849

צֵל shadow, shade 853

צלח to rush
to be successful, prosper 852
Hiph. to show experience, prosperity

צָעַק to cry, cry out 858
Niph. to be summoned
Hiph. to call together 1 Sam. 10:17
Pi. to cry aloud 2 Kings 2:12

צָפוֹן north 860

צַר adversary, foe 865

צָרָה straits, distress 865

צרר to bind, tie up
to be scant, cramped 864
Pu. to be tied up Josh. 9:4
Hiph. to make narrow, press hard,
cause distress

קָבַץ to gather, collect, assemble 867
Niph. (as Qal)
Hithp. to gather together, be gathered
together

קָבַר to bury 868

קֶבֶר grave, tomb 868

קָדוֹשׁ sacred, holy 872

קָדִים East, east wind 870

קֶדֶם front, east; ancient, of old; beginning
Prov. 8:22, 23 869

קָדַשׁ to be set apart, consecrated 872
Niph. to show oneself sacred, majestic

to be honored

to be consecrated Exod. 29:43

Pi. to consecrate, dedicate;

to keep sacred

to honor as sacred, hallow

Hiph. (as Pi.)

Hithp. to be observed as holy Isa. 30:29

to consecrate oneself

קֹדֶשׁ   apartness, sacredness 871

קָהָל   assembly, company, congregation 874

קוֹל   sound, voice 876

קוּם   to arise, stand up, stand

to be fulfilled 877

Pi. to fulfil Ezek. 13:6 Ps. 119:106

to confirm, ratify Ruth 4:7

to establish Ps. 119:28

to impose Esth. 9 (7 times)

Po'l. to raise up

Hithpo'l to rise up

Hiph. to raise, set up

קָטֹן   small, insignificant 882

קטר   *Pi.* to make sacrifices smoke 882

Pu. to be fumigated Song of Sol. 3:6

Hiph. to make (sacrifices) smoke

Hoph. to be made to smoke Lev. 6:15 Mal. 1:11

קְטֹרֶת   incense, sweet smoke of sacrifice 1 Sam. 2:28 (?) Isa. 1:13 Ps. 66: 15, 141:2 882

קִיר   wall 885

קָלַל   to be slight, swift, trifling 886

Niph. to show oneself swift Isa. 30:16

to be, appear trifling

to be lightly esteemed 2 Sam. 6:22

Pi. to curse

Hiph. to make light, lighten

to treat with contempt

Pilp. to shake Ezek. 21:26

to whet Eccl. 10:10

Hithpalp. to shake oneself Jer. 4:24

קָנָה   to get, acquire; buy 888

קָנֶה   stalk, reed; shoulder joint Job 31:22 889

קֵץ   end 893

קָצֶה   end; border, outskirts 892

קָרָא   to call, proclaim, read 894

Niph. to call oneself Isa. 48:2

קרא   to encounter, befall, often

with ל (לִקְרַאת)=toward, against

Niph. to meet unexpectedly Exod. 5:3 Deut. 22:6 2 Sam. 18:9, 20:1

Hiph. to cause to befall Jer. 32:23

קָרַב   to approach, come near 897

Niph. to be brought Exod. 22:7 Josh. 7:14

Pi. to cause to approach, bring near

קֶרֶב   inward part, midst 899

קָרְבָּן   offering, oblation 898

קָרוֹב   near 898

קֶרֶן   horn; hill Isa. 5:1; rays Hab. 3:4 901

קָרַע   to tear 902

קֶרֶשׁ   board, coll. boards Ezek. 27:6 903

קֶשֶׁת   bow 905

רָאָה   to see 906

to select 2 Kings 10:3 1 Sam. 16:1

to provide, furnish Deut. 33:21 Gen. 22:8, 14

to consider, reflect Eccl. 7:14

Niph. to appear

Pu. to be seen, detected Job 33:21

Hiph. to cause to experience Hab. 1:3 Ps. 60:5 71:20 85:8

Hithp.=reciprocal

רֹאשׁ   head, top; beginning, first; chief; sum 910

רִאשׁוֹן   former, first, chief; before, formerly 911

רֵאשִׁית   beginning, first, chief 912

רַב   much, many, great, chief 912

רֹב   multitiude, abundance 913

רבה   to be, become, much, many, grea 915

Pi. to increase, enlarge Judg. 9:29 44:13

to bring up, rear Lam. 2:22 Ezek. 19:

Hiph. הַרְבֵּה greatly, exceedingly

רֶגֶל   foot 919

רָדַף   to pursue, chase, persecute 922

Hiph. to chase Judg. 20:43

רוּחַ   breath, wind, spirit; quarter, side Ezek. 42:16, 17, 18, 19, 20 1 Chron. 9:24 Jer. 52:23 924

רוּם   to be high, exalted, rise 926

Po'lel to cause to rise

to erect, raise, exalt

Hoph. to be taken off Lev. 4:10

be abolished Dan. 8:11

Hithpo'l to exalt oneself Isa. 33:10 Dan. 11:36

רוּץ   to run 930

Po'lel to run swiftly, dart Nah. 2:5

רֹחַב   breadth, width 931

רָחוֹק   distant, far; distance 935

רָחַץ   to wash 934

Pu. to be washed Prov. 30:12 Ezek. 16:4

Hithp. to wash oneself Job 9:30

רָחַק   to be or become far, distant 934

Pi. to send far away

רִיב   to strive, contend 936

Hiph. ptc.=displaying contention 1 Sam. 2:10 Hos. 4:4

רִיב   strife, dispute 936

רֵיחַ   scent, odor 926

רָכַב   to ride, mount and ride 938

רֶכֶב   chariots; upper millstone Deut. 24:6 Judg. 9:53 2 Sam. 11:21 riders, troop 2 Kings 7:14 Isa. 21:7, 9, 22:6 939

רנן   to give ringing cry 943

Pu. "no ringing cry shall be given" Isa. 16:10

רַע   bad, evil; distress, misery, injury, calamity 948

רֵעַ   friend, companion, fellow 945

רָעָב   famine, hunger 944

רָעָה   to pasture, tend, graze 944

רָעָה   evil, misery, distress, injury 949

רֹעֶה   shepherd, herdsman 945 (רָעָה)

רעע   to be evil, bad 949

Niph. to suffer hurt Prov. 11:15, 13:20

Hiph. to do an injury, hurt to do evil, wickedly

רָפָא   to heal 950

Hithp. Inf. cstr. to get healed 2 Kings 8:29, 9:15 2 Chron. 22:6

רָצוֹן   goodwill, favor, acceptance, will 953

רַק   only, altogether, surely 956

רָשָׁע   wicked, criminal; guilty 957

שָׂבַע   to be sated, satisfied, surfeited 959

Niph. ptc. sated Job 31:31

Pi. to satisfy Ezek. 7:19 Ps. 90:14

שָׂדֶה   field, land 961

שִׂים, שׂוּם   to put, place, set 962

Hiph. (see BDB) Ezek. 14:8, 21:21 Job 4:20

Hoph. to be set Gen. 24:33

שָׂכַל   to be prudent 1 Sam. 18:30 968

Hiph. to look at Gen. 3:6

to consider, ponder

to have insight

to cause to consider

to give insight

to act prudently

to prosper

to cause to prosper Deut. 29:8 1 Kings 2:3

שְׂמֹאל   the left 969

שָׂמַח   to rejoice, be glad 970

Pi. to cause to rejoice

Hiph. (=*Pi.*) Ps. 89:43

שִׂמְחָה   joy, gladness, mirth 970

שָׂנֵא   to hate 971

Niph. to be hated Prov. 14:17, 20

Pi. ptc. only, enemy

שָׂעִיר   he-goat, buck 972

שָׂפָה   lip, speech, edge 973

שָׂר   chief, ruler, official, captain, prince 978

שָׂרַף   to burn 976

Pi. ptc. one burning Amos 6:10

Pu. to be burnt up Lev. 10:16

שֶׁ, שַׁ, שָׁ   who, which, that 979

שְׁאוֹל   sheol, hades 982

שָׁאַל   to ask, inquire 981

Niph. to ask for oneself 1 Sam. 20:6, 28 Neh. 13:6

Pi. to inquire carefully 2 Sam. 20:18 to beg Ps. 109:10

Hiph. to grant, make over to 1 Sam. 1:28, 2:20(?) Exod. 12:36

שָׁאַר to remain, be left over 1 Sam. 16:11 983

Niph. (as Qal)

שְׁאֵרִית rest, residue, remnant, remainder 984

שֵׁבֶט rod, staff, club, sceptre; tribe 986

שׁבע *Qal* ptc. pass. those sworn Ezek. 21:28 989

Niph. to swear

Hiph. to cause to swear

to adjure

שָׁבַר to break, break in pieces 990

Hiph. to cause to break out Isa. 66:9

Hoph. to be broken, shattered Jer. 8:21

שָׁבַת to cease, desist, rest 991

Niph. to cease

Hiph. to cause to fail Lev. 2:13 Jer. 48:35 Ruth 4:14

שַׁבָּת Sabbath 992

שדד to deal violently with, despoil, devastate, ruin 994

Niph. to be utterly ruined Mic. 2:4

Pi. to assault Prov. 24:15, 19:26

Pu. to be devastated

Po'el to violently destroy Hos. 10:2

Hoph. to be devastated Hos. 10:14 Isa. 33:1

שָׁוְא emptiness, vanity 996

שׁוּב to turn back, return 996

Po'l. to bring back

to restore Ps. 23:3 Isa. 58:12

to lead away Ezek. 38:4, 39:2 Isa. 47:10

to apostatize Jer. 8:5

Pu. to be restored Ezek. 38:8

שׁוֹפָר horn 1051

שׁוֹר a head of cattle (without reference to sex); bullock, ox 1004

שׁחה to bow down Isa. 51:23 1005

Hiph. to depress Prov. 12:25

Hithpa'lel to bow down, prostrate oneself

שָׁחַט to slaughter, beat 1006

Niph. to be slaughtered Num. 11:22 Lev. 6:18

שׁחת *Niph.* to be marred, spoiled Jer. 13:7 18:4 1007

to be injured Exod. 8:20

to be corrupted, corrupt Gen. 6:11, 12 Ezek. 20:44

Pi. to spoil, ruin

to pervert, corrupt

Hiph. (=*Pi.*)

Hoph. ptc. spoiled, ruined Prov. 25:26 Mal. 1:14

שִׁיר to sing 1010

Po'l. to sing

Hoph. to be sung Isa. 26:1

שִׁיר song 1010

שִׁית to put, set

to make 1011

Hoph. to be imposed Exod. 21:30

שָׁכַב to lie down 1011

שָׁכַח to forget 1013

Pi. to cause to forget Lam. 2:6

Hiph. (=*Pi.*) Jer. 23:27

Hithp. to be forgotten Eccl. 8:10

שׁכם *Hiph.* to start early, rise early 1014

שָׁכֵן to settle down, abide, dwell 1014

Pi. to make settle down, establish

to make to dwell Num. 14:30 Jer. 7:3

Hiph. to lay Ps. 7:6

to place, set, establish Gen. 3:24 Josh 18:1

to cause to settle Ezek. 32:4

to cause to dwell Ps. 78:55

שָׁלוֹם peace, completeness, soundness welfare 1022

שָׁלַח to send, stretch out

to let loose Ps. 50:19 1018

Niph. to be sent Esth. 3:13

Pi. to send away
to let go, set free
to shoot forth
to let down Jer. 38:6, 11
to shoot 1 Sam. 20:20
Hiph. to send

שֻׁלְחָן table 1020

שָׁלַךְ Hiph. to throw, fling, cast 1020

שָׁלָל prey, spoil, plunder, booty 1021

שׁלם to be complete, sound Job 9:4 1022
Pi. to complete, finish 1 Kings 9:25
to make whole
to make safe Job 8:6
to make good
to reward, recompense
Pu. to be performed Ps. 65:2
to be repaid, requited Jer. 18:20 Prov. 11:31, 13:13
Hiph. to make and end of Isa. 38:12, 13
to complete, perform Job 23:14 Isa. 44:26, 28

שֶׁלֶם peace offering; sacrifice for alliance or friend 1023

שָׁם there, thither 1027

שֵׁם name 1027

שׁמד Niph. to be exterminated, destroyed 1029
Hiph. to annihilate, exterminate to destroy

שָׁמַיִם heavens, sky 1029

שׁמם to be desolated, appalled 1030
Niph. (as Qal)
Po'. to be appalled Ezra 9:3, 4
to be appalling, causing horror
Hithpo. to be appalled
to cause oneself desolation, ruin Eccl. 7:16

שְׁמָמָה devastation, waste 1031

שֶׁמֶן fat, oil 1032

שָׁמַע to hear 1033
*Niph. to grant hearing 2 Chron. 30:27
Pi. to cause to hear 1 Sam. 15:4, 23:8

שָׁמַר to keep, watch, preserve 1036

Niph. to be on one's guard
to keep oneself, refrain 1 Sam. 21:5
to be kept, guarded Hos. 12:14 Ps. 37:28
Pi. to pay regard Jonah 2:9
Hithp. to keep oneself from Ps. 18:24 2 Sam. 22:24 Mic. 6:16

שֹׁמֵר watchman 1036 (שָׁמַר)

שֶׁמֶשׁ sun; pinnacle, battlement 1039

שֵׁן tooth, ivory 1042

שָׁנָה year 1040

שַׁעַר gate 1044

שִׁפְחָה maid, maid-servant 1046

שָׁפַט to judge, govern 1047
Niph. to enter into controversy, plead
to be judged Ps. 9:20, 37:33, 109:7
Po'el ptc. opponent-at-law Job 9:15 Zeph. 3:15 Ps. 109:31

שֹׁפֵט judge 1047 (שָׁפַט)

שָׁפַךְ to pour out, pour 1049
Pu. to be poured out, shed Zeph. 1:17 Num. 35:33
to be caused to slip Ps. 73:2
Hithp. to pour oneself out Job 30:16 Lam. 4:1, 2:12

שׁקה Hiph. to cause to drink, give to drink 1052
Pu. to be watered Job 21:24

שֶׁקֶל shekel 1053

שֶׁקֶר deception, falsehood 1055

שׁרת Pi. to minister, serve 1058

שָׁתָה to drink 1059
Niph. to be drunk Lev. 11:34

תְּהִלָּה praise, song of praise; renown, fame 239

תָּוֶךְ midst 1063

תּוֹעֵבָה abomination 1072

תּוֹרָה direction, instruction, law; custom, manner 2 Sam. 7:19 435

תַּחַת underneath, below, instead of 1065

מִתַּחַת from under, from beneath 1066

תָּמִיד continually, continuity 556

תָּמִים complete, whole, sound, healthful, wholesome, innocent 1071

Appendix

תמם to be complete, finished 1070

תִּפְאָרָה beauty, glory 802

תְּפִלָּה prayer 813

תָּפַשׂ to lay hold of, seize, grasp 1074
Pi. to grasp Prov. 30:28

תָּקַע to thrust, clap, give a blow 1075
Niph. to be blown Amos. 3:6 Isa. 27:13
to strike oneself into (pledge oneself)
Job 17:3

תְּרוּמָה contribution, offering 929